IRELAN
REVOLUTIONARY
ERA

IRELAND'S REVOLUTIONARY ERA

FIRST-HAND ACCOUNTS from the Easter Rising to the Anglo-Irish Treaty

EAMONN DUGGAN

Pen & Sword
MILITARY
AN IMPRINT OF PEN & SWORD BOOKS LTD.
YORKSHIRE - PHILADELPHIA

First published in Great Britain in 2026 by
PEN AND SWORD MILITARY
An imprint of
Pen & Sword Books Limited
Yorkshire – Philadelphia

ISBN 978 1 03614 891 1

A CIP catalogue record for this book is available from the British Library.

Typeset in Times New Roman 11/14 by
SJmagic DESIGN SERVICES, India.
Printed and bound in the UK by CPI Group (UK) Ltd.

The Publisher's authorised representative in the EU for product safety is Authorised Rep Compliance Ltd., Ground Floor, 71 Lower Baggot Street, Dublin D02 P593, Ireland.
www.arccompliance.com

For a complete list of Pen & Sword titles please contact
PEN & SWORD BOOKS LIMITED
George House, Units 12 & 13, Beevor Street, Off Pontefract Road,
Barnsley, South Yorkshire, S71 1HN, England
E-mail: enquiries@pen-and-sword.co.uk
Website: www.pen-and-sword.co.uk

or

PEN AND SWORD BOOKS
1950 Lawrence Rd, Havertown, PA 19083, USA
E-mail: uspen-and-sword@casematepublishers.com
Website: www.penandswordbooks.com

MIX
Paper | Supporting responsible forestry
FSC® C013604

Contents

Part One: A Stand Against the British

Introduction	Ireland Moves Towards a Rebellion, 1913–14	2
Chapter One	Republican Sentiment Grows, 1915	12
Chapter Two	Chaos and Confusion Reigns	19
Chapter Three	The 1916 Easter Rising, Monday, 24 April	28
Chapter Four	The Easter Rising, Tuesday, 25 April to Wednesday, 26 April	40
Chapter Five	The Easter Rising, Thursday, 27 April to Sunday, 30 April	49
Chapter Six	The Rising Outside of Dublin	58
Chapter Seven	The Aftermath of the Rising	67

Part Two: Irish Republicanism: Political Awakening and Military Reorganisation

Chapter Eight	Republicans Embrace a Political Agenda, 1917–18	84
Chapter Nine	Reorganising the Volunteers, Procuring Arms and Gathering Intelligence	98

Part Three: The War of Independence: Conflict with the British

Chapter Ten	The War of Independence, 1919	116
Chapter Eleven	The War of Independence, 1920	132

Chapter Twelve	The War of Independence, 1921	160
Chapter Thirteen	Cumann na mBan: The Unsung Heroines of the Revolution	186

Part Four: The Aftermath of the Revolution

Chapter Fourteen	The Truce, Peace Comes at Last	196
Chapter Fifteen	The Anglo-Irish Treaty	203

References	210
Reference Books	217
Index	218

PART ONE

A Stand Against the British

INTRODUCTION

Ireland Moves Towards a Rebellion

1913–14

On 25 November 1913 a meeting was called by a group of Irish nationalists with the sole intention of forming a military organisation in response to the recently formed Ulster Volunteers, an organisation committed to maintaining that province's place in the Union of Great Britain and Ireland. The Ulster Volunteers opposed the ideal of Home Rule for Ireland and, in order to preserve Ulster's place in the Union, it was prepared to resort to physical force to achieve that aim. During the latter half of 1912 some 250,000 male Unionists signed what was called The Ulster Solemn League and Covenant. Many, it was said, even signed the pledge in their own blood to affirm their resistance to Home Rule. The Ulster Volunteers came into being in January 1913 and the battle lines were drawn with the rest of Ireland. The Unionists made it very clear they were not for turning and would fight to the death to maintain Ulster's position in the Union.

In Dublin the republican fraternity took note of events in Ulster and a decision was made to form a force that might stand in opposition to the Ulster men. The initiative was taken by the Irish Republican Brotherhood (IRB) and a series of meetings took place within the executive of that organisation to discuss the type of response required. The main protagonist within the IRB was Bulmer Hobson, who was of the opinion that body should use the formation of the Ulster Volunteers as a means of persuading southern nationalists to form a military force of their own. The problem for the IRB was that it could not openly involve itself in the formation of a military force because its members were watched constantly by the authorities. The IRB was viewed by those in Dublin Castle as a physical force organisation in its own right and, if any of its members were seen to be publicly involved in the formation of a Volunteer force, action would be taken by the relevant authorities to suppress it before it even got off the ground. The IRB Supreme Council consequently took the view that it should, in time, encourage other nationalists to organise the new force.

In early January 1913 the IRB initiated the first steps towards the formation of a new Volunteers movement outside of Ulster by persuading the National Foresters to build a hall at the back of 41 Parnell Square in Dublin. Once that was up and running, foot drill classes were held under the watchful eyes of IRB member James Stritch, aided by members of Fianna Eireann. Some members of the Gaelic Athletic Association led by Harry Boland also participated in the classes. If the initiative was to be taken to the next level, the IRB leadership concluded it would need to find a highly regarded individual to act as a figure head for the new Volunteers force, thereby concealing the real control of it to the authorities and the general public. It did not take long for the right individual to be identified and an approach was made to Eoin MacNeill, the eminent Professor of Medieval History at University College Dublin. It was hard to argue against the choice because MacNeill was a well-known man of great integrity with impeccable academic credentials. It was agreed he would give the new Volunteers organisation an air of credibility and respect.

At that point, The O'Rahilly, who was the Assistant Editor at the Gaelic League newspaper *An Claidheamh Soluis*, got involved in the process and encouraged MacNeill to write an article for the publication on the wider question of Irish nationalism. Taking up the suggestion, MacNeill in his article, which appeared on 1 November 1913 claimed:

> There is nothing to prevent the other twenty-eight counties from calling into existence citizen forces to hold Ireland 'for the Empire'. It was precisely with this object that the Volunteers of 1782 were enrolled, and they became the instrument of establishing self-government.[1]

In the aftermath of the article, Bulmer Hobson encouraged The O'Rahilly to meet with MacNeill and suggest to him that a conference should be convened bringing together interested parties to work towards the ultimate goal of starting a new Irish Volunteers organisation. In his statement to the Bureau of Military History, Hobson recalled his conversation with The O'Rahilly:

> I went immediately to The O'Rahilly, who was then honorary editor of 'An Claidheamh Soluis', and proposed the formation

> of a National Volunteer Force. O'Rahilly said that if I could get fifty men he would join them. I said I could guarantee five hundred, and although he, like MacNeill, wasn't a member of the IRB, he realised what I had in mind and at once consented.[2]

In essence, MacNeill's article encouraged nationalists to match what the Ulster unionists had done in terms of organising themselves on a military basis. As it transpired, MacNeill was very much in the dark about what was going on in the republican background, though he was aware that Hobson had very militant tendencies. In effect, MacNeill knew why he had been tapped up by Hobson and his IRB colleagues but naturally enough he was determined not to be controlled by them. Hobson asked MacNeill to chair a meeting to discuss the formation of a Volunteer force and he quickly consented to do so. Hobson then sent out invitations to individuals and nationalist organisations to join the first Provisional Committee. Hobson saw great value in having MacNeill on board because of his immense intellectual ability and because he was a clear-headed individual who was sincere and well-liked. He also knew MacNeill would not quarrel with anybody and had the ability to throw oil on the most troubled of waters.

The first meeting was held in Wynn's Hotel on Abbey Street in Dublin on 11 November 1913. Hobson did not attend because, being an 'extreme nationalist', he felt his presence might have been problematic. As it transpired, the IRB was well represented at the meeting with two of its leading lights, Sean McDermott and Éamonn Ceannt, present. The irony here is that both McDermott and Ceannt turned out to be much more extreme than Hobson, who refused to take part in the Easter Rising on the basis that he felt it was a conflict republicans could not win. Several other meetings then took place over a short period of time, during which, plans for the formation of the Volunteers were drawn up.

On 20 November 1913 a circular letter signed by Eoin MacNeill and Laurence Kettle, a founding member of the organisation, was sent to all national organisations. The circular requested the organisations to put the aims of the Volunteers before their members and a copy was sent to the newspapers. The *Freeman's Journal* of 24 November 1913 printed a notice that the venue for the meeting had been changed from the Rotunda Concert Hall to the Rotunda Rink, which was then the biggest hall in Dublin and had a capacity for 4,000 people. Some 5,000 blank enlistment forms were brought along to the meeting and handed out in books of one hundred to appointed stewards. It was estimated that around 3,000 of the forms were filled in and signed on the night. With so many people outside the Rink there was traffic chaos on the streets, especially when Sean McDermott went out to address the crowd. Among those who spoke at the meeting were MacNeill, Laurence Kettle and P.H. Pearse, who went on to lead the Easter Rising. Hobson decided against speaking in the main hall because he felt his extreme republican views might turn prospective recruits away. Sean T. O'Kelly, the future President of Ireland, also addressed some members of the crowd in the adjacent Concert Hall. In his statement to the Bureau of Military History he recalled:

> It was decided then to hold an overflow meeting in the hall attached to the Rink which is now used as the Gate Theatre. I was sent for by John MacNeill and instructed to take charge of that meeting. I presided and a number of speakers who were on the platform in the Rotunda Rink where the main meeting was held were sent in to me as soon as they had delivered their speeches, to deliver addresses to the overflow meeting.
>
> I think every man at the overflow meeting before the end came had handed in his name for membership of the new organisation.[3]

The Irish Volunteers issued a manifesto that was primarily written by MacNeil with some amending contributions from Tom Kettle MP and barrister, and other members of the Provisional Committee that was set up to oversee the running of the organisation. The manifesto stated the Volunteers objectives were 'to secure and maintain the rights and liberties common to the whole people of Ireland', and that membership was open to all Irishmen 'without distinction of creed, politics or social grade'. The manifesto went on to state the Volunteers' duties were to be defensive, contemplating neither 'aggression or domination'. Though the 'rights and liberties' were never defined exactly, nor the means by which they would be obtained, the IRB, in the great Fenian tradition, construed the term to mean the maintenance of the rights of Ireland to national independence and to secure that right in arms. When the composition of the thirty-member Provisional Committee was eventually settled on, over half that number was made up of IRB nominees, with the remainder being of a more moderate nature such as the Sinn Fein nominees.

The Committee sat between November 1913 and October 1914 and it was augmented from mid-June to mid-September 1914, by an additional twenty-five nominees made by John Redmond, the leader of the all-powerful Irish Parliamentary Party. He was not inclined to allow a physical force organisation to have free reign across the country and, it came as no surprise when he demanded a controlling representation on the Provisional Committee. While the IRB committee men were completely opposed to Redmond taking control of the Irish Volunteers, the more moderate members were prepared to accept such a scenario, if only to prevent him from forming a rival organisation that would have drawn many men away from the Irish Volunteers. In the end, the IRB lost the argument to Redmond and his faction on the Committee and, with it, any chance of controlling the Irish Volunteers from the outset.

The Provisional Committee met in December 1913 to make arrangements for the publication of a manifesto setting out instructions for the formation of Volunteers companies around the country. The manifesto was a four-page publication titled *The Volunteer Gazette* and there was only one issue with little intention of continuing it as a periodical. A weekly newspaper called *The Irish Volunteer* came on stream by the end of January 1914 under the auspices of the *Enniscorthy Echo* newspaper. According to Bulmer Hobson, it offered the Volunteers organisation the advantage of being able to publish documents of all kinds. The newspaper continued to be published until November 1914, when the *Enniscorthy Echo* decided to discontinue it.

During the early months of 1914, Irish Volunteers companies emerged in many districts across the country as voluntary organisers took on the often-arduous task of recruiting young men into the ranks. A wave of nationalist enthusiasm swept many parts of the country as recruits signed up to drill and march as they prepared for a possible conflict with the British. One such young man was Dubliner Harry Colley, who joined the Volunteers in January 1914 and was assigned to 'B' Company, 1st Battalion at 41 Parnell Square. Colley went on to distinguish himself in the Easter Rising, during which he was badly wounded. He later became a Fianna Fail TD and was the father of future Tanaiste, George Colley. He recalled how the men in the company were drilled by an ex-British Army instructor. Colley also recalled how the tension was rising in the city and everybody expected to be in a fight with the British sooner or later. Though his new company was a relatively small one, numbering about thirty-two men in total, Colley maintained it did not lack in enthusiasm.

In April 1914, after one million pounds was raised by the Ulster Volunteers, a gun smuggling operation was launched and overseen by Major Frederick Crawford and Captain Wilfred Spender. Some 25,000 rifles and, somewhere in the region of 5 million rounds of ammunition were brought in from Germany. The shipments were landed at Larne, Donaghadee and Bangor on the 24th and 25th of the month and, motor cars were used to ferry the rifles and ammunition, without interference from the authorities, to many parts of the province. It was a real show of intent by the Ulster Volunteers, who were prepared to take on the British Army if the province was forced by the government in London to accept home rule. News of the arms shipment caused real alarm among the Irish Volunteers leadership. It was, by then, very clear the southern organisation needed to respond and take action to seriously arm itself in the event of it taking on the forces of the Crown.

By the summer of 1914 the number of members in the Irish Volunteers was variously estimated to be between 100,000 and 150,000 men but, the fact was it had little in the way of funds and virtually no arms. In order to improve the disastrous arms situation, which was endangering the whole Volunteers position, Roger Casement, on his own initiative, went to London in the early part of 1914 and, together with a few friends, raised a sum of £1,500. Casement was the retired British Consul to South America and Africa who was an anti-Imperialist and believed Ireland had every right to be a free and independent nation. Among his friends and contacts in London, it seems Mrs Alice Stopford Green, the historian and author, generously contributed about half this amount. Erskine Childers and his wife, the Honourable Mary Spring Rice, Captain Berkeley and Casement himself subscribed the rest of the money. With the exception of Casement, none of the subscribers had connections to the Volunteers. It was agreed the money should be used to purchase arms and transport them to Ireland. There they would be sold to the Irish Volunteers and the money reimbursed to the subscribers. It was an uncommercial risk taken by the subscribers and they must have been surprised when they did eventually get their money back.

This group selected the London-based nationalist Darrell Figgis to go to Belgium to purchase rifles. Erskine Childers and Conor O'Brien volunteered to bring the guns to Ireland in their yachts, *Asgard* and *Kelpie*. Figgis had no previous connection with the Volunteers, so he was unlikely to attract the attention of the authorities. He purchased 1,500 rifles and 45,000 rounds of ammunition and hired a tug at Antwerp to bring the guns to meet Childers' and O' Brien's yachts at an appointed time and place in the North Sea. The guns were Mauser rifles, old-fashioned and heavy but in perfect order. They were, it is believed, used by the German Army to rearm after the Franco-Prussian war.

News of the proposed project filtered out in June 1914, when Casement asked Bulmer Hobson if he could make arrangements for the landing of the two cargoes. Casement had already talked to MacNeill and The O'Rahilly about the matter but no working scheme had been put in place. Hobson agreed with the suggestion on the understanding that he was not to be hampered by any committee. He agreed to meet Casement and Childers in Dublin within a week and have some practicable plan ready. In his statement to the Bureau of Military History, Hobson recalled his initial thoughts on the matter:

> On thinking the matter over I decided that 1,500 rifles would not go very far in solving our problem, but that if we could bring them in in a sufficiently spectacular manner we should probably solve our financial problem and the problem of arming the Volunteers as well.[4]

Hobson went on to recall his next steps in the operation:

> With this in mind I decided to bring the guns in in daylight, in the most open manner and as near to Dublin as possible. I personally examined every harbour between Greystones and Balbriggan, cycling the whole way, and only turned down the North Wall in Dublin because I thought that we might not get time to unload before the authorities would appear.
>
> I decided that Howth was the best harbour, and that the best method was to march a large number of Volunteers to meet the yacht, to arm them on the spot and march them back. I felt that this could be done, provided the movement was executed with sufficient rapidity to enable us to get back past the narrow neck of land at Sutton before the Castle could intervene, and I felt that the task of seizing so many guns, from so many individual Volunteers, who would be scattered over a wide area, would be beyond the powers of either police or soldiery.
>
> I met Casement and Childers at Boswell's Hotel, Molesworth Street, Dublin, one Sunday about the end of June, and proposed my plan, with which they both agreed. Childers and I went out to Howth next day and looked at the harbour, and settled just where he was to come in. At that meeting it was fixed that Childers should sail into Howth harbour at twelve

> noon on 26th July and that I would have the Volunteers there to meet him.
>
> Childers then went off to keep his appointment with Figgis in the North Sea, and I did not see him again until he brought his cargo of guns into Howth harbour on 26th July.[5]

Some 900 guns and 24,000 rounds of ammunition were landed in Howth by Childers from his yacht. As the Volunteers marched from Howth back to Dublin with the guns they were met by a large patrol of the Dublin Metropolitan Police and the King's Own Borderers. The Volunteers escaped the confrontation largely unscathed, but when the Borderers returned to Dublin they clashed with a group of unarmed civilians who had been heckling them at Bachelors Walk. Though no order was given, the soldiers fired on the civilians, killing four and further wounding thirty-seven others. The incident was the first confrontation between the citizens of Dublin and the forces of the Crown, and was, of course, a precursor to what was to come.

On 2 August, O'Brien landed his cache of guns, numbering around 600 in total, as well as ammunition at Kilcoole in County Wicklow in the early hours of the morning. The only policemen in the area of Kilcoole were two individuals patrolling the railway line. They were put under arrest and when they were released they had several miles to walk to barracks before they could raise the alarm. There was no other interference of any kind from the authorities and the guns and ammunition were brought back to Dublin on a large motor charabanc that was so overloaded with men, guns and ammunition it broke a back axle in the middle of Bray. A motorcyclist was sent to Dublin to get help, and in a surprisingly short time a number of taxis and a couple of lorries arrived and the guns and ammunition were taken safely to Dublin.

By the middle of 1914 Ireland seemed on the verge of internal conflict and disaster. However, the outbreak of the First World War caused the introduction of Home Rule to be postponed for the duration of the fighting. Redmond secured a promise that Home Rule would be delayed 'not later than the end of the present war', which he said 'would be bloody but short lived'. He then called on the Irish Volunteers to join the British Army and, in his speech to them at Woodenbridge, County Wicklow, on 20 September 1914, he pledged his support to the Allied cause when he stated that:

> The interests of Ireland – of the whole of Ireland – are at stake in this war. This war is undertaken in the defence of the

> highest principles of religion and morality and right, and it would be a disgrace for ever to our country and a reproach to her manhood and a denial of the lessons of her history if young Ireland confined their efforts to remaining at home to defend the shores of Ireland from an unlikely invasion, and to shrinking from the duty of proving on the field of battle that gallantry and courage which has distinguished our race all through its history. I say to you, therefore, your duty is two-fold. I am glad to see such magnificent material for soldiers around me, and I say to you: 'Go on drilling and make yourself efficient for the work, and then account yourselves as men, not only for Ireland itself, but wherever the fighting line extends, in defence of the right, of freedom, and religion in this war.[6]

The majority of the Irish Volunteers reacted with great enthusiasm to the speech and formed a new organisation called the National Volunteers. Many went on to enlist in the Irish regiments of the 10th and 16th (Irish) Divisions of the British Army. The minority that stayed at home then became the IRB-dominated Irish Volunteers. Redmond genuinely believed Germany had to be stopped and that its military expansion threatened the freedom of Europe. Having secured Ireland's future self-government, he felt all Irishmen, nationalist and unionist, were duty bound to play their part in the war. That belief was also evident in his own family when his brother and fellow MP, Willie, joined up despite being over 50 years of age. While Redmond's call for Irishmen to take up arms was well meaning and had the support of so many, it did attract criticism from a minority, all of whom felt Ireland's real fight was with Britain rather than Germany. Redmond, like many others, assumed the war would last no longer than a few months and did not expect it to last as long as it did, bringing with it horrors and suffering on a scale never before experienced by mankind.

Those who refused to join Redmond were convinced the cause of Ireland's freedom was much more important than a conflict on the Continent. Those who remained at home retained the name 'Irish Volunteers' and continued to be led by MacNeill. Redmond's National Volunteers suddenly numbered 175,000 members, leaving the Irish Volunteers with an estimated 13,500 men. However, as the war progressed, the National Volunteers declined rapidly, and by October 1917 the organisation had virtually disappeared from the national scene. While the split in 1914 decimated the Irish Volunteers in terms of numbers, it did restore the IRB to a position of control.

The departure of Redmond and his followers meant the Volunteers were forced to reorganise and to adopt a constitution, which had been drawn up by the earlier provisional committee. It was ratified by a convention of 160 delegates on 25 October 1914. The constitution called for a General Council of fifty members and an Executive Committee, consisting of a President and eight elected members. In December 1914, a Headquarters Staff was appointed with Eoin MacNeill as Chief of Staff, The O'Rahilly as Director of Arms, Thomas MacDonagh as Director of Training, P.H. Pearse as Director of Military Organisation, Bulmer Hobson as Quartermaster, and Joseph Plunkett as Director of Military Operations. In 1915 they were joined by Éamonn Ceannt as Director of Communications and J.J. O'Connell as Chief of Inspection. By the end of 1914 the IRB was in control of the Irish Volunteers and, with Britain becoming further entrenched in a continental war that was showing all the signs of being a prolonged one, the Headquarters Staff believed it was the right time to plan for a rebellion. The term, 'England's difficulty is Ireland's opportunity' soon became a clarion call. Consequently, it was only a matter of time before a confrontation with the British became a reality.

It was around this time that the Volunteers leadership and the IRB concluded that in any conflict with the British it would be necessary to look for outside help. It was no surprise then that Britain's great enemy, Germany, was targeted as a potential ally. Contact was made with the German authorities in New York via the republican organisation Clan na Gael, and Roger Casement was dispatched to Berlin in November 1914 to speak with authorities there in the hope that an invasion force might be sent to Ireland in due course. The response was not exactly enthusiastic and the German commitment amounted to nothing more than an undertaking to send some guns and ammunition. While there, Casement was joined by Joseph Plunkett and both men endeavoured to form an Irish Brigade made up of German-held Irish prisoners of war. The attempt turned out to be a miserable failure, with fewer than sixty men agreeing to sign up. From then on, it was obvious if there was to be a rebellion in Ireland the Volunteers would have to fight the British without foreign help.

CHAPTER ONE

Republican Sentiment Grows

1915

By 1915 the Irish Volunteers were gaining a foothold in communities across the country, both rural and urban. Young men were recruited by organisers sent out by the Volunteers Headquarters in Dublin to engage with possible recruits and provide them with plausible reasons for signing up to fight for their country's independence. In many areas of the country, most especially in the south, there was an air of palpable enthusiasm, though it must be said there were other areas where it proved to be hard going when it came to drumming up support for the cause. It was, however, not uncommon to see groups of young men in the evenings or on Sundays marching and drilling under the watchful eyes of drill sergeants, many of whom were former members of the British Army. Though there was enthusiasm for the notion of being part of a new force, not all the young men involved were cut out for the life of a soldier. Many joined in the drilling and marching seeing it as a social outlet and soon discovered the discipline required of them by their superiors was something to which they could not commit. Indeed, Sean Moylan, the greatest of all IRA commandants in the War of Independence, made a salient point in his statement to the Bureau of Military History, when he said most of the young men who joined up had no idea about soldiering or the soldier's way of life and described them as:

> An irresponsible crowd of young men attracted for the moment by the drilling, marching and shouted orders.[7]

However, he went on to say that later during the revolutionary era many of the Volunteers recruits became first-class material for military purposes and, some went on to prove themselves as exceptional soldiers when they joined the IRA.

Often during the early months of 1915 many of the nightly drills and parades were attended by some of the more unionist-minded members of the community, who hoped the young men they were watching would eventually join the British Army and fight on the Western Front as well as in other theatres of war. Of course, they were to be disappointed because those who threw in their lot with the Irish Volunteers had little interest in fighting for Britain in a conflict that was not going to deliver independence for Ireland. Similarly, the high hopes Redmond had for his National Volunteers to play a significant role in the Great War never really came to fruition. The majority of the National Volunteers, probably about 80 per cent, did not enlist in the British Army. They did, however, stage a rally of over 20,000 men on Easter Sunday 1915 in Dublin's Phoenix Park, although even their Inspector General, Maurice Moore, saw no military future for them, saying:

> They cannot be trained, disciplined or armed, moreover, the enthusiasm has gone and they cannot be kept going … it will be of no practical use against any Army, Orange or German.[8]

As the war progressed the National Volunteers fell rapidly into decline and they involved themselves in very little activity; so much so, they eventually became an irrelevance. However, during 1915 the relevance of the Irish Volunteers continued to increase and, as an organisation, it became much more visible around the country despite many of its personnel's movements being watched carefully by the authorities. Organisers appeared in many communities and put in long hours travelling from house to house seeking recruits. They engaged in endless meetings, some in the open and, others of a clandestine nature, all held to spread the message of independence and set out the way forward to it.

One of the more prominent organisers was Ernest Blythe, an Ulster Protestant who was imbued with a sense of republicanism from a young age and who had travelled south to do his bit for an independent Ireland. Early in 1915 he set off for Cork with instructions from his superiors in Dublin to make contact with Terence MacSwiney and Tomas MacCurtain. Blythe firstly made contact with MacCurtain, finding him in Blackpool on the same day he opened a new business venture. Though very busy, MacCurtain did spare Blythe a couple of minutes and advised him to go to the Volunteers Hall that evening and attend a general meeting of the members. He did so and met with not only MacCurtain, but also with MacSwiney. They had a long discussion and Blythe set out his recruitment plans and took on board the views of two of the most important men in the organisation's southern leadership structure.

Blythe was officially introduced to the body of the meeting as the representative of Headquarters and in his speech assured those who were listening he intended to support the strategies of MacCurtain and MacSwiney. Blythe, like all other organisers, was particularly keen to ingratiate himself with the local leadership and once he achieved that goal he felt it would be easier to garner the confidence of the rank-and-file members. So, by the early months of 1915, the Irish Volunteers were clearly evolving into a well-run organisation with a well-defined and articulated vision for Ireland. The most important task at that stage was the necessity to bring the people on board in order that the aim of independence might be achieved in the not too distant future.

If having boots on the ground was important to drum up support for the Irish Volunteers, the written word also played its part in the recruitment campaign during 1915. Frank Henderson, who rose to be Commandant of the Dublin 2nd Battalion, recalled in his witness statement how the *Irish Volunteer* newspaper played its part in recruiting men into the ranks. Edited by Eoin MacNeill, it was a well-written publication and Henderson was of the opinion that it and a number of pamphlets written by P.H. Pearse succeeded in boosting Volunteer numbers. Many of the new recruits, he maintained, were of particularly fine quality and in time went on to become very dependable additions to the organisation. During the early months of 1915 a new drive for arms and ammunition began and soon revolvers and automatic weapons were imported and distributed. Rifles could be secured in many different ways, including the bribing of British soldiers or on the open market. In Dublin, for example, much of what a Volunteer needed could be bought in establishments like Lawlor's of Fownes Street or in Whelan's on Upper Ormonde Quay. In tandem with the increased supply of arms, training around the country was intensified as the year progressed with a lot of route marches and manoeuvres taking place.

Near the end of May 1915, the Volunteers leadership sought to give the organisation a more visible presence and made arrangements to stage a public display of strength with a parade in Limerick. In his witness statement, Ernest Blythe recalled how he cycled from Ennis to attend the event and, as he was not part of any formation, he stood on a pavement to watch the parade, which comprised of around 1,000 men. The parade, which was attended by P.H. Pearse, consisted of companies from Mitchelstown and other areas in Cork as well as those from various areas in County Limerick and Limerick city. They were joined by a sizeable contingent from Dublin. All went well until the parade was over and it was only then that trouble erupted. Blythe recalled the incident in his statement when he said:

> After the parade the rabble of the city, particularly the 'separation women', got into the mood to make trouble, and a large crowd of them gathered near the station to attack the Volunteers as they moved to the train. There was a certain amount of stone throwing, and blows were struck at Volunteers as they passed by. In a few instances the crowd pressed in and disarmed Volunteers. One Volunteer officer who lost his head ordered his men to load their rifles. Fortunately his instructions were countermanded, otherwise in the heat of the turmoil, irreparable damage might have been done. I was in civilian clothes in the middle of the crowd and saw the whole proceedings very well. A priest, an Augustinian Father, mounted a car and harangued the crowd about what they were doing. Summarily, from the car, he expelled various people from the Confraternity. Pearse was very much put out by the disturbances as we heard of its beginning in Daly's house in Barrington Street, but later he looked perfectly calm as he marched ahead in his place. Ultimately, all the Volunteers got into the station, and one could say that no damage was done. Some of them had been struck by sticks and stones, and some of them gave belts back to the crowd. One young fellow used his bayonet on an assailant, but fortunately did not do much damage. Beyond the loss of two or three rifles, the Volunteers suffered nothing. The occurrence afforded an indication, however, of the hostility that it was still possible to stir up against the Volunteers, the sort of hostility that was seen again when Volunteer prisoners were marching through Dublin after the Rising.[9]

The great Irish-American Fenian, Jeremiah O'Donovan Rossa died on 29 June 1915 in New York at the age of 84. An icon of Fenianism going back to the previous century, it was inevitable some form of commemoration would be held back in Ireland. As it transpired, the IRB leadership saw an opportunity to further showcase the growing strength of the Irish Volunteers by organising a grand funeral for the man who originally hailed from

Rosscarbery in County Cork. Rossa had been an advocate of physical force as the only way to achieve Irish freedom and during the previous century had organised a bombing campaign in Britain against both government and civilian targets. He was arrested in September 1865 on charges of treason and sentenced to penal servitude for life. He served his time in Pentonville, Portland, Millbank and Chatham prisons in England. He actually won a seat in Parliament in 1869 but was disqualified because he was a convict.

Rossa was released as part of an Amnesty for Fenian prisoners in 1870 and, after giving an undertaking he would not return to Ireland, he went to America. There he lived in New York City and joined the Irish-American republican organisation Clan na Gael. He also established his own newspaper and generally continued his agitation against British rule in Ireland. When his ban from the United Kingdom expired, he undertook lecture tours of Britain and Ireland but continued to live in New York until his death. When Rossa died, Tom Clarke of the IRB leadership cabled another great Irish-American, John Devoy, and requested that he send the body of the great patriot home.

So, on 1 August 1915 O'Donovan Rossa was buried in Glasnevin Cemetery in what turned out to be the biggest show of Irish Volunteers strength since the inception of the organisation. Both the Volunteers leadership and IRB Supreme Council took the view they could not pass up on the chance to place their respective organisations at the forefront of the occasion. The funeral provided them with an invaluable propaganda opportunity and the chance to defy the authorities' directives and regulations. In his witness statement to the Bureau of Military History, the future President of Ireland, Sean T. O'Kelly, recalled the funeral and his part in it:

> The remains of Donovan Rossa were brought to Ireland sometime at the end of July 1915. Previously it had been decided by the IRB that a public funeral of the most impressive character should be organised for the burial of O'Donovan Rossa's remains in Glasnevin Cemetery. I was instructed to select a spot somewhere near the O'Connell circle in Glasnevin Cemetery and to have the grave opened there. The money to be paid for the grave was given to me by Tom Clarke. The IRB nominated a committee to take charge of the organisation of the funeral. I was nominated as a member of the committee. The committee was divided into sub-committees to deal with the various aspects of the organisation of the funeral … The

> funeral was one of the biggest funerals that I have ever seen. It was probably the biggest that ever took place in Ireland with the exception possibly of the funeral of Charles Stewart Parnell in October 1891. As well as all the branches of the IRB, the whole Irish Volunteer organisation was mustered to take part in the funeral and the occasion was used by the Volunteers as an opportunity for showing their strength. As far as I remember, the Volunteers marched in uniform …
>
> The funeral procession on that day was certainly most impressive. As well as the Volunteers, public bodies of all kinds sent strong delegations from all parts of Ireland to take part in the funeral … Luckily the weather was particularly kind with the result that many thousands of people stood on the sidewalks to watch the funeral procession pass.[10]

O'Kelly went on to recall how P. H. Pearse was asked to deliver the graveside oration. He believed it to be one of the greatest speeches he had ever heard. The speech, he recalled, was essentially a call to arms and the last lines left a long and lasting impact on him and all republicans:

> They think that they have pacified Ireland. They think that they have purchased half of us and intimidated the other half. They think that they have foreseen everything, think that they have provided against everything, but, the fools, the fools! They have left us our Fenian dead, and while Ireland holds these graves, Ireland unfree shall never be at peace.[11]

O'Kelly went on to recall:

> I was standing alongside Pearse when he spoke and we all felt very proud of his impressive oratorical achievement. He evidently had his speech, which was not too long, well memorised for he used no notes on the occasion.
>
> After Pearse's oration the firing party, which had been quietly and privately arranged for by either some Volunteer Committee or the IRB Committee, were called on and they fired their volleys over the grave. This must have been one of the first if not the very first occasion on which this military demonstration took place in our lifetime and this too in its way

> made a deep impression not alone in all who were present but on all who read the report afterwards.
>
> The IRB and the Irish Volunteers were very proud of having been able to accomplish this military demonstration despite the orders of the British against the carrying of arms.[12]

The funeral of O'Donovan Rossa turned out to be a huge success in terms of advancing the public image of the Irish Volunteers and probably sent shock waves through the corridors of Dublin Castle and Westminster. It was clear from the turnout of men in military uniform that a new movement was emerging capable of taking the struggle for independence to a new level. The decision to move to that level was taken on 26 December 1915 when the IRB Military Council set Easter 1916 as the date to stage a Rising.

CHAPTER TWO

Chaos and Confusion Reigns

Having decided on Easter Sunday 1916 for the date of the rebellion, the IRB Military Council made up of Tom Clarke, Sean McDermott, P.H. Pearse, Joseph Plunkett, Éamonn Ceannt, Thomas MacDonagh and James Connolly, the leader of the Irish Citizen Army, resolved to maintain a strict secrecy around their plans for the conflict with the British. All seven men went on to sign the 1916 Proclamation prior to the Rising in the hope it would eventually bring about an end to centuries of British rule and subjugation.

Connolly was an interesting character and his working class and trade union background made him stand out in this group. Initially, he and his Irish Citizen Army had made plans to launch a workers rebellion looking for better wages and conditions in a new Ireland, which they hoped would be a socialist republic. The Citizen Army was a relatively small paramilitary group made up of members of the Irish Transport and General Workers Union. It was set up in 1913 to protect workers in Dublin from the Metropolitan Police whenever they engaged in demonstrations or strikes. Fearing Connolly and his Citizen Army would scupper their plans for a rebellion, the other six men, all members of the IRB decided to 'persuade' him over a period of three days of secret conversations in January 1916 to join forces with them and participate in the Rising they had been planning.

The Military Council plan called for Dublin to be the focal point of the rebellion while simultaneous rebellions were expected to break out across the country designed to attract the support of the civilian population. The Military Council also hoped a countrywide rebellion would overpower the British forces in Ireland, thereby ensuring a victory for the rebels. The problem was, however, the group of men who made up the Military Council, though brave, determined and intelligent, were not very experienced in military matters and strategies. Consequently, their best-laid plans on paper never materialised in practise.

On St Patrick's Day, 1916 a review of the Volunteers took place in College Green, during which the Chief of Staff, Eoin MacNeill, took the salute and all the Companies of the Dublin Brigade took part in the parade, which seemingly was a great success. The traffic in the city was held up for a number of hours and the review not only hardened the discipline of the men but also strengthened their spirit and, very importantly, garnered some new recruits. During the review, some British military officers leaving Dublin Castle attempted to make their way through the parade. They were held up by members of the 3rd Battalion under the command of Éamon de Valera. For a few moments it looked as if a real confrontation was about to take place. De Valera made it clear he and his men would use force if necessary and eventually the British officers moved off in a different direction.

Frank Henderson, Captain of 'F' Company 2nd Battalion, Dublin Brigade, recalled a meeting some two weeks prior to the Rising at No. 2 Dawson Street attended by every officer of the Dublin Brigade. The meeting was addressed by Éamonn Ceannt, who spoke about preparation for battle. Thomas MacDonagh also spoke and both men laid out for the meeting what they had done for themselves in preparation for the rebellion such as buying raincoats, leggings and marching boots. Interestingly, both men also revealed they had made their wills. Just as they finished speaking, P.H. Pearse swept into the room and dramatically asked the men if they were all ready to face their God. In the weeks leading up to the Rising, the Volunteers conducted raids for arms, ammunition and explosives. Henderson recalled one notable raid on the London North Western Railway at the North Wall that was carried out under the command of Captain Thomas Weafer of 'E' Company. The Volunteers managed to take a number of British military rifles, while other raids offered up some quantities of explosives.

The starting point for any rebellion or revolution, of course, is an adequate supply of arms and ammunition. Roger Casement, still in Germany in early 1916, negotiated a cache of 20,000 rifles, ten machine guns and about one million rounds of ammunition with the authorities there. On 9 April a ship called the *Aud* set sail from the Baltic port of Lübeck with its cache concealed under the camouflage of a timber cargo. The *Aud* was under the command of Captain Karl Spindler and had a crew of twenty-two. Spindler, hoping to evade a British blockade on German shipping, set a course for Tralee Bay, where it was planned to unload the cache at Fenit Pier with the help of a local pilot, Mortimer O'Leary. The *Aud* arrived in Tralee Bay on Holy Thursday, 20 April, which was three days earlier than the Volunteers in Kerry had expected. Unfortunately, the *Aud* had no radio on board so contact could not be made with Spindler to appraise him of the situation. In his witness statement to the Bureau of Military History, O'Leary recalled the confusion in Kerry over the arrival of the *Aud*:

> I was a member of the Castlegregory Volunteers Company and on Holy Thursday, Tadg Brosnan, the Company Captain, told me that a small steamer carrying arms was due to arrive on Easter Sunday night and arrangements for piloting her into Fenit Pier were to be made. He instructed me to come up to him on Saturday afternoon when he would give me final instructions. On Holy Thursday evening I saw a two-masted steamer of about 3,000 tons about two miles north of Leary's Island and about two miles east of Innistooskert. I watched her from nightfall until midnight. I did not see her make any signal during that time. She was much larger than the size of the boat which Tadg Brosnan's description had suggested to me that I did not connect her with the arms ship. It did not enter my mind that she was the expected arms ship … I watched the boat until dawn on Good Friday morning but did not see her make any signal during that period.
>
> At daylight she steamed east for Kerry Head. She turned inside Kerry Head, steamed west and dropped anchor north of Innistooskert about 8 a.m. No other vessels appeared in the Bay during the day and night, and none other did appear until 11 a.m. About 11 a.m. a British armed steam trawler came towards the anchored steamer from the east. He came alongside, stayed about an hour and a half, then steamed west for the Blaskets.
>
> About 3 o'clock I saw two big British destroyers coming from the west. One kept well off, the other circled the anchored steamer at a distance of about a mile.
>
> The destroyer was signalling … after a while the destroyer standing off steamed west, the other one slowly followed but the anchored steamer did not move.
>
> On Saturday I met Pat Ashe, who was Lieutenant in the Castlegregory Company, and sounded him to find out if he

> knew anything about the expected arms ship. He did not. He told me two or three men were arrested the previous day after coming ashore from a submarine, but we did not know who they were. I went to Tadg Brosnan to get final instructions. He expressed the view that the steamer I had seen might have been our ship. He instructed me to remain on Leary's Island on Sunday in case the arms ship should come in and to be ready to pilot her in to Fenit Pier.[13]

As we now know, the British discovered the true identity of the *Aud* and eventually three Royal Navy ships surrounded it. Spindler obeyed an order to proceed to Cork Harbour but rather than hand over his cache of arms, he decided to scuttle his ship. As a result, the guns and ammunition that were so vital to the Volunteers' plans for the rebellion ended up at the bottom of Cork Harbour.

Two of the three men O'Leary alluded to as having come ashore on 21 April, Good Friday, were Roger Casement and Robert Montieth. Montieth had helped Casement to form the Irish Brigade on the Continent. They were accompanied by a man called Daniel Bailey, who had been a German prisoner of war and who had signed up for the Irish Brigade. While Montieth and Bailey continued on to Tralee, a clearly ill Casement attempted to hide out in the hope he would be rescued by local Volunteers. The plan did not work out and Casement was eventually detained by the local Royal Irish Constabulary (RIC). In his witness statement, Bernard Reilly, who was a constable stationed in Ardfert at that time, recounted how Casement was apprehended. He recalled how news of the three men landing on the strand was spread through the village by a local girl, Mollie Gorman, who watched them come ashore. The police got to hear of the gossip and Reilly went on to recount what happened next:

> We called to houses making enquiries and continued thus until we came opposite McKenna's Fort. The Sergeant directed me to enter the Fort by the eastern side and he remained on the road smoking. As I entered the Fort a man approached me from the shrubbery. He was a tall gentleman … He wore a beard and had more or less an aristocratic appearance. I think I said 'Good morning' or 'Good day'. I asked 'What are you doing here?'
>
> He appeared to be a little excited. He said, 'I am an Englishman.' 'My name is Richard Morton and I come from Denham in Buckinghamshire.'[14]

Casement then went on to claim he was an author and was writing a book on St Brendan and was gathering some local information for it. It seems the sergeant then came on the scene and questioned Casement. He then asked the stranger to accompany Constable Reilly to the station to which, it seems, Casement raised no objection. On the way they called at Mollie Gorman's house, where she identified Casement as one of the men she saw landing on the strand. When they arrived at the police station they were met by detectives from Tralee and the District Inspector arrived soon after. It wasn't long before Casement was taken to Tralee and then on to Dublin. The authorities there believed they had arrested the leader of any rebellion that might be in the offing and concluded the danger to British rule in Ireland had passed. Their assessment proved to be wide of the mark. Nevertheless, Casement was transported to London, where he was tried for treason and eventually hanged in Pentonville Prison.

The loss of the *Aud* and the capture of Casement were serious and game-changing blows to the plans for the Rising and caused real consternation within the Military Council and the Irish Volunteers leadership and ranks. If the Rising was to go ahead, the Volunteers and the Citizen Army would have no option but to make do with the rifles they had begged, borrowed and stolen since their foundations in 1913, together with the rifles they brought in at Howth and Kilcoole. They also had access to bombs made in various bomb-making factories that had been set up during the previous year. One of the most productive of these outlets was in Kimmage on the Plunkett family estate, Larkfield, which was also used as a Volunteers training camp. As it happened, P.H. Pearse, in his capacity as Volunteers Director of Organisation, had, early in April, issued orders for three days of 'parades and manoeuvres' beginning on Easter Sunday. The order, which was published in the *Irish Volunteers* newspaper on 8 April, read as follows:

General Orders

1. Following the lines of last year, every unit of the Irish Volunteers will hold manoeuvres during the Easter holidays. The object of the manoeuvres is to test the mobilisation with equipment.
2. In Brigade Districts the manoeuvres will be carried out under the orders of the Brigade Commandants. In the case of the Dublin Brigade, the manoeuvres will, as last year be carried out under the direction of the Headquarters General Staff.

3. Each Brigade, Battalion or Company as the case may be, will on or before 1st May next, send to the Director of Organisation a detailed report of the manoeuvres carried out by the Unit.
   Headquarters: 2 Dawson Street, Dublin, 3rd April 1916. P.H. Pearse, Commandant, Director of Organisation.

It was hoped the IRB members within the ranks of the Volunteers would realise the orders were intended to signal the beginning of the rebellion. It was also hoped those in the Volunteers hierarchy who were not in favour of a rebellion at that time like Eoin MacNeill, Bulmer Hobson and The O'Rahilly would not question the order and take it at face value.

At a meeting of Dublin Corporation on 9 April, a Sinn Fein Alderman called Tom Kelly read out a document that he claimed was leaked from Dublin Castle. The document set out in great detail plans drawn up by the authorities to arrest the leaders of the Irish Volunteers, Sinn Fein and the Gaelic League. The document was quickly disowned by those in Dublin Castle. However, the Volunteers leadership and particularly Eoin MacNeill took the document seriously and he ordered his men to prepare to resist any coercive initiatives by the authorities. It transpired the document was a forgery drawn up by the Military Council designed to convince the more moderate of the Volunteers leadership to lend their support to a rebellion. The Military Council then informed some senior Volunteers officers that a rebellion was set to begin on Easter Sunday but declined to inform the Chief of Staff MacNeill and those close to him such as Bulmer Hobson and The O'Rahilly as well as the rank-and file members of the organisation. In his witness statement to the Bureau of Military History, Hobson provided a very revealing account of what next took place when he and MacNeill confronted Pearse about the rumours of a Rising. He went on to say:

> The first definite information I had that an insurrection was to occur in the immediate future was late in the evening of Holy Thursday, when J.J. O'Connell and Eimer Duffy came into my office and told me that an insurrection had been planned for the following Sunday. With them I immediately went to MacNeill's house at Rathfarnham, arriving a considerable time after he had gone to bed.
>
> We got MacNeill up and hastened then to St Enda's to see P.H. Pearse, arriving at about 2 a.m. knocking Pearse up.

> MacNeill, O'Connell and I went in to see Pearse, leaving Duffy, who was not a member of the Executive, outside.
>
> Pearse then admitted that an insurrection was to take place, and told us there was nothing we could do to prevent it. This was in striking contrast to the assurances which he had so recently and so frequently given, that he was acting loyally with his colleagues on the Executive Committee.
>
> MacNeill, O'Connell and I then returned to MacNeill's house, where MacNeill, as Chief of Staff, wrote an Order authorising me to take complete charge in Dublin, and to take all necessary steps to prevent the Volunteers being drawn into taking the initiative in an offensive action against the Government. MacNeill wrote a second Order directing O'Connell to proceed to Cork, and to take complete charge there, with the same object in view.[15]

Hobson then went on to say:

> I arrived early on Good Friday at the Volunteers office after this night-long activity, and immediately my office staff arrived, I set them all to work burning correspondence and lists of names, so that, whatever happened, the authorities should not come into possession of the names of our members throughout the country, and this is one of the actions which contributed to the absence of information on the part of the police during and subsequent to the insurrection.[16]

Apparently after MacNeill, Hobson and O'Connell left St Enda's, Pearse communicated with some of his Military Council colleagues and, early on Good Friday morning, Sean McDermott and Thomas McDonagh called to see MacNeill. It seems they reiterated Pearse's words and confirmed the Rising was inevitable. They somehow convinced MacNeill that he could do nothing to stop the Rising and he, there and then, sent a new Order to Hobson countermanding his Order of some hours previously. He also indicated he was on his way into the Headquarters office. Hobson then recalled:

> I waited for him in vain for several hours, and spent the time in hurrying on the destruction of our papers. I realised by this

> vacillation on MacNeill's part that it was impossible to take further definite action, and at any rate, events by then had got completely out of our control.[17]

Later that afternoon Hobson reluctantly yielded to a request from Sean Tobin, the Chairman of the Leinster Executive of the IRB, to attend a meeting at Martin Conlon's house in Phibsborough. In his statement he recounted what took place when he arrived:

> I was, therefore, not surprised when, as I entered the house, some members, who were armed with revolvers, told me that I was a prisoner, and could not leave the house. I felt that I had done all I could to keep the Volunteers on the course which I believed essential for the success and there was nothing further I could do.[18]

Hobson was held captive until Monday evening, when he was released. He made his way into the city with Sean T. O'Kelly, who asked him to join the Rising. Still believing the Rising was the wrong course of action taken by the Volunteers, he refused O'Kelly's request and instead made his way to Eoin MacNeill's house, where he remained for the following two weeks.

When news of the *Aud*'s capture and her eventual scuttling by Captain Spindler reached Dublin on Easter Saturday, MacNeill once again concluded a rebellion would fail and he moved to cancel it. That night he issued an order cancelling the so called 'manoeuvres' planned for the following day. He arranged for copies of the order to be despatched to Volunteers units throughout the country. It was around midnight when the majority of the Military Council learned of the cancellation and those in the ranks became aware of it when they opened the *Sunday Independent* the following morning, thereby adding to the wave of chaos and confusion.

In an effort to regain control, the Military Council convened in Liberty Hall later that morning. The members quickly agreed the publication of MacNeill's order meant there was very little point in proceeding with that day's plan. The likelihood was that few Volunteers would show up, so the Council decided to strike the next day, Easter Monday, at noon. In his witness statement to the Bureau of Military History, Captain R. Henderson of the Defence Forces and son of Frank Henderson, a senior officer in the Dublin Brigade IRA, laid out what then took place:

> The postponement necessitated immediate efforts by the Council to prevent any possible isolated offensive that Sunday by Volunteers in the provinces who might not have received, or who may have decided to ignore MacNeill's countermand; also to lull the British authorities into believing that the possibility of any immediate outbreak – which the arrival of the Aud and the proposed manoeuvres may have portended – had now passed. Despatches were issued at Liberty Hall about 1 p.m. signed by P.H. Pearse confirming MacNeill's cancellation and were sent by couriers to all main points. The next, and now all-important move, came later; additional couriers were summoned to meet Pearse that evening at the rooms of the Keating branch of the Gaelic League, North Frederick Street. By them went forth the final order for the Rising on Easter Monday.[19]

The result of all the last-minute conflicting orders to the Volunteers inevitably meant nothing less than chaos and confusion, not only in Dublin, but also around the country. In the provinces, important fighting units never saw action during the Rising and it inevitably became a Dublin-centric operation. In the capital itself, the confusion over mobilisation orders meant the early response from the men in the ranks was less than expected. Nevertheless, despite all the problems and confusion, when the Military Council eventually made its decision to stage the Rising on Easter Monday, it did so with a clear sense of purpose and with a definite national vision. Having made the momentous decision to strike out for independence, the men who made up the Military Council were, to a man, determined to bring the Rising to a glorious and patriotic conclusion.

CHAPTER THREE

The 1916 Easter Rising

MONDAY, 24 APRIL

Easter Monday, 24 April 1916, brought a fine and sunny morning, reflecting the bank holiday mood in Dublin. The people of the city were in a relaxed mood and some strolled about taking advantage of the fine weather. At Liberty Hall, hundreds of Irish Volunteers and the men and women of the Irish Citizen Army publicly assembled but their presence caused little in the way of consternation or apprehension to passers-by. Since 1913, the sight of armed men marching around the city had become a common occurrence to most Dubliners. However, unknown to those who passed by Liberty Hall that morning, the assembled Volunteers were very much in earnest as they prepared to march to various points across the city to take over designated buildings prior to the start of hostilities. Unbeknown to the majority of Dubliners, the Rising was only a matter of minutes away and their city and the rest of the country was about to be changed forever.

For the seven men of the IRB Military Council, the day had come to put their best-laid plans for an insurrection into action. Months of secret meetings and planning had brought them to this point and though they shared a sense of apprehension, especially as their plans had gone awry during the previous few days, they were all determined to start the rebellion and see it through to the bitter end. All seven of the men realised that what they were about to unleash upon an unsuspecting city and its population would ultimately cost them their lives, yet bravely they went ahead with the rebellion in the hope that it would inspire others after them to continue the fight for Irish independence.

That morning, Patrick Pearse, accompanied by his brother Willie, left their 'safe house' in Rutland Street and made their way to Liberty Hall but not before running the gauntlet of their sister, Mary Brigid, who urged them to go home and 'leave all the foolishness', and also The O'Rahilly's sister, who bitterly criticised Patrick saying 'this is all your fault'. Undaunted, both men continued on their fateful journey and were never to return home. James Connolly, the proposed Vice-President of the soon to be proclaimed Irish Republic and Commandant General, Dublin Division of the Army of the Irish Republic, led his Irish Citizen Army on an early route march that morning to St Stephen's Green and back to Liberty Hall via Dublin Castle. He intended to show the authorities that his small force was capable of acting independently of the Volunteers. Back at Liberty Hall, Connolly delivered his last public speech and told his men: 'You will not lay down your arms until you have struck a blow for Ireland.' He was, however, very disappointed by the turnout and was very pessimistic about the Rising's outcome, even telling his trade union colleague William O'Brien that they were 'going out to be slaughtered'.

During the morning, members of the Military Council and the officers and men and women of the Headquarters Staff gathered at Liberty Hall, where they agreed the final details of the plan for the Rising. Unfortunately, the numbers who did turn up fell far short of what had been expected mainly due to the confusion caused by MacNeill's countermand order of the previous Saturday night. Reports quickly came in to Pearse and Connolly that the turnout was much the same at other battalion centres around the city. It was clear to the leaders of the Rising that the pre-arranged positions around the city would not be manned adequately to ensure a prolonged defence. Nevertheless, the die had been cast and the decision to proceed with the Rising was not going to be rescinded.

At 11.50 a.m. a contingent of Irish Volunteers, Irish Citizen Army personnel and members of the 'Kimmage Garrison' gathered to ready themselves for the Rising. All told there were 150 men, some of whom were really not that well armed but still determined to do their part for Ireland. Nearby was a single cab loaded up with ammunition and explosives. As the men readied themselves to move off towards Sackville Street (now O'Connell St), a single individual in overalls carrying a bag of tools moved off quietly to disengage telegraph and telephone lines in the immediate area. James Connolly ordered the column to attention and into a quick march, which seemingly did not concern members of the public who happened to be in the vicinity at that time.

On arrival in front of the Imperial Hotel on Sackville Street, Connolly ordered the column to turn left and charge the GPO and the majority of the men entered the building through the main door. They took a few prisoners and ordered the post office staff and members of the public out of the building. About a dozen of the men entered through the door on Henry Street, allowing them to take control of the upstairs level. A small selected party of men rushed to the roof, while down at ground level every vantage point was manned. All the glass in the windows was smashed and books as well as other available materials were commandeered to be used as protection at the windows. Tom Clarke and Sean McDermott travelled together from Liberty Hall to the GPO, where they teamed up with Connolly, Plunkett and Pearse. On the steps of the GPO, Pearse, accompanied by his four Military Council comrades, read out the Proclamation of the Irish Republic watched by bemused members of the public. From that moment on the seven members of the Military Council effectively became the Provisional Government with Pearse as its President.

Clarke was clearly elated that at long last he was getting the chance to fight the British on Irish soil and, for him, it was the culmination of his life's work. Clarke's companion that morning, Sean MacDermott, radiated a real sense of happiness as the rebels took the GPO. Like his mentor, Clarke, the rebellion was also the culmination of MacDermott's life's work and one comrade later recalled his 'titanic' performance during the week of fighting was on a par with that of Connolly. The most flamboyant of the Military Council members was undoubtedly Joseph Plunkett and he left his sick bed on Good Friday to prepare for the Rising. On Easter Monday morning, Michael Collins helped him into his uniform, though he had to maintain a heavy bandage around his neck where tubercular glands had been removed during a recent operation. He was driven to Liberty Hall, where he joined the headquarters garrison behind James Connolly on the march to the GPO.

The two remaining members of the Military Council, Thomas McDonagh and Éamonn Ceannt, did not take up positions in the GPO. McDonagh issued the mobilisation orders to the entire Dublin Brigade and set the Rising in motion. He then joined the Second Battalion at St Stephen's Green and, at noon, he led his men to the Jacob's Biscuit Factory. Éamonn Ceannt joined his Battalion in Dolphin's Barn and proceeded to the South Dublin Union, a sprawling 50-acre complex, with just over one hundred men under his command. The Union bordered the Royal Hospital, which housed the British GOC and was near to the Royal Barracks and Kingsbridge Railway station, giving it a major strategic value. Other buildings taken that morning included the Four Courts, occupied by Edward Daly's First Battalion, Dublin Brigade, and the Mendicity Institute, which was occupied by Sean Heuston and his small band of men from 'D' Company, First Battalion,

Dublin Brigade. The 3rd Battalion of the Volunteers under the command of Éamon de Valera occupied Boland's Mills, situated about a mile south-east of the GPO. Just after midday, Michael Mallin and his Citizen Army cleared St Stephen's Green and occupied some nearby buildings, including the College of Surgeons.

At around 12.30 p.m. the republican tricolour was hoisted on the roof of the GPO at the Henry Street corner, while at the Princes Street side of the building a green banner bearing the words 'Irish Republic' was raised. Inside the building the sound of breaking glass could be heard above the general commotion. Foodstuffs that had been stockpiled began to arrive and were supplemented over the following days by raids on nearby hotels, warehouses and shops. Outside on the street some curious citizens of Dublin gathered, though they were unsure about what was actually taking place inside the GPO. They must also have noticed the absence of any members of the Dublin Metropolitan Police, all of whom had been recalled to their respective stations. Around that time, some Fianna Eireann boys arrived and, despite their young ages, were granted entry to the GPO, where they remained part of the garrison for the duration of the rebellion.

At 12.45 p.m. P.H. Pearse, in his capacity as President of the newly proclaimed Republic, emerged into Sackville Street and read the Proclamation of Independence. A few cheers rose up from the crowd watching on but most onlookers were somewhat bemused by what was unfolding before their eyes. Some, no doubt, were resentful of the fact their peaceful Bank Holiday was being inconveniently interrupted. It wasn't long before a group of Volunteers were despatched to take over Reis's shop at the corner of Abbey Street, where a wireless was installed and operated during the course of the conflict. Some Volunteers were despatched to hold the approaches from the Bridge (now O'Connell Bridge) leading onto Sackville Street while other men were sent to various points in the vicinity of the GPO for the same purpose. A barricade was thrown across Lower Abbey Street in the hope of impeding any advance of British forces from the north side of the city. Newspaper rolls, bicycles, furniture, all taken from nearby warehouses and shops, were used in the barricades. The upper stories of houses on Henry Street directly across from the GPO were also occupied. Copies of the proclamation were distributed around the city and telephone communications were disrupted. This forced a British Army officer in civilian clothes to cycle to Kingston Wireless Telegraph Station to transmit a message at 12.30 p.m. It began: 'Armed Sinn Fein Rising in Dublin today … Troops called out.'

Because of MacNeill's countermand order, the numbers mobilised were considerably fewer than anticipated, which forced the abandonment of some of the original plans, most notably the intention to capture Trinity College. However, at noon, a small group of Volunteers and some Na Fianna boys attacked the Magazine Fort in the Phoenix Park and disarmed the guards. They had intended to seize weapons and blow up the building as a signal that the rebellion had started. The rebels did manage to set off a small explosion but it did little in the way of damage. A force of Volunteers and Irish Citizen Army men and women under the leadership of Sean Connolly attempted to take Dublin Castle but failed. One policeman, Constable James O'Brien, was shot dead in the attack and the Under-Secretary, Matthew Nathan, helped close the Castle gates when he heard shots being fired.

Helena Molony, a member of the Irish Citizen Army, recalled in her statement to the Bureau of Military History what took place at the Castle gate and the subsequent events at the City Hall:

> I with my girls followed Sean Connolly and his party right up to the Castle Gate … just then a policeman came out and, seeing our determination, he thought it was a parade and that it would probably go up Ship Street. When Connolly went to go past him, the Sergeant put his arm out, and Connolly shot him dead. When the military guard saw that it was serious, he pulled the gates to … The sentry went into his box, and began firing … it breaks my heart –and all our hearts – that we did not get in.
>
> We would have captured the Under-Secretary having lunch in the Castle.[20]

Having failed to gain access to the Castle, the onus was on Sean Connolly to keep the action going and so he veered around holding his gun and ordered his charges to enter the adjacent City Hall. Molony, in her statement recounted what took place next:

> We met no opposition at the City Hall because it was a Bank Holiday, and the place was empty … I remember we climbed over railings; but I don't remember any difficulty at the doors. We took up various positions … my idea was to find out where there was a kitchen, and where there was a suitable place for a hospital. There was a kitchen upstairs.

> The firing had opened and there was a return of fire from the Castle. It was very heavy for the first hour. There was one young British soldier killed in Ship Street. About half-past-one Connolly sent me over to the GPO for reinforcements. I had no difficulty in getting in to the GPO. There was great excitement there. At the GPO I simply gave the request for reinforcements. I saw James Connolly himself. He said: 'We will send them as soon as we can.' I went back to the City Hall. Soon after that, at two o'clock, Sean Connolly, who was on the roof, was hit by a stray bullet and killed.[21]

Connolly was attended to by Dr Kathleen Lynn, a Captain in the Citizen Army, but there was little she could do for him as he was bleeding profusely from his stomach. Molony said an Act of Contrition into his ear as there was no priest among the party. To make matters worse, Connolly's younger brother, Matt, who was only 15 years of age, was also on the roof and Molony membered him crying bitterly as he watched Sean dying. The small Citizen Army group held out until evening, when a large group of British soldiers, probably numbering around one hundred men, stormed the building, coming in from Ship Street. Molony went on to recall how:

> At about half-past eight or nine o'clock, when nightfall came, there was a sudden bombardment … there were machine gun bullets pouring in. From the ceiling the plaster began to fall. It was dangerous. The bombardment went on and on. I had gone upstairs on a couple of occasions to see that the girls were attending to three or four wounded we had there – perhaps more. At this time, the firing was very intense.
>
> A window was smashed at the back, and then we knew they were pouring in.
>
> A voice said: 'Surrender in the name of the King'. 'Surrender', was called out again.
>
> Then we were taken.[22]

Molony and her female comrades were brought to the Castle, through the Castle grounds, and into Ship Street Barracks, where they were all put into a very old, dirty room and kept captive for eight days. Eventually, they were transferred to Kilmainham Jail. While there the women heard the executions shots being fired every morning as the perceived leaders of the

Rising met their deaths. The women were then moved to Mountjoy Jail and, in due course, were sent to English jails.

Once the Rising was under way the rebels expected a quick response from the British but Dublin Castle authorities only had four hundred troops available to confront the insurgents. They decided the priorities were to mobilise mass reinforcements, gather information on rebel strength, location and arms levels and to identify important strategic positions including Dublin Castle. The rebels failed to take control of the Telephone Exchange in Crown Alley as planned, though they did manage to sever many telecommunication lines across sixty locations in the city and in the suburbs. News emerged about fighting that took place at the north-western corner of the sprawling 50-acre South Dublin Union, where a group of men from the Royal Irish Regiment came into contact with an outpost of Éamonn Ceannt's men. The British took some casualties and then regrouped to launch several assaults before they forced their way inside and the small rebel force surrendered. The Union complex itself remained in the hands of the rebels for the duration of the Rising.

During the morning, a Citizen Army unit under the command of Michael Mallin occupied St Stephen's Geen and began digging trenches. Around 1.15 p.m. a troop of Lancers appeared on Sackville Street and staged a reckless charge past Nelson's Pillar, coming under fire from riflemen who were on the roof of the GPO and inside the building. Four Lancers lay dead after the volleys of shots. The remaining Lancers withdrew to the cover of the Parnell Monument, while their dead comrades were taken to Jervis Street hospital. Also, in the early afternoon, there was a series of communications between the GPO and the outlying posts that confirmed the general situation was deemed to be fairly satisfactory.

During the build-up to the Rising, arms and ammunition had been stored in a pavilion in Father Matthew Park in Fairview. The Companies of the 2nd Battalion were designated to stand guard over the cache and their mission on Easter Monday was to transport it into St Stephen's Green for use in the GPO and other locations. Around nine o'clock on Monday morning, Frank Henderson, Captain of 'F' Company of the 2nd Battalion, received a note ordering his men to parade with all arms and equipment to St Stephen's Green at ten o'clock. Feeling it was a very short time to get everyone to St Stephen's Green, Henderson decided all he could do was his best. Eventually, after getting around to most of the men, he returned home to get himself organised. On the way home, he passed Tom Clarke on the Tolka Bridge at Ballybough walking towards the city. Henderson, in his witness statement to the Bureau of Military History, recalled how he decided to send half of 'F' Company over to St Stephen's Green and he kept the remainder of the men in Father Matthew Park to guard the large amount of ammunition, equipment and medical supplies being held there. Other companies, under the command of his brother, Leo, and Thomas Weafer, took the same action.

The senior officers who were in the park held a conference as to whether they should lead the remaining men into city. Thomas Weafer travelled into the GPO to converse with James Connolly and get instructions from him. It wasn't long before word came back from Weafer to prepare to march into the city. Henderson and his fellow officers in the park quickly mobilised the men and a horse lorry was commandeered to carry the heavy equipment and supplies. With the men reassembled, Captain Weafer, on his return from the GPO formed the column, made up of about 100 men, for the march into battle. Henderson recalled as they were preparing to march into the city there was a:

> great stream of refugees coming out from the city. It was a very pitiful sight in many ways, because there were families carrying a few belongings, hastily put together. Many of them showed traces of terror. Some of these people gave us heartening news, saying that our people had the city and had already defeated the British in a couple of battles; others told us the direct opposite.[23]

When the column reached the junction of Bayview Avenue with Ballybough Road on its march into the city, news came through that British forces were moving along Summerhill and were about to launch an attack. Captain Weafer ordered Henderson and the men he had under his command at the back of the column to seize a position overlooking the Tolka Bridge at Ballybough. Henderson seized a two-storey house, part of which, was occupied by Gilbey's Ltd, as a shop and wine store. The house was also occupied by an old lady and her daughter, who were turned out, and it had a commanding view of Tolka Bridge and another window allowed for a view of the approach from Fairview. Henderson recalled while they heard heavy gunfire, they could not see any British troops. However, by the time the house had been readied for a fight, the gunfire ceased. There was nothing but silence and not a soul was on the streets.

Having lost contact with Captain Weafer, Henderson decided to keep his men where they were and hope to get in contact with GHQ. After a short while, his brother, Leo, arrived with his men. He had been to the GPO but James Connolly ordered him to take his men back and act as a reinforcement to Frank's garrison. He also ordered them to await further orders. It wasn't long before they were joined by Oscar Traynor, who confirmed Connolly's order to remain where they were. Traynor also confirmed the GPO, all of O'Connell Street and some adjoining streets were in the hands of the rebels. He also confirmed Captain Weafer and his men had arrived at the GPO and that he had spoken to him at a barricade in Abbey Street, near the Abbey Theatre.

In time Henderson's garrison was joined by men who had lost contact with their own companies. With it being clear that GHQ intended for the garrison to remain in Fairview, Henderson decided to occupy another house, so as to gain complete command of the bridge over the Tolka River. He decided on Lambe's public house, which gave the garrison a complete view of the approach from the direction of Drumcondra via the Richmond Road and it was about 50 yards from Gilbey's. The three officers, Henderson, his brother, Leo, and Oscar Traynor, all took up positions in Gilbey's, while Sean Russell, Adjutant of 'B' Company, was sent to take charge of the men occupying Lambe's.

Expecting to be in situ for some time, the officers set about finding food for the men. They sent some Volunteers to a nearby butcher to get some fresh meat, for which they offered to pay. The butcher refused to give the men any meat so they just took what they needed by force. They also held up a bread van and took whatever bread they needed but issued the friendly van driver with a receipt in the name of the Irish Republic. The garrison was joined later in the evening by some men from 'F' Company who had been disconnected from it during the day. Early on Tuesday morning they were joined by Harry Colley and Harry Boland and their presence was a welcome one because Henderson saw both men as individuals who led by example and were of a cheerful disposition, which was all important at a time of rising tension.

As it happened, Harry Colley had a story to tell his 'F' Company comrades. He had been part of a later mobilisation which came together at 2 p.m. on Easter Monday in Father Matthew Park. Under the command of Captain Liam Breen, the men had orders to escort arms, ammunition and medical supplies into the GPO. Once the march into the city began, word was soon put around that British troops were approaching from Dollymount.

Colley and his unit marched down Philipsburg Avenue, Fairview Strand and over Ballybough Bridge and stopped on the corner of Spring Garden Street on Ballybough Road. It was there the men in the first section were ordered to take possession of O'Meara's public house at the corner of the North Strand and Annesley Place. In his witness statement to the Bureau of Military History, Colley recounted what then took place:

> from the roof of the public house, they engaged the approaching military when they reached Annesley Bridge. I was informed that the military took cover down the East Wall but pushed out the two machine guns and crews on to Annesley Bridge and opened fire on our men. With his first shot one of our men got one of the machine guns and put it out of action. Immediately this happened the machine gunners also retired down East Wall. It was apparently decided our men should not pursue them as we were much weaker in strength …[24]

Colley and his comrades made their way along Ballybough Road to Summerhill Bridge, where he and a number of other men, under the command of Captain Breen, took over a large tenement building overlooking the bridge. In the process of doing so they turned the occupants out on to the street. It was Colley's and his comrades first unpleasant duty of the rebellion, though he said they carried out the task in a very kindly manner.

After about fifteen minutes in the tenement building, Colley and his comrades were ordered to accompany a lorry carrying ammunition and medical materials into the city. Under the command of Captain Breen, they made their way into Liberty Hall. In his statement Colley continued his recollection of the day's events:

> We were now under the command of the late Captain Breen and we proceeded down Summerhill Parade, Portland Road, North Strand, Talbot Street, to Liberty Hall.
>
> I remember seeing a number of policemen marching to Store Street Police Station, apparently being withdrawn off the streets, while we were passing through Talbot Street.
>
> At Liberty Hall we joined in with some Citizen Army men and a convoy of three or four carts laden with cabbage and other vegetables which had been commandeered at the North

> Wall, and proceeded to the GPO. There, James Connolly inspected us outside the GPO, and we then proceeded back to Fairview. This would be about 4 o'clock in the evening.[25]

As the day progressed the republican women of Cumann na mBan, Inghinidhe na hEireann and the Citizen Army became active. As arranged, the women mobilised in Wellington Street at noon. Disbanded temporarily, they were called in later in the afternoon. Some reported to Commandant Daly at Church Street, the others to Commandant Connolly at the GHQ in the General Post Office. The women posted to the GPO were assigned to nursing and kitchen duties as well as some outposts in Sackville Street. Some of the women were selected for despatch duties. When the medical supplies arrived at the GPO from Fairview, the medical personnel organised a 'red cross' station. Bedding was commandeered from the Metropole Hotel and, later in the week, additional supplies were brought in from the Imperial Hotel and Clery's Department store. During the afternoon the windows of the second floor of the GPO were barricaded and a special telephonic connection was established between Commandant Connolly on the ground floor and the men occupying the roof. The armoury was set up in what was the general sorting room of the post office.

The opening day of the Rising saw the chaos grow as the hours passed, leaving the citizenry of the city in a state of shock and bewilderment. More and more reports came in of incidents taking place in the city centre and the suburbs. Rebels took over buildings from very early in the afternoon; for example, just across from City Hall two supporting positions were taken in Parliament Street at the Mail and Express building and Henry & James Outfitters. At 1.30 p.m. a British counterattack took place at Ship Street, where there was close-quarter action between rebels and some 200 troops. Just before two o'clock in the afternoon intense fighting broke out on the Western Quays. The Royal Dublin Fusiliers suffered casualties under repeated volleys from across the river at the Mendicity Institute, where rebels were holed up under the command of Captain Sean Heuston. Around that time a policeman was shot dead in St Stephen's Green, where trenches were being dug by the rebels. Over at the South Dublin Union, a contingent of British troops came under fire from members of Éamonn Ceannt's unit holding the building and its surrounds.

By 2.30 p.m. the Marrowbone Lane Distillery, which was in the hands of the rebels, was on fire. By 4 p.m. British troop reinforcements were pouring into Kingsbridge Railway Station and, half an hour later, there was serious gunfire around Sackville Street. The spectacle was watched by hundreds of civilians seemingly oblivious to the dangers they had placed themselves in. By 5 p.m. the fighting had spread to Northumberland Road as well as along the Dublin–Kingstown railway line. Heavy fighting also took place in and around City Hall. The first reports of deaths started to come in around 6 p.m., including that of a young nurse in the South Dublin Union and a civilian on St Stephen's Green. There were also reports of civilians turning on the rebels by throwing stones and anything else they could lay their hands on at them.

Looting was widespread, most especially in and around Sackville Street. Some of the rebels fired over the heads of the looters in efforts to stop them in their tracks and force them off the streets. Just after 9 p.m. City Hall was beginning to fall into the hands of the British Army, while there were reports of sniping around Beggar's Bush Barracks. By 11 p.m. the southern part of the city was in darkness after the Gas Works on South Lotts Road was overrun by rebels who dismantled the machinery. Come midnight, the city of Dublin was engulfed in a conflict most of its citizens had not expected to ever witness. The question most were asking was, how long it was going to last and how much more chaos was in store?

CHAPTER FOUR

The Easter Rising

TUESDAY, 25 APRIL TO WEDNESDAY, 26 APRIL

Throughout the early hours of the following day, Tuesday, outposts were extended and fortified by the men occupying them and buildings were linked up by boring through walls. The authorities quickly declared martial law and thousands of British troops arrived to take up positions across the city. At 6 a.m. Volunteers at Annesley Bridge attempted and failed to blow up one of the Great Northern Railway bridges in a bid to obstruct any British advance from north of the city centre. A decision was then made by Captain Vincent Poole of the Citizen Army, who was commanding a unit that had taken over the Dublin Manure Company offices at Annesley Bridge, to blow up the railway line. In his witness statement, Harry Colley, one of the men ordered to carry out the task, recalled how they carried out the order:

> About 6 o'clock Harry Boland, who had been, I think, on duty somewhere in the meantime, the brothers Whelan who had accompanied him and myself were directed to blow up the railway line beyond the slob lands. None of us knew anything about gelignite. I certainly had never even seen a stick of it previously and I think my three companions were in the same position. Poole told us to dig a little hole in the ground under the tracks, to place the gelignite in it as he demonstrated for us, cover it again with soil, light the fuse and clear out. We were told it was a three-minute fuse. We did as directed, and in running down the embankment to get away I was so tired that when I tried to jump the small barbed wire fence at the foot of the embankment I muffed it and tore my thigh badly

> with the barbed wire. I had only got about twenty yards when the explosion occurred. The job was a failure though we had carried out our instructions to the letter.[26]

From About 4 a.m. on Tuesday morning the rebels in St Stephen's Green came under intense fire from British machine guns and rifles. The British had taken over the Shelbourne Hotel and the machine gun was fired almost non-stop from the fourth floor. By 8.30 a.m. the rebels had withdrawn from the Green into the Royal College of Surgeons and their snipers began returning fire from the roof of the building. Around 7 a.m. the Volunteers contingent that had marched overnight from Maynooth and had taken cover for a while in Glasnevin Cemetery arrived at the GPO. They were immediately ordered, together with men of the Hibernian Rifles, to make their way to the City Hall to reinforce the men there. It seems they got as far as the Exchange Hotel on Parliament Street, where they encountered and beat off attacks by the British. Short of ammunition and, with no hope of reinforcements, they eventually got back to the GPO that evening. Around 7.30 a.m., James Connolly ordered barbed wire to be erected across Sackville Street from each end of the GPO to keep curious citizens from getting too near the building. Around that time the British finally recaptured City Hall and cleared it of Citizen Army personnel, though the rebels in the outpost across the street were still holding out.

About an hour later a telegraphic operator from the Hibernian Rifles realised that wires connecting Dublin to some provincial centres were intact and he was able to communicate with the south and west of the country. As it transpired, the news from the provinces was not good and there was little indication the rebellion had spread outside the capital. The news was conveyed to Pearse and Connolly and, though disappointed, both men still hoped the provinces would join the rebellion in due course. The rebel positions in Boland's Mills and Jacob's Biscuit Factory saw no early action and remained quiet for the duration of the conflict. However, the 1st Battalion garrison at the Four Courts under the command of Commandant Ned Daly very quickly saw action when they fired on Lancers transporting munitions from the Docks at North Wall to the Magazine Fort in the Phoenix Park. The Four Courts and the surrounding streets such as Church Street, North King Street and North Brunswick Street saw some of the most intense fighting during the week of the conflict.

Tuesday saw some skirmishes at the South Dublin Union and there was serious looting in the centre of the city. In fact, it was so bad special squads of Volunteers were sent out to confront the looters and deal with the issue. Shots had to be fired over the heads of the looters to compel them to desist. The looters also set some buildings on fire and attempted to remove various items from the barricades that the Volunteers had set up. Tuesday also saw the arrest of the activist and pacificist Francis Sheehy-Skeffington in Portobello as he attempted to organise citizens to prevent the looting of shops and businesses. Later in the week, he was shot dead, together with five other civilians, by British troops under the command of Captain J.C. Bowen-Colthurst.

During Tuesday morning two rebel outposts in Grantham Street fell to the Royal Irish Rifles, who were advancing towards the city centre. British troops around Portobello Bridge came under rebel sniper fire from towers in Jacob's Biscuit Factory. The towers provided the snipers with a clear line of sight and there was constant firing between them and Dublin Castle. Over in the South Dublin Union, a contingent of British infantry men, unable to dislodge the rebels, pulled out, under fire from members of the Volunteers 4th Battalion. Meanwhile, in Sackville Street, sniper firing continued and, though it was deserted of civilians, a number of bodies could be seen lying here and there. In the early afternoon a gun battle erupted near the City Hall as the Royal Dublin Fusiliers attempted to storm the Evening Mail offices occupied by the rebels. The Fusiliers took a number of casualties before being forced back into the Castle, from where a machine gun was deployed. British troops also attempted to flush out rebels on Marrowbone Lane on Tuesday afternoon, where again they suffered a number of casualties.

Around mid-afternoon artillery fire erupted on the North Circular Road where 18-pounder guns were used in an attempt to dislodge Volunteers from the 1st Battalion from a barricade built close to Charleville Road. Over in Broadstone, the Dublin Fusiliers in the Railway Terminus came under attack from other members of the Volunteers 1st Battalion. The Fusiliers were able to beat off the rebel onslaught. Meanwhile, in St Stephen's Green, fighting continued, with the British bringing in a Vickers machine gun and a Lewis gun. Sometime around 8 p.m. the Dublin Fusiliers eventually took control of the Mail and Express office from the rebels and then advanced into Parliament Street. It seems they were not aware the Exchange Hotel on the street was occupied by rebels and they walked into an ambush. Some reports claimed more than twenty soldiers lay on the ground either dead or wounded as the rebels retreated across the river to the north side of the city.

As noted earlier, Frank Henderson and his fellow Volunteers in 'F' Company of the 2nd Battalion in the Dublin Brigade had taken over two buildings in Fairview on Easter Monday as the fighting raged a short distance away in the city centre. Henderson, in his witness statement, confirmed James Connolly directed the unit to remain where it was until new instructions were issued to it. There was nothing for the men to do but sit tight and wait to be called into the city centre at some stage during Tuesday. On Tuesday morning, Henderson sent scouts out to check for any enemy movements in the area as there had been some rumours overnight the British were advancing on Dublin from the north. Henderson ordered scouts to cycle out as far as Malahide and it was there they observed the arrival of British troops. Later that day, the scouts observed two contingents of troops advancing towards the city, one along the Malahide Road in the direction of Fairview and the other along the Swords Road towards Drumcondra.

Henderson informed GHQ. of everything the scouts were reporting in relation to the movement of British troops. About six o'clock on Tuesday they reported two columns of troops were closing in on Fairview. Henderson, in an address to his men, ordered them to prepare a defence of their position as a confrontation appeared to be imminent. He claimed his men were all in good spirits and were determined to put up a good show. A messenger was sent into the GPO to appraise James Connolly of the situation. He sent back a reply ordering Henderson and his men to make their way into the GPO, if at all possible. He also asked Henderson to get the same message to the Volunteers under the command of Captain Craven at the North Strand.

Acting on the order, Henderson formed his men up, all sixty-six of them, outside Gilbey's with their arms, ammunition and equipment and began the march into the GPO. They eventually joined up with Craven and his twenty-five men but were forced to take a circuitous route as they had to avoid British troops who were massing at various junctions. Henderson sent scouts ahead of the main body of men and they were able to find the best way into the city centre. It seems the British could have opened fire on the Volunteers at some point along the way but decided against it, most probably because Craven had somehow earlier managed to capture a number of British soldiers and he had brought them along with him.

In his statement, Henderson recalled the march into Sackville Street:

> We proceeded along Ballybough Road. I marched at the head of the column, with Lieutenant Oscar Traynor on one side of me and Captain Leo Henderson on the other.
>
> As far as I can recollect Sean Russell was in the rear. We were preceded by scouts on bicycles. These were young boys

> who were able to cycle around without exciting suspicion, and they kept us informed of the best line of advance ... The danger point in Marlborough Street was the crossing over at Talbot Street, on account of the British forces being in the G.N.R. station. However, we got across without any casualties, turned right into Sackville Place, at the Sackville Street end of which we encountered the barricades which had been erected by the Republican forces.[27]

When the Volunteers arrived into Sackville Street, firing was incoming from the British stationed around the Parnell Monument and the Bridge direction. Oscar Traynor dashed across the road in a zig-zag fashion to the GPO and returned a little later with orders for the men to make their way into the building in small groups. They managed to do so and gathered under the portico of the GPO without suffering any casualties. Henderson, in his statement, recalled what happened next:

> When we arrived under the portico where the front entrance then was, we were fired on by our forces who were in possession of the Imperial Hotel over Clery's. This was apparently due to the fact that we still had prisoners in British uniforms, and these had to dash across the road, the same as ourselves, and some of the men who were at the windows assumed the British were attacking. A few of our men were slightly injured, and some confusion ensued as some of our men replied, without waiting for an order, to the fire which was coming from the Imperial Hotel. At this point, James Connolly rushed out of the GPO stood out on the road, held out his arms and shouted, to the men in the Imperial Hotel, that we were friendly troops and not to fire any more. The firing then stopped. James Connolly was dressed in the dark green uniform of his Citizen Army. We then proceeded into the GPO, where we were addressed by Pearse, who was also in uniform. Pearse stood up on a large table in the public hall of the GPO, congratulated us on what we had done, and prepared us for what was to come. We were all deeply moved by his address.[28]

Connolly then took charge and sent about ten of Henderson's men across the road to reinforce the garrison in the Imperial Hotel and ordered some twenty men to the Metropole Hotel under the command of Oscar Traynor. Henderson and his brother, Leo, together with another twenty or so men were ordered into Henry Street, where they were to enter the building flanking the GPO. They were also ordered to erect two barricades, one at the Sackville Street side of Moore Street and the other at the far side of Moore Street. They were also ordered to enter McDowell's jewellery shop and Bewley's provision shop and make sure any civilians who happened to be there were sent away. Once all that was done, they were to bore through the walls to create a passageway directly back into the GPO.

The Imperial Hotel, which was situated above Clery's Department Store, was the focus of intense activity on Sackville Street for the duration of the fighting. On the Tuesday morning, Frank Thornton and his Citizen Army unit had occupied the hotel on the order of James Connolly. In his witness statement to the Bureau of Military History, Thornton recalled his entry into the hotel:

> I took over the Imperial Hotel about mid-day on Tuesday and proceeded to bore through walls connecting the buildings on our left and right. Later on, that night we connected Brennan Whitmore, who was on my right flank, towards Talbot St.[29]

Thornton and his Citizen Army unit spent the rest of the Rising in the hotel with orders to hold it until it was either blown down by shell fire or burned down. During their time there they came under a constant barrage from the British. As mentioned above, some members of Frank Henderson's unit arrived on Tuesday night to bolster the numbers holding the hotel. Included in Henderson's unit were Noel Lemass, brother of the future Taoiseach, Sean Lemass, and Ned Boland, brother of Harry Boland. That same night, Thornton recalled, other men arrived from the GPO to requisition blankets, mattresses and food. He also recalled how:

> a communication wire had been fixed by us to the GPO and messages were hauled backwards and forwards across the street. The box was riddled with machine gun bullets in its passing back and forth, and the rope severed later in the week.[30]

While in the hotel, Thornton also received an order from Connolly to erect the Irish Citizen Army flag, 'The Plough and the Stars', on the roof of the hotel, a task he managed to carry out even though he was under constant fire from the enemy.

While all that was going on it was relatively quiet in Sackville Street, with no danger from enemy gunfire. Henderson detailed some of his men to fill all available vessels with water and other men were sent out to collect all the food they could find in the Henry Street shops. They found so much they were able to send a lot of it over to the GPO. They also procured tools to help with the boring of the walls and managed to take large rolls of cloth from a tailor's shop to use in the barricades. By that time, looters had again gathered and Henderson ordered shots to be fired over their heads. However, as the crowd was not fazed by that, Henderson ordered his men to fix bayonets and charge the crowd but on no account use the bayonets. The fixing of bayonets had the desired impact and the looters dispersed. All of the men worked through the night and their task was made easier by the fact that some of the them were builders by trade. By Wednesday morning they had bored a passage between Bewley's and the GPO.

Throughout the early hours of Wednesday morning machine gun and rifle fire grew in intensity in the area around Trinity College, Tara Street and Amiens Street. Eventually, a fierce barrage swept through Sackville Street, Marlborough Street and Lower Abbey Street, which the rebels bravely countered. Meanwhile, in the GPO some men were busy making bombs but were running out of fuses and detonators. A decision was made to send a number of men out in a car to an establishment on Bride Street that sold those items. They somehow managed to reach the premises and return to the GPO with the fuses and detonators on a journey that took them past Trinity College and St Stephen's Green, where danger lurked at every turn.

Wednesday morning saw the murder of Francis Sheehy-Skeffington and two journalists, Thomas Dixon and Patrick McIntyre, in Portobello Barracks by Captain J.C. Bowen Colthurst. The incident proved to be one of the most controversial incidents of the conflict. Bowen-Colthurst was later found guilty of the murders in a military trial but was declared insane, much to the anger of very many people. Around midday, the Volunteers garrison holding out in the Mendicity Institute, under the command of Sean Heuston, surrendered in what was the first real blow to the rebel cause. A force of about three to four hundred Royal Dublin Fusiliers surrounded the building and opened up with machine gun and rifle fire as well as grenades. Hopelessly outnumbered, the Volunteers had no alternative but to surrender. Unfortunately, as they came out of the building with one of their number carrying a white flag, a distant British sniper shot and wounded one of Heuston's men. Heuston, unfortunately, had on his person an order from

James Connolly and that document eventually sealed his fate in front of a subsequent military tribunal, which ordered his execution.

On Wednesday the British decided to bring up their heavy artillery and use it on the major rebel strongholds. It wasn't long before Liberty Hall came under a bombardment and the arrival of the gunboat *Helga* on the Liffey was an ominous sign for the rebels. Very quickly it began to shell a number of rebel strongholds, including the GPO. The pressure on the rebels was increased with the arrival of a large contingent of Sherwood Foresters at Kingstown (Dun Laoghaire) and they wasted no time in making for the city centre. However, on their way, they encountered the Volunteers in what turned out to be the largest battle of the Rising.

As the Foresters approached Mount Street Bridge on their march into the city centre, they were confronted by rifle fire from seventeen Volunteers occupying four posts commanding the approach. The first of these was the house at No. 25 Northumberland Road, which was occupied by Captain Michael Malone and James Grace and controlled the junction with Haddington Road. Closer to the Grand Canal was St Stephens Parochial Hall, which was occupied by four other Volunteers, while seven of their comrades occupied the seven-storey Clanwilliam House on the far side of the canal, overlooking Mount Street Bridge. Four other Volunteers were positioned at Robert's Yard, a building contractor's premises located at the corner of Lower Grand Canal Street. The plan also called for additional supporting fire from the men in Boland's Mills, where Éamon de Valera and his 3rd Battalion were positioned. The northern approach to the area was protected by posts based at Boland's Bakery, the Railway Workshops and Horgan's shop.

The Foresters, numbering around 1,700 men, had advanced through Ballsbridge and encountered their first gunfire from rebels at the Junction of Haddington Road and Northumberland Road. Inexplicably, because alternative routes could have been taken, the Foresters made a number of charges, which were easily beaten back by the rebels. Malone and Grace, in 25 Northumberland Road, kept up their barrage until the Foresters eventually overwhelmed them. Malone lost his life and Grace was captured. Once that house had been secured, the Foresters then moved forward but came under fire from the Volunteers in the Parochial Hall and Clanwilliam House. The men in the Parochial House used up all their ammunition and then made a tactical withdrawal but not before inflicting more casualties. The Volunteers in Clanwilliam House continued to fight for some hours before finally succumbing to the overwhelming odds against them. Three

Volunteers died and the house caught fire. All in all, the battle lasted some ten hours, with the British taking 224 casualties wounded and killed in their costliest single engagement of the conflict.

As Wednesday came to a close the rebellion was taking its toll on the citizens of Dublin, all of whom had their lives and routines severely upended. Food supplies began to run low and workplaces and businesses were badly impacted. In a significant military move, Sir John Maxwell was sent from England to take charge of British troops in Ireland. His mission was to put an end to the rebellion and he and the authorities were granted power to court martial any prisoners taken into custody. During the day, Liberty Hall came under a constant artillery barrage from the *Helga*, which was still on the Liffey. Buildings on Lower Sackville Street and on Lower Abbey Street also felt the full force of the gunboat's might. Fighting erupted on St Stephen's Green between Citizen Army snipers and British troops who were sent out from the Shelbourne Hotel. Over on Marrowbone Lane, the Distillery held by the rebels was also under constant sniper fire from the British. The Four Courts came under heavy fire during the afternoon as well as a rebel barricade on Church Street, while, the Linenhall barracks was also set on fire. In the early evening, Liberty Hall was stormed by British troops, who found the building empty. The starting point of the rebellion on Easter Monday fell into the hands of the British and from then on the writing was on the wall for the rebels. It was only a matter of time before other important strongholds, one by one, would fall into the hands of the British.

CHAPTER FIVE

The Easter Rising

THURSDAY, 27 APRIL TO SUNDAY, 30 APRIL

On Thursday, artillery was again deployed around Sackville Street from an early hour and the heavy shelling resulted in fires and much in the way of destruction. Unfortunately, looting became much more widespread, which placed many civilians in great danger. Thursday evening saw James Connolly wounded when he was hit in the ankle as he inspected rebel positions in Lower Abbey Street and Princess Street. He was so badly wounded it was a real struggle for him to make his way back into the GPO. Though in great pain, he insisted on continuing to direct operations from a hastily constructed bed placed near the front door of the building while being treated by medical student James Ryan. The rebel's plight was, by the hour, becoming desperate and P.H. Pearse ordered the women to vacate the GPO but they refused and returned to their duties.

Sackville Street and the centre of the city was, by Thursday morning, almost unrecognisable with burnt-out tram cars littering the boulevard, as well as, grimly, human bodies and dead horses. Rubble was strewn everywhere and fires were burning while buildings were destroyed and on the point of collapse. During mid-morning there were several probing attacks by the British at various points in the city centre but all were beaten back, while, across at the Four Courts, the garrison there had to contend with unrelenting sniper fire from the enemy. At around 3 p.m. a huge assault on Sackville Street began from Lower Abbey Street by the Ulster Composite Battalion. The attack ended in failure and the Ulstermen suffered some casualties as they retreated, while the entire block between Lower Abbey Street and Eden Quay was left ablaze.

Around mid-afternoon the South Dublin Union came under sustained attack and the fighting developed into some serious close-quarter incidents. Despite that, the British eventually withdrew, believing the rebel garrison was much larger than they had anticipated. It may also have been the case that the troops were needed to fight in other areas of the city deemed to be more pressing. As it happened, one of the Volunteers in the Union was W.T. Cosgrave, the future leader of Cumann na nGaedheal and, President of the Executive Council during the Free State's first ten years in existence. In his witness statement to the Bureau of Military History he recalled that fateful afternoon:

> On Thursday a sustained attack was made on the Nurses Home. During this engagement the plaster was shot off the walls and ceilings. Holes were breached in the walls from one to the next to permit more freedom of movement when the attack increased in severity. Explosions went on repeatedly and every now and then a shower of bricks would fall from the Nurse's Home. Vice-Comdt. Brugha was on the top floor, while I occupied the ground floor. Late in the evening Captain ffrench-Mullen came down to tell me that the Vice-Comdt. had been wounded, that the British were in, and that we were to retire. We hesitated to accept this order, regarding it as premature. The attack was easing off – breaking off … However, we obeyed orders and retired along the passage.[31]

At that stage the British withdrew from the complex, much to the surprise of the rebels. Cathal Brugha was found by Éamonn Ceannt and, though badly wounded, he still had his revolver in his hand and was singing 'God Save Ireland'. Cosgrave went on to say:

> Vice-Comdt. Brugha was suffering from a number of wounds. He got such first-aid treatment as we had available from Volunteer Doolan, whom I assisted for some 5 or 6 hours. Both Doolan and I were much fatigued as Brugha required a lot of attention and was becoming delirious.[32]

By the early evening Sackville Street was ablaze and buildings were being systematically destroyed. The noise of incoming shells was deafening together with the sounds of breaking glass and flying metal. The British took control of Capel Street around 8 p.m., cutting off the GPO from the

Four Courts garrison and, it was around that time James Connolly sustained his ankle wound.

By 9 p.m. the noise and chaos in Sackville Street could only be described as both terrific and frightening, with the shelling becoming incessant. Frank Thornton and his unit were still holding out in the Imperial Hotel despite the onslaught being delivered by the British. In his witness statement he recounted in detail the events of that evening:

> On Thursday, during the shelling by the battery in Tara St, a H.E. shell came right over our building and hit the front of the Freeman's Journal office, now the Capital Cinema, and blew a huge hole in the upper portion of the building. On the same afternoon a shell came through one of the back windows of the Imperial Hotel and hit the side wall, exploding in the room. A sniper sitting at one of the three windows in the room furthest from the explosion was found still at his point, not wounded, but stunned.
>
> The shellfire intensified and the number of incendiary bombs increased and, what with the disaster of the falling barrels of methylated spirits, turpentine, etc from the Hoyte's explosion, we were now a cauldron of flames. However, acting on our specific instructions, we relentlessly held on until only six of us remained on the first floor, holding both the rear and the front, mainly the rear ... We remained until the ceiling of the first floor was falling all around us in flames and then retreated through Allen's, which was now one huge wall of flames. We had to come down a ladder about 16 ft. which was on fire, and gradually worked our way out, having received severe burns, and having our uniforms very badly burned, we reached Talbot St. The buildings at this end had not yet gone on fire ... all efforts on our part to contact the Post Office for further instruction failed, as the building was in flames. The fire gradually enveloped all our corner and we were forced to retire to the far side of Talbot St. and got out to the back of Cathedral Lane through a billiards hall, the name of which I cannot remember.
>
> I distinctly remember, however, that we went through a billiards hall and finally occupied a building on the corner of Gloucester St and held on there until the surrender.[33]

Note. Hoyte's was a chemical store situated beside the Imperial Hotel.

By midnight the net was closing in on many other rebels in Sackville Street and in the streets adjacent to it. They had no other choice but to leave their outposts and make their way to the GPO, where they were confronted by chaos and panic. The building itself was under a constant artillery barrage and those inside were looking for shelter wherever they could find it. In essence, the rebels were trapped and had no means of escape during what turned out to be a long and torturous night. Friday saw Sir John Maxwell officially take charge of the British troops and his appointment had a profound impact on the course of the Rising and its aftermath. In time, he ordered the executions of the rebellion's leaders, a decision that changed public opinion in favour of the rebels to the point of elevating all who died or participated in the conflict to the status of martyrs and heroes. By that day, the outlook for the rebels was very grim and the reality of defeat was dawning on them as they faced into what were to be the final hours of the conflict.

Having assessed the deteriorating situation the rebels found themselves in, P.H. Pearse issued a statement as President of the Irish Republic and Commander of the Army of the Republic. Pearse acknowledged the difficult situation his forces found themselves in and went on to pay 'homage to the gallantry of the soldiers of Irish freedom who have during the past four days been writing with fire and steel the most glorious chapter in the later history of Ireland'. He went on to say, 'Let me, who have led them into this, speak, in my own, and in my fellow-commanders and in the name of Ireland, present and to come, their praise, and ask those who come after them to remember them. For four days they have fought and toiled, almost without cessation, almost without sleep, and in the intervals of fighting they have sung songs of the freedom of Ireland.'

By that stage it was obvious to the five members of the Military Council that the time had come to begin an evacuation of the GPO and The O'Rahilly, the much-revered founding member of the Volunteers, undertook to lead a sortie along a route to Williams and Woods, a factory on Great Britain Street (now Parnell St) but he and some of his comrades were cut down by a British machine gun situated at the intersection of Great Britain and Moore Streets. Badly wounded, The O'Rahilly made his way back towards Sackville Street, where he lay for many hours, dying, having given his life for a cause he had passionately believed in.

One of the major battles of the Rising took place around North King Street, behind the Four Courts, where the British tried to take well-held rebel positions under the command of Edward (Ned) Daly. By Thursday, the British had closed in on the Four Courts and taken up positions in the streets surrounding the building and communication lines to the GPO in Sackville Street were cut. Daly and his men believed there was nothing left for them to do but make their final stand in the face of an all-out British assault. That onslaught began around 6.45 p.m. on Friday evening when a cordon was thrown around the Four Courts. Desperate fighting ensued and was probably heavier than anywhere else in the city during the week of the rebellion, with the exception of the action that took place on Mount Street Bridge. The gun battles were particularly vicious in nearby North King Street, where a strong British contingent was backed up by armoured cars. Rebel snipers took up positions in almost every house, aided by a sympathetic local civilian population.

Unfortunately, civilians died during the gun battles, which lasted over a period of fourteen hours, and some sixteen British soldiers lost their lives with thirty-one wounded. By around 8.30 on Saturday morning most of the rebels had retreated into the Four Courts and remained there until the surrender ordered by P.H. Pearse later that day. After the Rising, allegations of British brutality were centred on the Four Courts area. It was claimed by local civilians that British soldiers had killed fifteen innocent and unarmed men and boys in a block of roughly ten houses in North King Street during fierce house-to-house gun battles over the two days of fighting. The killings were later discounted by the British, who maintained the men and boys had been caught in the crossfire. The claims were disputed by their womenfolk who had also been in the houses. It was only when the bodies of two men were discovered buried in the cellar of 177 North King Street that the British admitted responsibility for the killings.

As far as nationalists were concerned, this episode came to be regarded as a 'massacre' by British troops overseen by their officers. At a later coroner's enquiry, Lieutenant Colonel H. Taylor, the officer in command of the unit involved, claimed 'no persons were attacked by the troops other than those who were assisting the rebels, and found with arms in their possession'. Unsurprisingly, the jury did not find the military explanation satisfactory. A later court of enquiry concluded, 'it was unlikely that any persons were shot or killed unless the men had reason to think that they had been fired on, whether they were mistaken or not'. However, on this occasion, Taylor did concede, while referring to some of the deaths, 'I think it very possible that these men might have been shot or killed by soldiers at sight.'

Maxwell later admitted publicly that, 'possibly some unfortunate incidents, which we should regret now, may have occurred'. Privately, it seems, Maxwell was greatly bothered with these cases where soldiers were accused of having murdered innocent civilians in cold blood. However, the official explanation of the deaths was that they had occurred, 'during rebellion and active armed resistance to his Majesty's troops in the execution of their duty', implying that the rebels were really responsible for their own deaths. The incident was discussed in the House of Commons and the Prime Minister, Herbert Asquith, accepted that, 'There could be little doubt that some men who were not taking an actual part in the fighting were, in the course of the struggle, killed by both rebels and soldiers.'

By 8 p.m. on Friday evening the majority of the garrison in the GPO had vacated the building. The Volunteers tunnelled through the walls of neighbouring buildings, so the evacuation was completed out of sight of the British and safe from their rifle and machine gun fire. Michael Staines, Quartermaster of the Dublin Brigade of the Irish Volunteers, recalled in his witness statement to the Bureau of Military History the last moments of the evacuation:

> We all got orders to prepare for evacuation and to remove all explosives, etc. to the basement. This took some time. As fire was coming down the lift we had to remove all the stuff to the courtyard. A number were employed on this work while the others were evacuating. When this work was done, I reported to Pearse and with him were Connolly, Willie Pearse and Judge Law Smith's chauffeur. Pearse inquired if every man had left and I replied in the affirmative. He insisted on me going down through the Henry Street houses where we had broken through the walls. I went and searched them.
>
> When I reported back, Pearse himself went down to ensure that no one was left, either dead or alive. P.H. Pearse, Willie Pearse, the chauffeur and myself brought Connolly on the stretcher. Although there was firing down Henry St, we got across safely to Henry Place. Before we reached the 'L' of Henry Place we found some of the men in a panic as Henry Place at the end of Moore Lane was under machine-gun fire from the Rotunda Hospital.
>
> Sean McLoughlin lined the men up and steadied them. Joe Plunkett drew his sword and stood exposed in the middle

> of the machine-gun fire and allowed two men to rush across each time he dipped his sword. All got over safely, including Connolly on the stretcher. We went into a house, No. 10, in Moore Street at the corner of Henry Place.
>
> We placed Connolly in a bed and made his room the headquarters. I placed the green flag with harp, which I had taken from the GPO with me, over his bed. We then cut through the walls along Moore St. until we reached Sackville Lane. It was there reported to us that O'Rahilly's body was laying in the lane.[34]

Throughout his evacuation, Connolly was accompanied by his trade union secretary, Winifred Carney, and once out of the GPO all the Volunteers took up new positions in Moore Street and awaited further developments.

The following day, Saturday, April 29, the leaders of the Rising were forced to make the definitive decision to surrender. Jim Ryan, later recalled how, when he was dressing Connolly's wounds, he 'saw a sight I shall never forget. Lying dead on the opposite footpath on Moore Street were three elderly men.' Soon afterwards, Sean MacDermott told Connolly and Ryan that the sight of the dead men convinced Pearse it was time to surrender in order to spare the lives of Dublin's innocent civilians. It was also reported that Pearse watched a man, his wife and daughter being killed in the crossfire, further convincing him the Rising should be brought to an end. Early that afternoon, Pearse and the other rebel leaders in Moore Street met to discuss the situation and decided to surrender.

Many of the Volunteers in Moore Street were enraged by the decision to surrender and even went as far as to make plans to fight their way out of the city to the Dublin mountains. It fell to MacDermott to pacify them in a powerful speech that witnesses later recalled was filled with passion. He strongly argued that by surrendering they would save the lives of countless citizens of the city and it would prevent the city from being burned down. He went on to praise the men for their bravery and assured them their gallant fight would inspire generations to come to carry on the struggle and finish what they had started. He memorably ended his speech with the words, 'We who will be shot will die happy knowing there are plenty of you around who will finish the job.'

One man who dissented from the decision was Thomas Clarke and he attempted to rally the men, urging them 'to die fighting as they would in any case be executed if they surrendered'. Clarke was devastated by the decision to surrender and the failure of the rebellion. It was later reported that when Elizabeth O'Farrell of Cumann na mBan left the building with the white flag of surrender, 'Clarke turned his face to the wall and broke down sobbing.' General Lowe of the British Army informed O'Farrell that he would only accept an unconditional surrender. Pearse, after meeting with Lowe, was taken to British Army headquarters, where he signed an unconditional surrender that read:

> In order to prevent further slaughter of Dublin citizens, and in the hope of saving the lives of our followers now surrounded and hopelessly outnumbered, the members of the Provisional Government present at headquarters have agreed to an unconditional surrender, and the commandants of the various districts in the city and the county will order their commands to lay down their arms.[35]

Though sporadic gunfire did continue until Sunday, when news of the surrender reached all the rebel garrisons, the Rising was, to all intents and purposes, over. The garrison at the Four Courts under the command of Edward Daly surrendered soon after, though Daly, as he said himself, 'was very cut up about it but accepted it as a soldier should'. Many of his men took the news badly but followed the orders of their commandant and laid down their arms. On Sunday morning, Elizabeth O'Farrell delivered the surrender note to Jacob's Biscuit Factory, where Thomas MacDonagh initially rejected the order stating it was invalid because its author, when writing it, was a British prisoner. He maintained that as Pearse and Connolly had been taken into custody, chief command had devolved to him and, he insisted on negotiating with the British GOC. Eventually, MacDonagh met General Lowe, who made the rebels' position very clear to him and so MacDonagh was left with little option but to surrender. A tearful MacDonagh told his men he was unhappy at the thought of surrender but they had to follow Pearse's order and accept the sad fact that the rebellion was over.

That afternoon, MacDonagh arrived at the South Dublin Union to confirm to Éamonn Ceannt and his garrison the news of Pearse's surrender. Though several of the men there broke away, the majority marched to Jameson's Distillery after an agreement with General Lowe. Over at Boland's Mills, Éamon de Valera was equally sceptical about the surrender and, when he and his men did lay down their arms, they did so with a heavy heart. They had seen little in the way of action during the week and had been somewhat isolated from the rebel headquarters in the GPO. Elizabeth O'Farrell delivered the surrender order to Michael Mallin at the College of Surgeons at 11 a.m. that Sunday morning. He consulted his officers before addressing the rest of his garrison, recommending acceptance of the order saying that, 'as a soldier he must obey and as soldiers they must obey also'. His decision was supported by his second in command, Countess Markievicz, and one Volunteer later confirmed how he had been struck 'by the awful gloom that had settled over the place'.

By Sunday, 30 April the Easter Rising was over and the centre of Dublin had been reduced to rubble. As well as causing extensive damage to the capital, the Rising claimed the lives of many individuals on both sides of the fighting. The British Army eventually reported 116 soldiers dead with a total of 368 wounded. Rebel and civilian casualties amounted to 318 dead with 2,217 wounded or injured. It is important also to note that all sixteen police fatalities and twenty-two of the British soldiers who died were Irishmen. The majority of the casualties, both killed and wounded, were civilians and it has to be accepted that both sides, British and rebel, shot civilians deliberately on occasions when they refused to obey orders such as refusing to stop at checkpoints. We also cannot overlook the fact that there were two instances of British troops killing civilians out of revenge; at Portobello, where six were shot, and at North King Street, where fifteen were shot.

After the Rising, the city of Dublin and the country in general was changed forever and, though the strike for Irish freedom had failed in terms of a military victory, the men of the Military Council had every reason to be satisfied. They could be confident in the knowledge, as they faced their own deaths, that their gallant efforts and the efforts of the men and women they commanded had not been in vain and the struggle for Irish independence, though stalled, was far from over.

CHAPTER SIX

The Rising Outside of Dublin

The Easter Rising was essentially a Dublin-centric rebellion and never really spread beyond the confines of the capital. Much to the disappointment of the rebellion's leaders, very few Volunteers companies across the provinces mobilised and those who did basically waited around for most of Easter Sunday for orders to arrive from Dublin. The fact is, those orders, if they arrived in an area, were so confused it left company commanders unsure of what to do and they eventually gave up on the notion of rebellion. By the end of the day, there was nothing left for the men to do but reluctantly and sadly return to their homes, having never fired a shot for the cause of independence.

In Cork, around 1,200 men mobilised early in the day at various locations across the city and county. The Volunteers headquarters in Shears Street in the city was a hive of activity from early morning, while other Volunteers mobilised in places like Barley Hill just outside Newmarket where the company was commanded by Sean Moylan. In his statement to the Bureau of Military History, Moylan recalled what transpired on Easter Sunday:

> Then came our mobilisation orders for Easter, 1916. For the first time we met Companies from adjoining areas. The mobilisation point was Barley Hill, near Newmarket. The officer sent to take charge of the Volunteers was the late Captain David Barry. In the evening of Easter Sunday, we were ordered to return to homes and we were not again called upon. Many of those who paraded on Easter Sunday emigrated in the following years, some played minor parts in the movement, some disappeared from it, a few were faithful to the end.[36]

Despite the lack of activity on Easter Sunday at Barley Hill, and the subsequent diminution of the Newmarket Company over time, Moylan went on to express an opinion in his statement, saying:

> The faith of the few was rooted in a refusal to disbelieve. Irishmen, they could not accept the view that they were a lesser breed, that their country was fated to remain a Province. Blindly, instinctively, they held to this refusal; out of it, because they were blindly, intuitively right, came light and guidance and strength to achieve. 1916 proved one thing – that Irishmen could fight and die for their own country. It proved, too, that, the first breath-taking shock past, Irishmen's allegiance was still to their own land; that they were proud of the men who made manifest that allegiance. The spell of national inanition was broken. Ireland would never again be quiescent under foreign rule.[37]

Across County Cork on Easter Sunday the Castletownroche, Mallow, Blarney and Grenagh companies mobilised at Bweeng, the Ballingeary Company marched to Kealkill, while the Ballinhassig Company and other Volunteers from the city marched through Crookstown and Kilmurray and on to Macroom, where as many as 400 men were dismissed by their officers around 4 p.m.

One of the main shows of republican strength during the Rising manifested itself in County Wexford and, in particular, in Enniscorthy, where the tricolour flew proudly for the week. The town had a strong IRB tradition and many of those involved in that organisation joined the Irish Volunteers in 1913. Companies were also in existence in Wexford town, Gorey, Ferns, New Ross and other centres. P.H. Pearse visited Enniscorthy in March 1916 and urged all republicans in the town to ready themselves for the independence struggle. Like most other places outside Dublin, there was utter confusion in Enniscorthy as to whether the Volunteers should rise up on Easter Sunday. Paul Galligan, a Cavan man, who had been sent by Thomas MacDonagh to organise and train the Enniscorthy men some months earlier, travelled to Dublin late on Easter Saturday to ascertain if the Rising was going ahead. On Easter Sunday, he met with Pearse, Connolly and Plunkett and was ordered to return to Enniscorthy to mobilise the Wexford battalion and take over the railway line to prevent British troops travelling from Wexford to Dublin.

Galligan was forced to cycle back to Enniscorthy, only arriving on the following Wednesday, avoiding the British on his journey. While he was cycling back to Enniscorthy, Seamus Doyle, another officer, received an order on Easter Monday from Pearse stating, 'We start at noon today, obey your orders.' Doyle, however, was unsure of what the orders were and he communicated with the Brigade Commander in Wexford Town, Sean Sinnott, who was reluctant to make any decision because of the conflicting orders. When Galligan got back to Enniscorthy he decided to take action and, in the early hours of Thursday, the Volunteers seized the town. Thomas Doyle, a member of the IRB and a Volunteer, recalled in his witness statement to the Bureau of Military History what transpired that morning. After rounding up as many men as he could, they all congregated at Captain Pat Keegan's house on Irish Street, where rifles and shotguns were handed out. Doyle went on to recount what happened next:

> With about 90 men we marched over to the Athenaeum, took it over, hoisted the Republican flag over it, fired a salute and made it our headquarters. Commandant Rafter was in command with Captain Sean Etchingham, Captain Seamus Doyle, Commandant Paul Galligan and Bob Brennan. The first order issued was to place Volunteers on all the principal points of the town. When the people of the town woke up in the morning and saw the Volunteers, all armed, they did not know what was after happening.[38]

That morning some of the banks were taken over by the Volunteers and guards were placed in them, while the managers locked up everything. Posters were displayed around the town ordering anyone in possession of firearms to hand them over before noon. Those who wished to leave the town had to apply for permission to do so and a recruiting office was opened in the old police barracks. Initially there were very few willing to enlist but a rumour quickly spread around the town that conscription was about to be introduced, which resulted in many recruits eventually showing up. A proclamation was issued ordering a 10 p.m. curfew and warning that anyone caught looting would be shot. Public houses in the town were forced to close.

By Saturday, one thousand rebels had mobilised in Enniscorthy and it wasn't long before the British made preparations to launch an assault on the town. The British recruited retired officer Lieutenant Colonel G.A. French to take command of the one thousand troops who were assembled in Wexford town equipped with a naval gun and two field guns. Some of the rebels took up positions on Vinegar Hill, which overlooked the town and, as they held a meeting, a blank shell from the first armoured train used in Ireland was fired among the men, quickly scattering them. Many of the fleeing Volunteers were captured by the British, while others just laid down their arms. The rebels voluntarily laid down their arms once they had verified the veracity of the surrender in Dublin. Some 375 alleged 'Sinn Feiners' were arrested in County Wexford, with 319 of them sent to Dublin. The police recovered arms and ammunition as well as gelignite and other explosives. Most of the prisoners were sent to prisons in England and to Frongoch in Wales, where they were held until at least December 1916 before being released.

While the republicans in Enniscorthy were making a stand against British rule, their Volunteer comrades in Meath were engaged in an operation that was, in essence, the bloodiest outside of Dublin. It was, arguably, one the most successful republican attacks on the forces of the Crown during the whole of Easter week. The offensive was carried out by the 5th Battalion of the Dublin Brigade, sometimes known as 'the Fingal Volunteers', and the group consisted of about sixty men under the command of Thomas Ashe and Richard Mulcahy.

On Easter Monday, James Connolly sent an order to Ashe to send some of his men into the GPO and deploy the remainder of his men attacking any RIC barracks in his area as he saw fit. Ashe subsequently raided the barracks in Donabate and Swords, with the forays providing him and his men with a substantial cache of arms and ammunition. They also went on to destroy rail and telegraph communications in the north Dublin area. By Thursday, the decision was made to release the older men of the battalion and anyone else who was not in a position to commit to further action. What became known as the Battle of Ashbourne took place on the following day, Friday, when, having split the battalion into four units, Ashe sent his men into action. One of the units remained behind to protect the camp and gather supplies while the other three units set off on bicycles to destroy the Midland Great Western Railway line that passed through Batterstown in order to disrupt the movement of British troops travelling from Athlone to Dublin. The men were accompanied by the battalion's Medical Officer, Dr Dick Hayes, who travelled by car with his medical supplies. In his witness statement to the Bureau of Military History, Michael McAllister, a Volunteer in Ashe's unit, recalled the battle:

> On Friday morning, Ashe detailed a party of which I was a member and of which Charles Weston was in charge and

to proceed to Ashbourne and take the R.I.C. barracks there. Ashbourne was only a few miles from our camp. Our party consisted of eight men all told. Mounted on bicycles, we set off for Ashbourne. When we reached the bend on the bye-road which we were travelling and about a quarter of a mile from the junction with the main road at the cross of Rath we came across a policeman armed with a rifle and, apparently, guarding a barrier which was comprised of a pole laid across the road.

We sent him back with an escort of one of our men to our main body at Borranstown while we proceeded on to Ashbourne. On reaching the road junction at the Rath crossroad we dumped our cycles and proceeded along the main road in single file towards the barracks. We kept well under cover of the road bank so that our approach could not be seen from the barrack window. There was no sign of activity around the barracks which was set back from the road. We now shouted to the police to surrender.

There was no reply so we fired a volley through the windows and Blanchfield, who was with us, threw some kind of a home-made bomb. This made a terrific noise and let off a lot of smoke but otherwise did no damage.

The police now shouted out to us that they would surrender. We shouted back at them to come out with their hands up. Immediately, after telling the police to come out we were the recipients of a volley of rifle fire from the cross of the Rath which was a few hundred yards in our left rear. On looking in that direction we could see a number of cars pulled up on the side of the main road just short of the crossroads. More cars were in the act of pulling up further back along the road and we could see figures of men jumping from them and, apparently, taking cover on the side of the road … We jumped up and ran across the road and jumped into the field at the opposite or west side. From here we made our way under cover of the roadside hedge back to the Rath crossroads where the firing was coming from. On getting to the crossroads, we took up a firing position behind the banks of the roadside fence there. This position gave us a good view of the main road in the Kilmoon direction. There appeared to be about one hundred cars pulled up along the road leading back towards Kilmoon and the leading cars were only a short distance from the crossroads with the remainder close up in the rear. We immediately opened fire on the cars. We could see that a number of enemy forces had taken cover underneath the cars and we also realised that it was a big force of R.I.C. we were up against. We proceeded to deal with the policemen underneath the cars and those that exposed themselves on the roadside. We opened up with rapid fire on them and soon my rifle was burning my hands.

This pinned the police to the ground and what fire was coming from them now became very erratic … As I said before, our men were good natural shots and at this range I knew we were decimating the enemy in their positions. After the initial burst of fire by us, our men settled down very calmly and, although this was our first experience under fire, they were behaving as veterans … deliberately picking their targets and dealing with them very cooly in their own time. I was satisfied that whatever would be the outcome of the fight, the R.I.C. would have a lot of casualties.

Dick Mulcahy, who was with the main body of our force back on the Borranstown road, had come up to us prior to this and asked Charlie Weston how many policemen were up the road. Charlie replied that there were about a hundred. Mulcahy said, 'Pity it is not a thousand. I will deal with them fellows. Do not let them get down below the crossroads.' He then crossed the ditch and road as if nothing was happening and disappeared across country towards Borranstown. We continued to engage the enemy, whose fire now became spasmodic. They were apparently hugging mother earth for dear life. Some of them realised their mistake in getting under the cars and tried to get out of that position but were promptly dealt with by us, while those that remained were either dead or so badly wounded as to be incapable of any movement.

This was the position for a long time … At any rate it took some considerable time for Mulcahy to get back to the main body and take them across country to outflank the enemy.

Meanwhile, eight of us were holding up the big force of R.I.C. After a long time we could hear the commotion starting

> near the top of the incline in the Kilmoon direction and could hear the fire of rifles and shotguns and we knew our main body was engaging the police at the other end of their position. Soon we could see some of the police leaving their positions and running towards our position. All this time they were presenting beautiful targets to us and were crowding in on their comrades who were nearest to us and who were not in a happy position. It was soon apparent that the police were in a state of confusion, and some of them had already discarded their rifles. We now ceased firing and got up from our position and advanced up the road. The enemy fire had died out completely now and there seemed to be no further fight left in them.
>
> The police now came out their positions with their hands up and we herded them in together to a central position, where we were joined by Mulcahy and Ashe and the remainder of our men. Their arms and equipment were now collected up and Doctor Hayes, who had now come up, set about tending their wounded. They seemed to have a big number killed and wounded … All told, the police numbered seventy-five including dead and wounded. County Inspector Gray of Meath, who was in charge of them and who was killed, was in civilian attire, or at least he wore a light civilian coat over his uniform. The survivors of the police were put into any of the cars which were still running and sent home to their stations. Doctor Hayes did all he could to relieve the suffering of the wounded, using our medical equipment to do so. They had no medical equipment of their own. We had two men killed and three wounded. I cannot remember what the police casualties were, but from what I saw they were very heavy. There were quite a few dead and a large number wounded. Our Quartermaster had a bread van which we had commandeered in Swords and we loaded it up with the captured arms and ammunition and we all returned to Camp at Borranstown.[39]

The Battle of Ashbourne lasted some five and a half hours and the final number of deaths was reported as eight RIC men, two civilians driving RIC cars, two innocent civilians caught in the crossfire and two Volunteers. Three other Volunteers were wounded together with many policemen in an engagement that ended in a decisive victory for the rebels.

Over in County Galway some 2,000 men had joined the Irish Volunteers under the command of Liam Mellows. In the first instance the Galway men were led to believe the Rising had been cancelled in the days prior to Easter Sunday. However, word eventually filtered through from P.H. Pearse to proceed with the operation. The Volunteers in Galway were ordered to attack as many police barracks as they could. They were also to collect about 3,000 rifles in Tralee once they had come ashore from the ill-fated *Aud.* With the rifles lost to the bottom of the sea, the Galway Volunteers accepted the situation and still proceeded to attack police barracks in Oranmore, Gort and Clarinbridge. Owing to the confusion over orders emanating from Dublin, the number of men who turned out was much smaller than anticipated, with about 600 of the original force in county available to fight in the rebellion. They gathered in Athenry on the Tuesday armed with just a small number of rifles, handguns, ammunition and pikes.

Once mobilised, the men retreated south to Moyode Castle and to Limepark as the Royal Navy vessel HMS *Gloucester* began firing artillery shells from Galway Bay into the Athenry area. The indiscriminate shelling of the Galway coast continued up until Saturday. While the majority of the Volunteers gathered in Athenry, the Claregalway and Castlegar companies stayed in the village of Carnmore on the Tuesday night, where they waited on orders from Mellows. Aware of the Volunteers presence in the village, a unit of Special Constables and other RIC personnel travelled in convoy out from Galway city to Carnmore to confront them. Michael Newell, an Intelligence Officer with the Volunteers, recalled in his witness statement to the Bureau of Military History what then transpired:

> It was about 5 a.m. on Wednesday. I noticed a girl on a hill at Kiltullagh waving a white apron, apparently in order to attract our attention. I looked to see what was wrong and saw a number of motor cars about half a mile away, coming in our direction from Galway City. We first thought it was the Galway city Volunteers coming to join with us. Captain Molloy ordered us to take cover behind the walls. Just as we had taken cover, fire opened on us. The cars proceeded to about one hundred yards from our position and then halted. The enemy advanced on foot on our position, firing all the time. Captain Molloy ordered us to open fire which we did, but the enemy fire was so intense and the bullets striking the top of the walls, we were compelled to keep down, and we were only able to take an

> occasional shot. The enemy advanced up to the cross roads and Constable Whelan was pushed by District Inspector Heard up the wall which was about four foot high, the District Inspector standing behind Whelan and holding him by the collar of his tunic.
>
> Constable Whelan shouted, 'surrender, boys, I know ye all'. Whelan was shot dead and the District Inspector fell also and lay motionless on the ground. The enemy then made an attempt to outflank our position but were beaten back. The enemy then retreated and continued to fire until well out of range of our shotguns. They then got back into their cars and went in the direction of Oranmore ... We suffered no casualties. The company then fell in and marched to Athenry.[40]

Because of the severe lack of arms there really was little else for the Volunteers to do and, as such, they basically just waited out the week and disbanded the following Saturday in Moyode Castle. The pity of it was, had there been no confusion over the orders and had the arms from the *Aud* being secured, there is little doubt the Volunteers in Galway would have been capable of making a significant stand against the forces of the Crown. As it transpired, many of the Volunteers were arrested and eventually deported to jails in England. Mellows and two of his officers, Frank Hynes and Alfie Monaghan, escaped into County Clare, where they managed to remain at large for a number of months.

Unfortunately, in many other counties, despite some intense preparations for it, the Rising failed to materialise and there was nothing more than a few skirmishes and minor confrontations here and there. Many hundreds of Volunteers who mobilised on Easter Sunday and in the days after as news of events in Dublin filtered through to the provinces were left to bide their time due to the confusion over orders emanating from the leadership in the capital. The failure of the *Aud* to deliver the expected supply of arms and ammunition to the Volunteers outside of Dublin was, in essence, the death knell for what would have been a national rebellion. Nevertheless, had the men of the provinces received some clear guidance and orders from Dublin they would, despite the lack of arms, almost certainly have made a better stand against the forces of the Crown even if only to show solidarity with their comrades bearing the brunt of the fighting in Dublin.

CHAPTER SEVEN

The Aftermath of the Rising

P.H. Pearse issued the order to surrender on Saturday, 29 April 1916. With most of the men from the GPO and nearby outposts all cornered into Moore Street, there was no possibility of carrying on the conflict. Pearse had seen enough destruction and, having personally witnessed civilian deaths, took the view there was nothing more to be gained in continuing the fighting. Some of his men were adamant they would carry on the fight even if it meant an attempt to break out of the city in order to head for the Dublin mountains. They still held fast to the ideal of a 'blood sacrifice' in the hope it would inspire future generations to continue the struggle for Ireland's freedom. However, the impassioned speech delivered by Sean MacDermott eventually held sway and, with a sense of sadness and despair, the gallant Volunteers of the rebellion reluctantly laid down their arms.

So, on that fateful Saturday afternoon, the survivors of the GPO garrison, having left their wounded to be picked up by a British Medical Unit, emerged into the open from Moore Street and its surrounds and marched to Nelson's Pillar. There they piled up their guns and readied themselves for whatever the British had in store for them. This was not the outcome the Volunteers had hoped for but they were safe in the knowledge they had struck a mighty and significant blow for Ireland and the independence struggle was, in reality, just beginning. In his witness statement, Frank Henderson recalled how he and his comrades surrendered reluctantly and recounted what then transpired:

> Later in the afternoon, Sean MacDermott told us that agreement had been reached and that we were surrendering as

prisoners of war. I believe he said that we were surrendering unconditionally, but this has been disputed. Accordingly, we filed out into Moore Street with our arms and ammunition, formed up under our officers, and marched off with our rifles at the slope, through Moore Street, Henry Place into Henry Street and Upper O'Connell Street (Sackville St), as far as the portion extending from the Gresham Hotel to Parnell Street corner. We were all lined up on the East Side of O'Connell Street.

I happened to be beside Joseph Plunkett; beside him were Tom Clarke and Sean MacDermott. We were ordered to throw down our arms and ammunition in a heap on the road …

Our names were taken by British officers, many of whom were very truculent. There was one of them who behaved like a soldier and a gentleman. Joseph Plunkett was singled out by one British officer for particular insult. When he had been maltreated by the officer, he stepped back into the ranks … There were no citizens on the street at this time, but I noticed there were some people in civilian dress in the Gresham Hotel who were at the windows looking on at what was taking place. We were marched over to the green plot inside the railings of the Rotunda Hospital, in front of the main entrance. We were not long there until we were joined by the garrison of the Four Courts area. Amongst them was Ned Daly, the Commandant of the area and Fionan Lynch. The area of the green plot was extremely small, and we were ordered on no account stir off the grass but to keep lying down there.

The night spent there can be described without any exaggeration as a night of horror.

Tom Clarke was maltreated shortly after we arrived at the plot … I noticed Michael Collins protesting vigorously to the British officers at the maltreatment of Tom Clarke. The conduct of the British officers during the night can only be described as savage. Some of the Dublin Metropolitan Police also uttered sundry threats during the night, but one or two of them were inclined to be rather decent. There were three of four women amongst the prisoners, and they also had to spend the night along with the rest of us on the green plot. We received no water and no food during the night.

Early in the morning, sometime after daybreak, we were ordered to stand up and to get ready to march off … We marched down O'Connell Street, which was still burning on both sides. When we reached O'Connell Bridge there appeared to be a gaping hole in the centre of the Bridge. We continued down Westmoreland Street, College Green and Dame Street. In Dame Street I noticed there were a few civilians about, and these people cursed us as we went by … We continued via Kilmainham to Richmond Barracks. When we got to the barrack square we were halted and searched several times. After standing in the square for a long period … we were brought into a room which they called 'the gymnasium' where every man was scrutinised by DMP and military officers, who picked out the leaders and other men against whom they were about to bring charges. These men were put in a corner of the room separate, to the main body. Amongst those picked out were Tom Clarke, Joe Plunkett, Sean MacDermott, Sean McGarry, Fionan Lynch and my brother Leo Henderson. We were kept lying on the floor for a long time and eventually water was brought in to us in buckets, and we got some hard biscuits to eat.

As it was getting dusk, in the evening we were all – except the special group which had been picked out by the British military and police – ordered out to the barrack square, and were told we were about to be moved off somewhere. They served us with bully beef and a few more hard biscuits, and told us that we were to be careful with this food as it was all we would get for some time. While we were in the barrack square, some more Republican prisoners were marched in, including the garrison from Jacobs and the College of Surgeons.

It was getting dark when we marched off. We marched out of the barracks and turned towards Kingsbridge. We crossed the Liffey either at Kingsbridge or at the next bridge nearer the city and marched along the North side Quays until we got to Grattan Bridge. By this time, it was completely dark and there were no street lamps lighting. All the houses and shops were in darkness and the streets were deserted. We re-crossed the Liffey at Grattan Bridge and continued as far as Butt Bridge, where we crossed again and proceeded along the North Wall

> as far as the L&N.W.R. station, whence we proceeded by the underground passage to a steamer which was waiting for us … When we got to the steamer, we had a very good view of the burning city. We were immediately put down into the cattle lairs. British soldiers were posted all-round the ship and challenged us any time we made a move. There was talk of submarines being in the Bay. I fell asleep soon after the boat left the Quay, and I do not remember anything more until we arrived at Holyhead.[41]

On arrival at Holyhead the prisoners were divided into two groups, one of which was sent to Knutsford Jail in Cheshire while the second group, including Henderson, travelled on to Stafford Jail. A few months later many of the prisoners who made that journey across the Irish Sea found themselves in Frongoch prison camp in Wales, where they were to remain until just before Christmas 1916 when they were released to make a triumphant return to their homeland. In total, some 3,430 men were arrested after the Rising and 79 women and, of these, 1,841 men were deported to Britain. All of the prisoners had erroneously been labelled as 'Sinn Feiners' by the British press and consequently the rebellion became known as the 'Sinn Fein' Rising. Most of the remaining prisoners, numbering around 1,400 or so, were released within weeks of the conflict's ending on the grounds they were believed to pose no threat to the state. Many of the prisoners who ended up in British jails played no part whatsoever in the rebellion but had been picked up by the authorities on suspicion of being sympathetic to the republican cause.

Some seventy-seven women were taken prisoner after the Rising and, though most of them were released quickly, a number of them were held in prison until early in June 1916. The women were members of Cumann na mBan and the Irish Citizen Army but a small number were not of any organisation but simply turned up on Easter Monday to help out in the fight for their country's independence. One such woman was May Gibney, who recalled how:

> On Easter Monday 1916 I volunteered for service at the GPO I was not a member of a Republican organisation at that time but as a reference I mentioned the name of a Volunteer whom I knew was on duty at one of the points. I asked to be allowed to remain at the GPO and was lucky enough to be accepted as a member of the garrison.[42]

While in the GPO the women tended the injured and wounded and prepared and served food. Some were asked to carry messages to outposts in and around the city, which they bravely did and without question. Not all of the women found themselves in the GPO for the week of the fighting. Some were ordered to other outposts at Stephen's Green, the City Hall and Marrowbone Lane, where they all performed admirably with determination and conviction. Rose McNamara was typical of the women who played their part in the Rising. She was in command of the women in the Marrowbone Lane garrison and she recalled how, in addition to providing first aid to the men, they loaded the rifles and acted as spotters for the snipers. During the week the women managed to locate a cow with her two calves and made bread and butter for the entire garrison with the milk. When the garrison did eventually surrender, the women made the decision not to evade capture and McNamara went to the British officer and informed him that she and her female comrades were part of the garrison. They then proudly marched out with the men to Kilmainham Gaol. She later recalled:

> The men gave each of us their small arms to do as we liked with, thinking we were going to go home, but we were not going to leave the men we were with all the week to their fate; we decided to go along with them and be with them to the end, whatever our fate might be.[43]

Nora Daly was a Cumann na mBan nurse in the St Stephen's Green garrison and when she and her comrades, under the command of Michael Mallin, retreated to the College of Surgeons, she set up a first aid station and treated all of the wounded. After the garrison's surrender she was sent to Richmond Barracks before being transferred to Kilmainham Jail. She recalled:

> The order was given to lodge us in Kilmainham Jail and hither we were finally marched, arriving after dusk and being received by the light of candles, which only served to intensify the gloom. Finally, our quarters were allotted, one cell to each four prisoners, and one blanket and one 'biscuit' doled out to us. Our cell doors were banged shut and we were left to make the best we could of the means at our disposal.[44]

Probably the most famous woman who served during the conflict was the Countess Markievicz, who was part of the St Stephen's Green garrison and second in command to Michael Mallin. Though from an Anglo-Irish background, she was totally dedicated to the republican ideal and a loyal member of the Citizen Army. While there are conflicting accounts of her shooting a policeman, there is no doubting her participation in the conflict. She reluctantly surrendered with her garrison and, ironically, the British officer who accepted the surrender, Captain de Courcy Wheeler, was married to Markievicz's first cousin. Once in Kilmainham Jail, she spent some of her time there in solitary confinement, the only woman to do so. She was court-martialled on 4 May and sentenced to death for her actions during the conflict. She had her sentence commuted to life in prison solely on account of her sex. Markievicz was released in June 1917 and continued to play a role in Irish politics, becoming the first female to be elected to the British House of Commons. She did not take her seat on account of Sinn Fein's abstention policy. She went on to become Minister for Labour in the First Dail of 1919–21, but spent much of her time in prison having been arrested once again. She went on to oppose the Anglo-Irish Treaty and was a founder member of Fianna Fail but died soon after in 1927.

One of the most impressive of the women who served was Dr Kathleen Lynn, a captain in the Citizen Army as well as its Chief Medical Officer. She began her participation in the Rising by delivering medical supplies to the various garrisons in her own car helped by Countess Markievicz. She then joined the City Hall garrison and, early on in the attack on Dublin Castle, she had to tend to her dying commanding officer, Sean Connolly. He died in her arms and, it is said, she wrapped him in the green flag from the play *Under Which Flag*, in which he had starred only a week earlier. Later that afternoon, Lt Sean O'Reilly was killed in action and Lynn took command of the garrison. She remained in command until the garrison surrendered and, when searched, she was found to have a revolver and 50 rounds of ammunition in her apron. In her witness statement to the Bureau of Military History, she vividly recounted her own and her female comrade's experiences after their surrender:

> Then we were brought to Kilmainham. Miss ffrench-Mullen, Miss Molony and I had a cell to ourselves in the old part of Kilmainham. We were more comfortable there than in the other place. At Kilmainham I remember we were given one basin of water for the three of us to wash in. It was more than we had in the other place. We had wardresses there and conditions were decidedly better. It was a very trying time for us because

> Madame Markievicz was overhead in the condemned cell and we used to hear reports that she was to be executed. We also heard about the other people that were being executed.
>
> We could hear shootings in the mornings, and we would be told afterwards who it was.
>
> It was a very harrowing experience.[45]

Lynn then went on to describe that after six days she and the other women who continued to be held as prisoners were transferred to Mountjoy Jail. She recalled in her statement how:

> We were then removed in 'Black Marias' to Mountjoy, where we had cells to ourselves.
>
> Countess Plunkett was in the next cell to mine. She was in a terrible state about her son having been executed … after a while we were allowed visitors and parcels. The only thing we longed for was clean bread and butter. We were allowed after a little while to have association. We would be walking in the grounds and talking to each other. In the afternoons we went to a room where laundry work was done. We had not too bad a time in Mountjoy. Then I was deported to England.[46]

After the Rising, Lynn remained active in politics and joined Sinn Fein before taking part in the War of Independence and opposing the Anglo-Irish Treaty. She later devoted her time to running St Ultan's Infant Hospital, which she founded in 1919 together with her friend and fellow republican, Madeleine ffrench-Mullen. It was the first hospital of its kind in Dublin.

Another woman of note was Winifred Carney from Belfast ,who was James Connolly's secretary during his time in the Labour and Trade Union spheres. Prior to the Rising she received a telegram from Connolly asking her to travel to Dublin. When the GPO was stormed on Easter Monday, she was the only woman present and was one of only three women in the building when it was evacuated. She left with Connolly when the men relocated to Moore Street. After the Rising Carney was imprisoned in Kilmainham, Mountjoy and Aylesbury jails until Christmas 1916.

The role played by women in the Rising has come under scrutiny in recent years and the releasing of military archive material allows for a reassessment of their contribution. We now know the names of approximately 300 women who took some part or other in the conflict. Many of them remained active in politics after the Rising and participated in the War of Independence and Civil War. The Easter Rising may have been a male-dominated event, but the sources now available to historians clearly show the extent of female participation in the conflict. Just as we honour the men of 1916 for their bravery and dedication to the cause of Ireland's independence it is right that we take time to remember and honour the courageous and committed women of the revolution. The republican women certainly played a notable and significant role in the conflict, displaying a militancy that surprised the British and the civilian authorities. In essence, however, the Rising was in many ways just a precursor to their much more organised participation in the War of Independence that followed almost three years later.

Very early on in the conflict, the British response to the Rising was made clear, leaving the rebels and the general public in no doubt that any act of rebellion against the Crown would be dealt with severely. The main architect of the British response to the Rising was General Sir John Maxwell, Commander-in-Chief of the British forces in Ireland. He was also placed at the head of the country's civil administration and Irish administrators were ordered to place themselves at his disposal and carry out his instructions. He issued an order instructing his men to shoot any individual suspected of being a rebel, uniformed or otherwise, who was armed and not surrendering. On Thursday morning during the week of fighting, he ordered the military to introduce 'free fire zones' in parts of the city where any civilian on the streets was assumed to be an enemy and treated accordingly.

On his arrival in Ireland, Maxwell decided to adopt a hard-line response to the Rising, proclaiming martial law not only in Dublin but across the country. He also decided by means of court martial to make examples of the leaders of the Rising, the seven signatories of the Proclamation, and ordered the arrests of those who had surrendered with them. He also ordered a nationwide sweep of all known or suspected republicans to be conducted by the army in tandem with the RIC and Intelligence Service. Some 3,500 people were arrested, with most having played no part in the conflict and taken into custody merely for being suspected of having republican sympathies or tendencies.

The most visible British response to the Rising was the holding of military courts and by the time they had finished their business some ninety-three individuals were sentenced to death, of which fifteen were confirmed by Maxwell. It was only in 1999 that the official British government records of the trials were released to the public. Though they appear to be comprehensive, there are some anomalies, especially in relation to the actual times and dates of the executions. All but two of the cases were heard in Richmond Barracks, the exceptions being James Connolly, who was in bed in the Red Cross hospital in Dublin Castle as a result of his injuries, and Thomas Kent, who was executed in his native County Cork. Brigadier General Charles Blackadder of the 177th Infantry Brigade presided at seven of the cases between 2 and 4 May. He was described by a friend as a 'charming, sympathetic person, half-French, very emotional and terribly affected by the work he had to do'.

From 3 to 5 May, Brigadier Maconchy of the 178th Brigade, Sherwood Foresters and a native of Rathmore, County Longford, presided over the trials of four of the leaders. Though less emotional than Blackadder, he was reputed to have found the whole process very stressful and actually protested against his appointment on the basis that he was an Irishman. He was replaced on 5 May by Colonel D. Sprate, who presided over the final three cases that resulted in executions. The man chosen by the Attorney General, James Campbell, as prosecution counsel was the Dublin-born William G. Wylie, the son of a presbyterian clergyman from Ulster. He had considerable sympathy for the men on trial and constantly voiced his disapproval of the speed and secrecy of the trials, maintaining they should have been held in public. Initially, he suggested the men were entitled to defence counsel, but his opinion was rejected by the Attorney General. Wylie did succeed, after MacDonagh's trial on 2 May, in ensuring defendants were permitted to call witnesses if they so wished. It seems Wylie was courteous to all the accused and John MacBride expressed his gratitude to him at the end of his trial.

The first three men to face the firing squad on 3 May were P.H. Pearse, Tom Clarke and Thomas MacDonagh, all signatories of the Proclamation and dedicated to the republican ideal. All three were to the forefront in the planning and carrying out of the conflict. Another signatory of the Proclamation, the terminally ill but very brave Joseph Plunkett, faced the firing squad a day later on 4 May. He was joined by Ned Daly, who commanded the Four Courts garrison during the conflict. Also executed that day were Michael O'Hanrahan, second in command to MacDonagh in Jacob's Biscuit Factory, and Willie Pearse, who was put on trial and executed for no apparent reason other than he was the younger brother of P.H. Pearse.

The following day, 5 May, saw the execution of John McBride, who had taken part in the Boer War on the side of the Boers and had been commissioned with the rank of major. McBride, the estranged husband of Maud Gonne, was well known to the British and consequently had been kept out of the planning of the Rising. He found himself involved in the conflict really by accident. He was in the city on Easter Monday to meet his brother and, as he walked up Grafton Street, he saw MacDonagh in uniform and offered his services to him there and then. He accompanied the garrison to Jacob's Biscuit Factory, where, by all accounts he acquitted himself very well and won the admiration of the men. On surrender, it seems, he proudly marched out from the factory with his comrades still attired in his best suit and bowler hat.

On 8 May four more executions took place and included in those who faced the firing squad was Éamonn Ceannt, a signatory of the Proclamation and Commandant of the South Dublin Union garrison. Also shot was Con Colbert, who had fought at Watkin's Brewery, Jameson Distillery and Marrowbone Lane. He was known to the Dublin Metropolitan Police detectives, who had often watched him drilling Fianna Eireann boys prior to the Rising. The third man shot that day was Sean Heuston, who commanded the garrison at the Mendicity Institute on the south side of the city. The fourth man shot was Michael Mallin, Commandant and second in command of the Irish Citizen Army. He commanded the St Stephen's Green garrison that eventually retreated to the College of Surgeons and held out there until the surrender.

On 9 May, Corkman Thomas Kent was executed after a gunfight with the RIC at his family home, Bawnard House, Castlelyons, in County Cork. Kent and his three brothers planned to take part in the fighting had it broken out in Cork. They held off the police in a four-hour gunfight, during which one policeman, Head Constable William Rowe, was killed. Eventually, the brothers surrendered and two of them, Thomas and William, were put on trial for armed rebellion. William was acquitted while Thomas was found guilty and sentenced to death. He was executed by firing squad in Cork and was the only person outside of Dublin to be shot for his role in events surrounding Easter Week.

On 12 May the final two men to be executed were Sean MacDermott and James Connolly, both signatories of the Proclamation and both equally committed to the rebellion. MacDermott was prominent throughout the planning process and was a major driving force, not only in the Irish Volunteers but also in the IRB. Deeply committed to the ideal of independence, he saw the Rising as the culmination of his life's work and willingly faced the firing squad for a cause in which he believed passionately. James Connolly, the leader of the Citizen Army and a Scotsman by birth, was another man committed to the cause of independence and the ideal of an Irish socialist republic. He went to the breakers yard in Kilmainham on a stretcher having sustained bullet wounds to his leg during the fighting, and he faced his executioners bravely and with no regret for the part he played in the conflict. In the days prior to his death, Connolly struck up an unlikely friendship with the Capuchin priest from Church Street, Father Aloysius. The priest ministered to Connolly and was with him when he died. In his witness statement to the Bureau of Military History, Aloysius poignantly recounted those last few hours with Connolly, a man he came to admire greatly. He was asked by a British officer, Captain Stanley, on the evening of 11 May, to make himself available to minister to Connolly during his last hours. Aloysius awaited the call and at one o'clock the following morning a car duly arrived to take him to Dublin Castle, where Connolly was being held in the hospital wing. He recalled:

> I heard Connolly's confession and gave him Communion again. Then I left while he was given a light meal. I had a long talk with Stanley in the Castle Yard and he told me he had been very impressed by Connolly.[47]

Connolly was laid on a stretcher and brought to a car and Aloysius travelled with him. Once in the yard in Kilmainham Jail, Connolly was placed on a chair in front of the firing squad and the order to fire was given. Father Eugene McCarthy, who was also in attendance, anointed him. Father Aloysius recalled:

> I had stood just behind the firing line. It was a scene I should not ask to witness again. I had got to know Connolly – to wonder at his strength of character and marvellous power of concentration. I got to regret that I had not known him longer and now, I had to say goodbye. All I could do was to return home with a heavy heart and to offer the holy sacrifice for his soul.[48]

At the end of the Rising the prevailing mood among the people of Dublin was one of indignation and anger. For one full week their lives had been turned upside down by the actions of a small few. As the citizens milled around the centre of the city during the days after the Rising, many found it difficult to come to terms with the devastation inflicted on their city. There was, of course, a great degree of mourning because around 250 of the

450 deaths during the conflict fell into the civilian category, including some 38 children. Added to the human misery of death and injury was the clearly visible infrastructural damage that enraged many Dubliners, causing them to vent their anger against those who had taken part in the rebellion.

The Rising brought about a great deal of dislocation and disruption for the ordinary citizens of the inner city. Many, who were living in houses within the fighting zones, eventually had to be evacuated, while a huge number of business properties were destroyed or badly damaged. During the week of fighting the transport system collapsed and the gas supply was cut off by the rebels hoping to reduce the risk of their strongholds catching fire. There was no postal, telephone or telegraph services and most newspapers did not go to print. In the days following the Rising, all these services had to be reinstated to bring some semblance of normality back to the city.

With all the inconveniences the people of Dublin had to endure during the week of fighting, it was no surprise there was little in the way of sympathy for the rebels. For many Dubliners, the Rising was badly timed as the city was prospering economically. There was also the worry the rebellion might harden the British attitude towards Ireland and they would renege on their promise to introduce home rule once the war on the Continent was over. Also, very importantly, thousands of Dublin families had menfolk serving in the British Army, which meant there was a welcome and much-needed flow of 'separation money' into the city and they viewed the actions of the rebels as nothing short of treachery.

By the time the conflict ended, the prevailing mood among the citizens of Dublin was one of unhappiness and that mood did not go unnoticed by the Volunteers as they surrendered at different point around the city. For example, at the College of Surgeons, the surrendering Volunteers encountered fierce verbal abuse from members of the public. In fact, it was so vitriolic the British forces taking the surrender had to set up a protective cordon in Grafton Street to restrain the mob at bayonet point. Similar scenes ensued at Jacob's Biscuit Factory, when the rebels were forced to run the gauntlet of further abuse as they were escorted to Richmond Barracks. It was no coincidence the route to the barracks took in areas scarred by abject poverty and inhabited by families who had loved ones fighting for King and country in the trenches on the Western Front and elsewhere.

One Volunteer, Robert Holland of 'F' Company, 4th Battalion, Dublin Brigade, who was part of the Marrowbone Lane garrison under the command of Con Colbert, recalled in his witness statement to the Bureau of Military History how he and his comrades were treated upon their surrender:

> Colbert then announced that we were surrendering unconditionally and that anyone wishing to escape could do so … I have a distinct recollection of Joe McGrath saying, 'Toor-a-loo, boys, I'm off.' He crossed the wall. Some others broke also. Then Colbert reformed us up, numbered us off and we 'sloped arms' and marched out of the Distillery through the front entrance with Colbert at our head. We fell in behind the South Dublin Union ambulance which was in the rear of the South Dublin Union garrison. The Cumann na mBan girls were formed up in our rear … On our route we were subjected to very ugly remarks and cat-calls from the poorer classes … When we were almost at the Coombe Maternity Hospital, two drunken men insisted on falling in with us. They were ejected from our ranks several times on the route but eventually must have got into the ranks in my rear … about two months later I saw these two men taking their exercise in Knutsford Prison.[49]

Holland recalled how he and his comrades were ordered to lay down their arms at the Iveagh Baths and were then searched by British Army personnel. Once that was completed, they were ordered to form up and make ready to continue their surrender march. Holland went on to recall what happened next:

> We were ordered into fours and we got a 'right turn' and marched back into Patrick Street and then turned into Nicholas Street, then into Christ Church Street, High Street, Thomas Street, James's Street, Mount Brown and Kilmainham. There were few people on the Streets up to Kilmainham Cross, but at this point a crowd had gathered. It would be about 8 p.m. and was falling dusk. At Kilmainham we were jeered at and as we passed by Murray's Lane both men, women and children used filthy expressions at us. 'F' Company, which was mainly made up of men from Inchicore, heard all their names called out at intervals by the bystanders. They were, 'shoot the Sinn Fein b…s'. My name was called out by some boys and girls I had gone to school with and Peadar Doyle was subjected to some very rude remarks. The British troops saved us from manhandling.[50]

However, it would be unfair to say all Volunteers met a barrage of verbal and physical abuse from the people of Dublin. As he emerged with his men from Boland's Mills, Éamon de Valera was struck by the generous and spontaneous greeting they received from the local people, though he was angered by the fact that he and his men had been unable to join the rebels in the fight against the British. Éamonn Ceannt was also pleased with the reception he and his men received from the local people as they marched out of the South Dublin Union. They sensed the mood of the people was clearly turning in their favour at that time. Indeed, all indications suggested that many members of the public were in the process of changing their views and were starting to regard the rebels as very brave individuals, all of whom had fought an honourable and a clean fight against a formidable and imposing enemy. One observer, John Clarke, a shop owner who lived near the Four Courts, wrote after witnessing the surrender of Edward Daly and his men:

> This ends the last attempt for poor old Ireland. What noble fellows! The cream of the land. None of your corner-boy class.[51]

The rebels, in the aftermath of the conflict, also found support in the medical community, especially within the staff of the Richmond Hospital who tended to the gravely wounded and recognised their bravery and dedication to the independence cause. Support was also forthcoming from many of the religious orders in the city. Some priest and nuns provided support and assistance during the fighting and were on hand to help the men after their surrender. One order that was particularly involved in looking after the needs of the rebels during and after the fighting was the Capuchin community in Church Street. To the very end, as we just saw, in the case of James Connolly, the Capuchins stood by the Volunteers and extolled their virtues to all and sundry. Oscar Traynor recalled the moment when he and his comrades were being escorted from the Rotunda to Richmond Barracks:

> Outside the gates of the barracks, I saw a Capuchin priest who, as we were entering, kept saying, with tears in his eyes, 'Misneach' (Courage), which was completely unintelligible to the enemy forces.[52]

In the immediate aftermath of the Rising, as the executions were carried out and news of them filtered into the public domain, the mood of the people in the city and across the country changed dramatically. The hostility and ambivalence of the general public, which had so clearly been on display, quickly dissipated. Many began to question the response and the actions of the British Army and the Castle authorities, believing they were disproportionate to the actions of the rebels. Almost overnight, the people of Ireland stopped viewing the rebels as renegades and troublemakers and recognised them as martyrs and heroes, all of whom had pursued a just and noble cause, that of Irish independence and freedom from British rule. Though the Easter Rising of 1916 was a military defeat for those who espoused the republican ideal, it did without any shadow of doubt change the course of Ireland's history and set the foundation for a greater and a much more profound struggle to come.

PART TWO

Irish Republicanism

Political Awakening and Military Reorganisation

CHAPTER EIGHT

Republicans Embrace a Political Agenda

1917–18

In the days immediately following the Rising, a Royal Commission under the auspices of Lord Hardinge of Penhurst was set up to investigate the causes of the conflict. The Commission started work on 18 May and Hardinge, together with two judges, heard evidence over nine days, five in London and four in Dublin. They interviewed twenty-nine people, including key figures such as Augustine Birrell, the Chief Secretary for Ireland, Nevile Chamberlain, the Inspector General of the Royal Irish Constabulary, and Sir Matthew Nathan, the Under-Secretary for Ireland. The remit of the enquiry was essentially to gain an understanding of why the Rising actually took place and why it was such a surprise to the authorities in Ireland. The Commission's report was published on 26 June 1916 and it criticised the administrative and intelligence systems that were in place in Ireland. It concluded the main cause of the conflict, 'appears to be that lawlessness was allowed grow up unchecked, and that Ireland for several years past has been administered on the principle that it was safer and more expedient to leave the law in abeyance if collision with any faction of the Irish people could thereby be avoided'.

Essentially, the report suggested the root cause of the conflict had its origins in the 1913 Strike and Lockout with the creation of the paramilitary Irish Citizens Army. The formation of that organisation, the report concluded, inspired the founding of the Irish Volunteers. The report also concluded that Birrell and Nathan had permitted the republican organisation to flourish unhindered by the authorities. In his evidence to the commission, Birrell blamed the uncertainty over home rule as the main reason why the republican ideal garnered the support it did among a cohort of Irish men and women. The report was so damning it left Birrell and Nathan with little option but to resign their positions.

Many of the republicans arrested in the aftermath of the Rising were released from mid-June onwards. However, a cohort of those who continued to be detained found themselves in places like Reading Jail, while some 1,836 men were eventually incarcerated in the Frongoch internment camp in Wales. Over the following months, until their release in December 1916, the seeds for a future conflict were sown by the men in the camp while, at the same time, a new political approach to the issue of Ireland's independence was formulated. Over time, the numbers in the camp were eventually whittled down to around 600 inmates, most of whom had no intention of walking away from the independence struggle. During those months, a new and younger breed of republican leaders emerged, many of whom were destined to chart a new political course as well as take a leading role in a future military conflict with the British.

Frongoch is situated about 2½ miles from the small town of Bala and today one could drive past the village without really noticing it. Yet, it unwittingly played an integral role in the struggle for independence. In 1916 the village was something of an economic backwater because some years earlier a fairly successful whiskey distillery that had provided the locals with employment and had underpinned the area's economy went out of business. Its premises remained derelict until the Great War, when they were converted into camps for German prisoners of war. When the Irish prisoners arrived, the camp was divided into two sections; the South Camp based in old buildings of the distillery and the North Camp situated on higher ground. Between the two camps there was a road leading to the railway station and nearby was an open field that had the distinction of hosting the first ever hurling match played in Wales by teams selected from the prisoners.

The prisoners included young farm boys and labourers as well as teachers, tradesmen and trade unionists, military strategists, poets, artists, authors, songwriters, singers and actors and, they all had one thing in common, a fervent belief in Irish independence. During their months of captivity, the younger men sat and listened to the senior men, most of whom had taken part in the Rising. Michael Collins, who was to become one of the dominant voices in Frongoch, later reckoned very few of the younger men had any real awareness of the Rising. However, because of Collins's influence and a coterie of other prominent individuals, the seeds of the War of Independence were sown and the new tactic of guerrilla warfare was devised as the best way to take on the forces of the Crown in any future conflict.

During the months of incarceration life was not always easy in conditions that were, in essence, appalling, but it seems the vast majority of the men accepted their fate and made the best of the situation they found themselves in. They went on route marches to maintain their fitness and organised the playing of sports. They exercised their minds through classes and talks on a wide variety of subjects, while some men learned to play musical instruments and others took part in drama productions. Collins even took to learning the Welsh language, impressed by the locals who were fluent in it. There was much in the way of political discussion and many ideas were kicked around about the direction a future independent Ireland should take. The lessons of the military failure that was the Easter Rising were revisited and innovative new military strategies to advance the independence struggle were put forward and discussed. By December 1916, when the British authorities decided it was no longer feasible to keep the men locked up, they had regrouped under a new leadership regime ready to strike out once again in pursuit of Ireland's freedom and her right to self-determination.

From the early weeks of 1917 the political activists in the republican movement embarked on a new and far-reaching programme designed to bring the independence ideal to the forefront of people's political thinking. At the same time, the unionist population in Ulster, under the leadership of James Craig, was still railing against the proposed introduction of home rule on the island of Ireland. On the other hand, the Irish Parliamentary Party, under the leadership of John Redmond, continued to believe its long-held and much cherished ambition of sitting and ruling in a Dublin parliament would materialise once the war on the Continent ended. That ambition was never realised and instead what emerged between 1917 and 1919 was a united and coherent separatist political party that eventually attracted the support of the majority of voters across the country. That process started in earnest during 1917 and reached its conclusion in January 1919 with the first sitting of a Sinn Fein-dominated Dail Eireann in Dublin's Mansion House. What follows here is the story of how the different elements purporting to act in the name of republicanism eventually came together to form a single party called Sinn Fein that went on to dominate the political scene in Ireland from December 1918 to the signing of the Anglo-Irish Treaty in December 1921.

Up to and including the Easter Rising, the Irish Parliamentary Party enjoyed the overwhelming support of Irish nationalists and, at first, it seemed the actions of a few radicals in Dublin had little hope of endangering the political ambitions of many moderates. However, the disproportionate response of the British to the Rising, when sixteen men were executed and over 3,000 republicans were arrested, brought about a change of attitude across the country as resentment of the rebel's actions was replaced by a genuine concern for their fate. Many observers noticed a change in public attitude in the early weeks after the Rising. As the executions came to an end, one commentator was moved to intimate that, 'if the military executions do not stop … Ireland will be driven into sympathy with Sinn Fein'. The original Sinn Fein party founded by Arthur Griffith in 1905 had no involvement in the Rising, yet, remarkably, the term 'Sinn Fein' was universally applied to the conflict by all and sundry. It was to prove a very perceptive observation. What is even more extraordinary is that the Sinn Fein party itself had made very little impact on Irish politics since its inception and had reached its peak of influence around 1909, when some 100 Sinn Fein clubs were in existence. By the outbreak of the First World War, the party's membership had declined significantly and its future looked anything but bright. However, the political landscape changed dramatically in 1917 when the Irish Volunteers, Cumann na mBan and the IRB, all republican organisations committed to the use of force to achieve independence, found themselves in league with nationalist organisations like the Gaelic Athletic Association and the Gaelic League. They all came together under the Sinn Fein name, thereby giving Arthur Griffith's party an unexpected new lease of life.

So, how did the Sinn Fein dominance of Irish politics take root in 1917? By that time the Sinn Fein movement, as we will now call it, had huge numbers of enthusiastic foot soldiers but it was in need of a new and vibrant leadership in order to give it a sense of direction and purpose. The release of young and more aggressive-minded men from places like Frongoch and Reading Jail had a tremendous impact on the republican movement and within months they brought Sinn Fein to an unprecedented level of national predominance. Men like Michael Collins, Cathal Brugha, W.T. Cosgrave and Arthur Griffith positioned themselves to play leading roles in the Sinn Fein movement in the early months of 1917 and were, in time, joined by Éamon de Valera.

Their chance to engage the movement in political activity came very quickly in 1917 when a parliamentary seat became vacant in the constituency of North Roscommon. Local Sinn Fein activists, led by Father Michael O'Flanagan, decided to run a candidate in the ensuing by-election and they turned to Count Plunkett, a well-known separatist, to contest it on behalf of the party. He was a surprise choice, being, it seems, an unlikely revolutionary, but he was the father of Joseph Plunkett, one of the executed leaders of the Easter Rising. His two other sons had been held in British captivity after the conflict, so Plunkett himself was viewed as a man of republican credentials and above reproach. He was, at that time, 65 years of age and a wealthy property owner with a reputation for being well read in the arts. He was a supporter of the Gaelic League and had been a director of the National Museum from 1907 to 1916, when he was dismissed from his post and interned in England on account of his son's activities.

The election took place on 3 February 1917 and Plunkett was ably assisted and supported by members of the Volunteers as well as Sinn Fein party activists. He went on to secure a fine victory with a majority of 687 votes over his Irish Parliamentary Party opponent and kick-started what turned out to be a series of Sinn Fein victories throughout 1917. Plunkett's victory was a seismic moment in Irish politics and, for the first time, the mighty Irish Parliamentary Party found itself in the shadow of a new and potentially powerful political opponent. One of the most important aspects of the by-election was the realisation by all republicans and nationalists of the need to close ranks in order to advance the independence cause. Before they all left Roscommon they held a meeting, during which it was agreed all contacts made during the campaign would be renewed once they were back in Dublin.

Some eleven days later, Count Plunkett hosted a meeting in his own home that was attended by Griffith and Rory O'Connor together with fifteen other Sinn Fein members, 'for the purpose of finding some basis of co-operation, some agreement as to policy, that would weld together all the genuine nationalist forces as to make their efforts more cohesive'. A committee was set up to co-ordinate the activities of all republican organisations and, though it did not prove to be an effective one, the notion of consultation among all republicans was well and truly established. During the following months after the by-election, Sinn Fein began to build up an efficient, energetic grass-roots organisation, making it the dominant political force in the country. However, it was not all plain sailing as there were numerous arguments and disagreements, many of which revolved around Count Plunkett, who was proving to be a very divisive, intolerant and dogmatic individual.

Younger men such as Collins and Brugha, both of whom represented the Volunteers, were not overly enamoured with some of the views of the older men, and Plunkett's often erratic behaviour only served to complicate matters and accentuate the differences that were clearly evident within the republican family. Plunkett's tendency to summon public and private meetings without proper consultation, as well as making speeches promoting views that were often at variance with others, did not help the cause of unity. His by-election victory seemed to give him a false sense of self-importance and he failed to realise his role was that of an accidental stopgap leader. He was, in essence, much more suited to the role of a figurehead rather than the self-appointed leader of the emerging movement that had adopted the Sinn Fein name. As the year progressed, the debate in Sinn Fein revolved around the question of whether the party should aim formally at establishing an Irish republic and whether Plunkett and future republican members of parliament should take their seats in Westminster. As the months passed the usual moderate and radical wings began to take shape, as they would in most political parties.

Plunkett announced a convention to be held in Dublin's Mansion House on 19 April 1917 and he invited representatives from county councils and other authorities as well as numerous other nationalist-minded organisations. The differences in opinion between Plunkett and others in attendance quickly surfaced and Arthur Griffith, realising the negative impact of the discord, did his best to mediate between the differing factions despite his own well-known antipathy towards the venerable Count. However, the manifesto Plunkett issued was a divisive document and was seen by many as an egotistical one, casting him in the role of unquestioned leader of Irish republicanism. In his witness statement to the Bureau of Military History, Liam de Roiste, a member of the Irish Volunteers and a member of Dail Eireann from 1918 to 1923, recalled the gathering as the 'Plunkett Convention', saying:

> There was a very large attendance. I attended as delegate from Cork Sinn Fein Executive. It was apparent there were many cross-currents of opinion among those present as to the line of action to be taken and to the personnel of an Executive that may be formed. There was a clash between Count Plunkett and Griffith. It was apparent, however, that there was no general support for the Count as leader of 'a new movement'.
>
> Griffith advocated the old Sinn Fein policy of 'passive resistance', but this did not commend itself to certain militant sections whose only idea was that of 'physical force' through the Volunteers. Also, Griffith was said to have opposed the Rising. There was unanimity regarding the presentation of Ireland's case at the Peace Conference.[53]

The majority of the county councils ignored the invitation to the meeting and failed to send representatives to the Mansion House, and only sixty-eight of the 227 public bodies circularised were represented. The meeting passed motions in relation to the Paris Peace Conference as well as on the issue of conscription for Ireland. It also issued a proclamation affirming Ireland's right to independence.

In his address to the gathering, Plunkett ignored the existence of Griffith's Sinn Fein and called for the setting up of a completely new organisation that he wanted to call the Liberty League. This, he claimed, would operate along the same lines of the original Sinn Fein with clubs established across the country. Plunket clearly attempted to outmanoeuvre Griffith and his party at a level that mattered most; that is, in the villages and parishes around the country. Griffith reacted angrily, claiming his party would not allow itself to be swallowed up in any new body or give up its policies or its constitution. Eventually, a compromise was reached, with all republican elements reporting to what became known as the Mansion House Committee based in Dublin, which was tasked with co-ordinating all republican political activities. It was an honest attempt to bring unity to the various factions making up the republican family.

The spring and summer of 1917 saw the Sinn Fein movement spread country wide, mainly due to the enthusiasm of the younger cohort of Volunteers and Griffith's clever use of propaganda. By July 1917 the RIC estimated 166 Sinn Fein clubs with a membership of 11,000 were up and running and by mid-August, the figures had increased to 336 clubs and 21,000 members. By October, 1,200 clubs were operating with a membership of 250,000 and clearly Sinn Fein was the most popular and dominant political organisation in the country. The massive increase in numbers during that summer can also be attributed to many spontaneous local initiatives; more so than any assistance from the Dublin leadership, though it did become more actively involved in the autumn in an effort to consolidate all the gains.

While the Sinn Fein clubs were flourishing, Plunkett attempted to establish the Liberty League around the country and found a modicum of support, especially in Cork and Kerry. The League was opposed by prominent separatists, who doubted the wisdom of setting up an organisation in districts already well served by a Sinn Fein club. The Liberty League failed to compete with Sinn Fein clubs because it lacked all its rival's advantages. Sinn Fein had come into existence earlier and had a well-known name and a tradition, as well as a very efficient central office with two full-time paid organisers and two influential newspapers, *Nationality* and *The Irishman*. It wasn't long before Plunkett threw in the towel and abandoned his Liberty League, with its clubs merged with those of Sinn Fein.

The decision to merge both organisations was taken at a meeting of the Mansion House Committee held at the home of Cathal Brugha in the Dublin suburb of Rathmines. Griffith was retained as President of the new organisation, again to be called Sinn Fein, with the constitution to be left in place until the convening of a convention set for October 1917. On 10 May, Sinn Fein won its second seat in Parliament when Joseph McGuinness was victorious in the South Longford by-election in what was another disaster for the Irish Parliamentary Party. In June, Éamon de Valera and Thomas Ashe were released from prison and arrived back into the country, re-engaging with a republican movement moving from division to unanimity. Though not inclined to support the political path during their incarceration, the former prisoners lost their aversion to political activity soon after their release and when they joined the Sinn Fein party they found it to be an efficient and energetic organisation. On 10 July, De Valera stood for election in the East Clare by-election and won impressively. In August 1917, W.T. Cosgrave won the Kilkenny by-election. The party was surging in popularity and the writing was on the wall for the Irish Parliamentary Party. By October 1917, Thomas Ashe was dead and de Valera was well placed to assume the leadership of the party.

Before the October convention, Griffith continued to act as the leader of Sinn Fein but he had no real desire for personal power or authority and was content to confine himself to the writing and dissemination of propaganda. Griffith did admire de Valera because of his participation in the Easter Rising, which he believed gave him a legitimate claim to high office. In the days leading up to the convention, Griffith was aware de Valera intended to challenge him for the leadership of Sinn Fein. Both men had a good body of support but Griffith decided not to contest any election and he confirmed that decision to de Valera, though he did not announce it publicly and did not do so until the convention was under way. Realising he had little chance of winning a leadership contest, Plunkett also stepped aside in favour of de Valera, who was duly elected as President. The Sinn Fein republican movement was at last unified under one popular leader.

With the leadership question settled, the focus of the convention shifted to agreeing on policy matters, which had been left very vague during the previous months. The question of abstention from Westminster was agreed upon before the meeting turned its attention to the writing of a constitution. The meeting eventually agreed on a constitution that called for the establishment of a republic and, when achieved, the people would decide on a form of government. It should be noted the convention ignored the very pressing social and economic issues like poverty and unemployment, which were rampant in the country, and the delegates offered no view on how the problems could be resolved. Nevertheless, the convention was a triumphant conclusion to a process that culminated in the unification of various republican organisations under the banner of Sinn Fein.

In May 1917 in a response to the changing political scene in Ireland, David Lloyd George, the British Prime Minister, suggested to John Redmond, leader of the Irish Parliamentary Party, that an Irish Convention be set up to give Ireland the opportunity to agree a form of self-government with the country remaining part of the Union. The convention met for the first time in June 1917, made up of delegates representing different political parties and organisations from other elements of society. The Sinn Fein party was, of course, conspicuous by its absence. The convention met over a number of phases and the final one took place in Trinity College between January and April 1918 but it struggled to make any real progress. The final report, which was published on 8 April 1918, recommended that home rule be implemented as quickly as possible. With the British Army struggling in the war on the Continent, the government in London took the decision to implement both home rule and conscription in Ireland at the same time.

Needless to say, the convention report fell by the wayside very quickly when it became apparent the introduction of conscription would have caused serious public disorder and discontent across the country. Sinn Fein and the Catholic Church and, even the Irish Parliamentary Party, vehemently opposed conscription and they all did a fine job in mobilising the majority of the population against it. There was even a general strike in opposition to it in April. As it turned out, the conscription crisis dissipated as the British fortunes on the Western Front took a turn for the better when the Germans' final military onslaught of the war petered out. By the time convention issued the report, John Redmond was dead, having suffered heart failure following a routine operation in a London hospital in early March.

In May 1918 the British made a further attempt to discredit the republican movement when the authorities arrested seventy-three prominent Sinn Fein personnel, including de Valera, Griffith, Kathleen Clarke and Constance Markievicz. The British claimed they had discovered a 'German Plot' to import arms for Sinn Fein. It backfired spectacularly as no one in Ireland gave any credence to the claim and it only served to convince the majority of people the government feared the continuing rise of Sinn Fein. The consequence of the government's action was to increase support for the party rather than diminish it. Near the end of June, Arthur Griffith won a by-election in East Cavan. It was Sinn Fein's first election victory since their four victories of the previous year and it provided the party with another timely boost. In July, the authorities, still determined to put the shackles on the republicans, proclaimed both the Irish Volunteers and Sinn Fein as 'dangerous organisations' in certain areas of the country.

Despite British attempts to curtail the influence of the republicans, there was little doubt that by December 1918, the political landscape in Ireland had changed dramatically from that which had prevailed prior to the Easter Rising in 1916. The five by-election wins garnered by Sinn Fein over the previous two years started a political momentum that showed no signs of slowing down. After the signing of the Armistice in November 1918, the Prime Minister, Lloyd George, decided to call a general election to seek a mandate from the people of Britain and Ireland to continue with his coalition government and oversee the transfer from a state of war to peacetime. It turned out to be a momentous political decision for Ireland and the impact was profound in the sense that it widened the already gaping political divide in existence across the country at that time.

The 1918 general election was unique in a number of ways. It was the first general election to be held on one day, Saturday, 14 December, though the votes were not counted until 28 December in order to allow time for the ballots cast by the many soldiers still on active duty in Europe to be transported back to Britain. It was also the first general election to be held after the passing of the Representation of the People Act of 1916, which extended the franchise to include women over the age of 30 and all men over the age of 21. The election is also notable for the fact that it was the last ever held in Ireland on an all-island basis as just two years later the Government of Ireland Act set up the state of Northern Ireland and, two years later still the Irish Free State emerged out of the Anglo-Irish Treaty of 1921. The election was taken very seriously all across the country and the Irish Volunteers were out in force to ensure that every ballot was counted. In fact, that organisation went to great lengths to secure the ballot boxes once the voting closed. In his witness statement to the Bureau of Military History, Thomas Donnelly of the Newbliss Company in Monaghan recalled how he and his comrades guarded the ballot boxes for two weeks:

> The General election of 1918 aroused considerable activity of a political nature in the Volunteer organisation. Ernest Blythe

> was the Sinn Fein candidate. The main part of the election was carried out by the Volunteers. After the closing of the polling, on the day of the election, the ballot boxes had to be guarded by Volunteers for two weeks until the count took place. The police authorities at first attempted to prevent the Volunteers guarding the ballot boxes. When a Volunteer guard was first posted, by Seamus Stack of Kerry, who was in charge in Monaghan, Mr Stack carried his point and a guard of Volunteers remained on duty night and day from the 14th December date of polling up to the 28th December, when the counting of votes took place.[54]

The election resulted in a landslide victory for Lloyd George's coalition government but in Ireland there was an equally dramatic result as Sinn Fein swept to an overwhelming win in terms of seats over the once-mighty Irish Parliamentary Party, by then under the leadership of John Dillon. It was a watershed result, setting the country on a new political course that eventually brought it into conflict with Britain in the form of the War of Independence. The result confirmed Sinn Fein won 73 of the 105 seats reserved for Ireland. During the campaign the party placed an emphasis on the unbroken history of Irish resistance to British rule and particularly focussed on recent events like the Easter Rising and the anti-conscription campaign as examples of that very same resistance.

The Sinn Fein manifesto stressed the importance of nationhood and unity as well as the Irish people's possession of a distinctive national culture and social order. It also stressed the Irish people's moral courage and praised their dignity in the face of centuries of alien aggression. The manifesto also committed the party to using 'any and every means available to render impotent the power of England to hold Ireland in subjection by military force or otherwise'. During the campaign the Sinn Fein candidates openly called for the setting up of an Irish republic, and the same demand was also to be found in the pro-Sinn Fein press despite attempts by the authorities to supress the various publications under the Party's and its supporters' control.

On the other hand, the Irish Parliamentary Party stuck rigidly with its long-held view that the best way forward for Ireland was to follow the path of home rule. The Irish Party's candidates argued Ireland would be much better off as part of a strong and stable union with Britain with all the economic and social benefits it brought with it. This view, of course, proved to be outdated and unacceptable to so many voters, especially those of the younger generation. It was the younger generation that went on to provide the mandate for Sinn Fein to take the country away from home rule and on a path to independence and the breaking of the link with Britain.

With 70 per cent of Irish adults eligible to vote in 1918 instead of the previous figure of 25 per cent in past elections, Sinn Fein's voter constituency increased dramatically. In round figures the numbers eligible to vote rose from 698,000 to 1,932,000 and Sinn Fein received 47.5 per cent of the votes cast. Undoubtedly, the Sinn Fein vote was boosted by the successful anti-conscription campaign but the party also appealed to women voters, especially the younger generation who saw it as a platform from which they could air their political views. The fact that the party put forward two female candidates in the election made it the most progressive and radical political party in Britain and Ireland. The rise of Sinn Fein had a hugely detrimental impact on the Irish Parliamentary Party, which held a view diametrically opposed to the republicans. Having dominated Irish politics for the previous forty years with its home rule policy, it was unused to trading political blows with another party, and especially so during election campaigns. Though it would never accept it as being the case during the 1918 election campaign, the party was clearly out of step with the new culture of political activism introduced by Sinn Fein. By the time the results of the election were confirmed it was a demoralised party with just six candidates returned to Westminster.

Sinn Fein also had to contend with the Labour Party in 1918 and its radical election manifesto. Led by the highly competent and likeable Englishman, Thomas Johnson, it put forward a manifesto promising to adopt the same principles of the Russian Revolution. However, divisions within the party ranks soon emerged over whether it should contest the election or not. Eventually, the party hierarchy decided against contesting the election and allowed Sinn Fein a free run in return for the promise that, should it form a government, it would introduce a programme of social and economic reforms. Once in power, Sinn Fein unashamedly reneged on its promise to do so. The only sector of the country where Sinn Fein failed to make an impact was in Ulster, where the unionists continued to hold sway. Sinn Fein's victory was all the more remarkable when one considers the authorities did everything in their power to impede the party's progress. Many of its leaders, including de Valera and Griffith, were jailed as early as May 1918. This drastic action by the government actually backfired spectacularly as some forty-seven Sinn Fein candidates were elected from their prison cells. It seems the party's election clarion call to the public, 'Put them in to get them out' resonated with the voters, who responded by casting their votes at the ballot boxes.

So, who were the successful candidates in the election? It is fair to say many of those who were elected in 1918 went on to contribute to Irish public life for the following twenty years or more. Victorious candidates Arthur Griffth, Michael Collins, Robert Barton, George Gavan Duffy and Éamonn Duggan had the hopes of the people thrust upon their broad shoulders as delegates to the Anglo-Irish Treaty negotiations in 1921. Others, including Éamon de Valera, Harry Boland, Austin Stack and Sean Moylan, found themselves unable to accept the Treaty. Terence MacSwiney eventually gave his life for the cause he passionately believed in as a result of a very public hunger strike in 1920. W.T. Cosgrave, Ernest Blythe, Kevin O'Higgins, Desmond Fitzgerald and Eoin MacNeill cut their political teeth in the election and all went on to be part of the first Cumann na nGaedheal government in the fledgling Irish Free State. The men of 1916 were not forgotten and Count Plunkett was elected, as was Sean T. O'Kelly, who later had the honour of becoming the Second President of Ireland between 1945 and 1959. One woman, Constance Markievicz, was elected, thus becoming the first to be elected to the Westminster parliament. Like the rest of her Sinn Fein colleagues, she did not take her seat due to the party's abstention policy.

The election marked the end of the road for the Irish Parliamentary Party and the result confirmed the majority of people outside Ulster were no longer interested in the political concept it had long championed, that of home rule. The consequences of the election result were enormous and far reaching for the whole island of Ireland. The result copper-fastened the unionists' view that their future was best served by being part of a union with Britain, in which their Protestantism would be respected and their undoubted economic well-being would not be endangered. Within two years of the election, the Government of Ireland Act of 1920 legitimised Northern Ireland as a separate state, bringing with it the contentious and long-enduring issue of partition. The response of the London government to the election result was, as expected, a negative one and the prevailing view was that Irish republicans would soon come to their senses and see the error of their ways. Until then, Ireland would continue to have military rule and the Sinn Fein MPs who languished in jails would remain there for the foreseeable future. This hard-line approach from London only served to cement the separatist attitude of Sinn Fein and the party took the decision to ignore the British administration in Ireland. Within weeks of the general election, Dail Eireann was established and its first meeting was held in Dublin's Mansion House on 21 January 1919. That day marked a defining moment in modern Ireland's political history as the country was enthusiastically and proudly set on a new and exciting journey of self-determination by the representatives of the country's revolutionary generation.

CHAPTER NINE

Reorganising the Volunteers

PROCURING ARMS AND GATHERING INTELLIGENCE

In November 1916 Cathal Brugha was released from hospital, still dealing with the wounds and scars of the Easter Rising. The authorities released him in the belief he had been seriously disabled as a result of his wounds and posed no danger to the political and military status quo that prevailed throughout the country after the failed rebellion. In the months after the Rising, the Volunteers, who were not in Frongoch or English jails, made some attempts to meet in their local areas. However, on a national basis, there was little to note until Brugha's release, when he became the catalyst for the Volunteers' renewal and reorganisation. Not long after his release, Brugha held a meeting at his home with Sean O'Muirthile and Diarmuid O'Hegarty, who were both prominent members of the IRB. Brugha told his visitors he was done with the IRB and he wished to discuss the future of the Irish Volunteers. They agreed to call a meeting in Fleming's Hotel on Gardiner Street for later that month to plot a way forward for the organisation. About fifty representatives attended the meeting, chaired by Brugha, who was still getting around on crutches. A decision was made to establish a provisional committee under the direction of Brugha and it was tasked with making contact with the areas not represented at the meeting with a view to bringing them on board.

The following month, just before Christmas, prisoners were released from Frongoch and other British jails and those who emerged were, in effect, a ready-made group of freedom fighters. Once back in their homeland they found, to their surprise, a different Ireland emerging from the ruins of the Rising. The majority of the people were no longer willing to accept the limitations of home rule and the dominance of the Irish Parliamentary

Party. They were switching their allegiance to the reinvigorated Sinn Fein Party with its promise to pursue a fully independent Ireland free from all ties with Britain. A new campaign against Britain was called for and the men of Frongoch and those who had been held in other British prisons were ready and willing to answer that call.

Having spent Christmas at home with their loved ones, most republicans began 1917 with a renewed vigour and determination to continue the independence struggle. One such individual was Michael Collins and, after spending the festive season at home in Woodfield outside Clonakilty, he relocated to Dublin in order to be at the centre of republican activities in the capital. The coming year saw the reorganisation of the IRB under the direction of Collins and by that stage he was also Secretary to the National Aid Association, set up to help former prisoners and the families of those who lost their lives in the Rising. That role brought him into contact with many individuals who were active in the republican movement. Together with his good friend Harry Boland, he went to see Kathleen Clarke, widow of Tom Clarke, who, realising he would probably be executed after the Rising, gave the secrets and details of the IRB's membership to his wife. The information she passed on was invaluable and it enabled Collins, with help from Thomas Ashe, to set about reorganising the secret society that had been responsible for the Rising. With Ashe as President and Collins as Secretary, the IRB then adopted a new constitution later that year.

While Collins was reorganising the IRB, Cathal Brugha continued his quest to revamp the Volunteers and he made it very clear they were planning to resume the fight against the British. In August 1917 a meeting was held in the Conradh na Gaeilge offices in Parnell Square attended by Éamon de Valera, Brugha, Thomas Ashe, Diarmuid O'Hegarty, Diarmuid Lynch, Michael Collins, Michael Staines and Richard Mulcahy. The meeting decided to hold an Army Convention to establish a National Executive of the Irish Volunteers or Oglaigh na hEireann in the Irish language. The meeting chose 27 October as the date for the Convention, which coincided with the Sinn Fein Ard Fheis being held in Dublin on 25 and 26 October. The date chosen was a deliberate one and the Volunteers hoped to use the Sinn Fein gathering of republicans as a cover for their own meeting. It was hoped the much larger political gathering in the city would draw the attention of the police and other authorities, thereby leaving the military gathering to pass almost unnoticed.

Not long after the meeting in Parnell Square, the Volunteers hierarchy suffered a major blow when three prominent leaders, Thomas Ashe, Fionan Lynch and Austin Stack, were arrested for making speeches the authorities regarded as subversive and designed to cause disaffection and incite violence. The three men, together with forty others, were also charged with illegal drilling and imprisoned in Mountjoy Jail, where they all demanded political prisoner status, a demand that was refused. The prisoners began a hunger strike and the authorities attempted a mass force feeding. Ashe was moved to hospital after five days and died a few hours later, elevating him to the status of a martyr in the eyes of the 30,000 people who turned out to file past his body as it lay in state.

Ashe was given a military funeral and it represented the first real opportunity for the revamped Irish Volunteers to display their new-found enthusiasm for the independence cause. In his impressive witness statement, Colonel Joseph Lawless, a member of the Irish Volunteers Fingal Brigade and later a Commissioned Officer in the National Army, recalled the funeral of Thomas Ashe and its implications for the republican movement. He went on to say:

> Ashe's death, tragic though it was, became another milestone in the march to freedom. The national leaders determined to make full use of the occurrence to further the cause for which he died. This occurrence was a tactical blunder on the part of the British authorities, which the Irish leaders were bound to exploit to the full; while, on the other hand, I fancy that the more moderate elements in the British Councils were not slow to point out this to their colleagues whose policy was responsible for the situation. This latter, however, is pure surmise on my part.
>
> I learned of Ashe's death on the same evening, 25th September 1917, and, having got in touch with some of the Fingal Volunteers and also the Dublin Brigade Staff, it was arranged that a uniformed guard of honour of his old Fingal Battalion should be mounted over his body in the Mater Hospital pending further arrangements. The nuns and other members of the hospital staff were most co-operative, and so I, with about ten or twelve other Fingallians who could still boast of the possession of Volunteer uniform, mounted that guard that night over the body of our dead commander. This

also was dressed in the uniform he had so proudly worn at Ashbourne.

There was some difficulty in getting a sufficient number of uniformed men from Fingal to provide for guard reliefs, and, in any case, the city battalions were anxious to have the honour of supplying guards, so when the body was removed from the hospital to the City Hall the guard of honour there was augmented by detachments from all of the four City battalions.

Ashe was no longer merely the commandant of the Fingal Volunteers. He had joined the ranks of the immortals and his name was written on the national escutcheon. The manner of his death shocked the feelings of large numbers of people who, up to then, had little sympathy with the national cause, while those who had already had some national leanings threw caution to the wind in their resentment of the outrage.

As the body lay in state in the City Hall, I was reminded of the previous lying in state where I had also been present as a member of the guard of honour. The lying-in-state and the funeral of O'Donovan Rossa in 1915 had been such an active stimulus to national thought and feeling that it, no doubt, paved the way for the Rising of 1916.

Here was another such occasion, but in conditions where considerable progress had already been made in the development of a national consciousness. As Rossa's dead body had served to advance the Fenian ideals for which he had lived, even by one step, would not the body of Ashe move the people to yet another effort to reach the goal of freedom.

Thousands of people from city and country came to the City Hall to view the body of the latest martyr and to pay their respects. I am sure that amongst them were many who, coming for the satisfaction of their idle curiosity, went away convinced that a cause which claimed the adherence of so many reputable people, and where death was so readily accepted, was worthy of their respect, if not their active co-operation.

The public funeral which took place from City Hall to Glasnevin Cemetery on Sunday, 30th September 1917, was a re-staging of the O'Donovan Rossa funeral in its effect.

For the first time since the Rising, uniformed and armed Volunteers paraded through the streets of Dublin, while Trades

Guilds and social organisations helped to swell the procession. So great were the numbers that the British authorities hesitated to take any action further than the posting of parties of police here and there along the route of march. The police, however, did attempt to bar the way of the Volunteers on the return march

The position must have been rather embarrassing to the Dublin Castle authorities who, on one hand found bound to enforce the British edict banning the wearing of uniforms and the carrying of arms, while on the other, it was manifestly impossible to take any effective action against such numbers without the employment of considerable military force. It was not the policy of the Volunteers to invite a clash of arms just then. Volunteer arms were much too scarce to be really effective and the reorganised movement was still in its infancy. Yet, displays of moral force, constituted by the public defiance of the British orders and the numbers of the people who signified their attachment to the national cause by following the coffin of the dead leader, was a significant milestone in the long road to freedom.

As one who formed the guard of honour marching beside the hearse, I could not see the whole procession at any point, but from what I was told at the time, I believe that the procession was at least a mile long and that the groups of trades guilds and suchlike towards the end of the procession were unable to reach the cemetery grounds, which were densely packed before they could arrive. A firing party rendered military honours at the graveside and the oration, if it might be called such, was given by Mick Collins.

Collins merely spoke a few sentences to the effect that 'the volleys just fired are the most fitting tribute to a dead soldier of Ireland'.

There was some apprehension at this point that the British authorities might try to disarm and arrest the firing party as some police parties had tried to force their way into the cemetery but had so far been prevented by Volunteer guards at the gates.

The firing party, therefore, departed secretly and left the cemetery by a back way while the remaining Volunteer units formed up to march back to the city. Finding their route barred by a strong cordon of police at Binn's Bridge, they did not attempt to force a way through, but wheeling left down Whitworth Road dispersed to their respective battalion areas.[55]

On Saturday, 27 October 1917, the day after the Sinn Fein Ard Fheis, a Convention was held in the GAA Pavillion on Jones's Road in Dublin to elect a National Executive of the Irish Volunteers or Oglaigh na hEireann. The Dublin Brigade leadership put in place very stringent security precautions in and around the meeting venue but, as it transpired, there was no real need for them and the convention took place without disruption. The meeting agreed that any decision by the Executive should be carried by a clear majority. Meetings of the Executive were to be held at least once a month, while the Directors were required to meet on a weekly basis. At that time some 390 Companies were affiliated to the Volunteers organisation, though the authorities had a much lower figure. Hundreds of representatives from around the country attended the meeting, while others who would have been there were still in jail. Éamon de Valera presided over the meeting just one day after being elected President of Sinn Fein.

De Valera was elected President and, the meeting decided the National Executive of the Army would be based on provincial representation, with Dublin regarded as a province. The representatives from each province then elected their own National Executive representatives, all of whom were then ratified by the full meeting. Once that task was completed, the meeting went on to elect individuals to oversee specific areas of the organisation. Michael Collins was elected Director for Organisation, while Diarmuid Lynch was appointed Director for Communications. Michael Staines was elected Director for Supply and Rory O'Connor was appointed to the post of Director for Engineering. Sean McGarry was appointed as Secretary General, while Cathal Brugha became Chief of Staff under the rather grand title Chairman of the Resident Executive. Eighteen other men from all around the country were also elected to the Executive, including Austin Stack, Éamonn Duggan, Dick McKee, Eoin O'Duffy and Sean McEntee.

Six members of the National Executive were also members of the Sinn Fein National Executive and, with de Valera president of both organisations, they were then inextricably linked. The fact that some prominent individuals in the pan-republican movement held positions in both the political and military factions was often advantageous as they helped to define and nurture a common agenda, though, like any movement, tensions did arise between both factions at times. The Convention went on to define its main objective as, 'to carry on the reorganisation and direction of the Irish

Volunteers throughout the country, and put them in a position to complete by force of arms the work begun by the men of Easter Week'. While this clearly opened up the possibility of a return to hostilities against the British, the meeting took the view it would not happen until the Executive was satisfied the Volunteers or the IRA, as the organisation became commonly known, was in a well-equipped position to do so.

By the time of the military convention there were many indications around the country the new-found enthusiasm for the independence cause was gathering momentum. In his witness statement, Frank Henderson, who became Commandant of 'F' Company in the 2nd Battalion of the Irish Volunteers, Dublin Brigade and later Adjutant of the Brigade, recounted how men once again came together to prepare for another conflict with the British. He and his comrades encapsulated that enthusiasm, which manifested itself not only in Dublin but across the whole country. He went on to recall:

> As soon as we came together in 'Clonliffe Hall' there began in the Companies of the 2nd Battalion – as there began likewise in the other Dublin Battalion areas – a period of unremitting intensive organising, training and planning which did not cease until the Truce in July 1921 … It was hard, tedious work, but a spirit of great devotion and self-sacrifice, together with faith in the righteousness of the cause, succeeded in knitting the members of the Battalion together in a disciplined and trained force which, when the time came for action, played an efficient part in breaking down foreign domination in the country.[56]

It was no different out in the rural areas of Ireland as many individuals continued to hold the ideal of an independent republic dear to their hearts and were willing to fight for it on another day. In his witness statement, Sean Moylan, who by then had become Captain of the Newmarket Company of Volunteers in County Cork, recalled how once the prisoners arrested after the Easter Rising had been released in December 1916, it did not take long for what had initially been an insurrection to quickly evolve into revolution. He went on to recall how life for him and other Volunteers changed dramatically in a few short months, saying how:

> They began to engage in a physical training regime, which he believed played an important role in developing each man's character. They all enthusiastically took part in long-distance cycling on bad roads as well as punishing sessions of drilling, marching and training as they prepared for what would essentially be the fight of their lives.[57]

In order to instil a more professional approach, the Executive set up a General Headquarters in March 1918 with Richard Mulcahy, who was at the time Minister for Defence in de Valera's Provisional Government, as Chief of Staff, thereby cementing the link between the political and military factions of Irish republicanism. In April, Cathal Brugha took over as Minister for Defence, with Mulcahy taking up the role as his assistant. The Volunteers or the IRA, in effect, became answerable to Dail Eireann. Collins was, at the same time, confirmed in the post of Director of Organisation and Intelligence of the IRA. The men of the General Staff possessed outstanding ability and were of the highest integrity. They were, if required, prepared to give up their civilian occupations to devote all of their time to the IRA. Around the country, the IRA was divided into companies, battalions and brigades, each with its own officers elected by the men. It was clear the members were determined to continue the military campaign against British rule in Ireland but the general consensus of opinion was the new campaign would have to embrace far different tactics to those adopted by the leaders of the Easter Rising.

With the administrative structure being put in place, the National Executive turned its attention to raising funds to purchase arms and ammunition as well any other equipment deemed necessary to sustain a campaign against the British. A sub-committee that included Collins, Brugha, Rory O'Connor and Michael Staines was set up to explore fundraising methods, going beyond the usual holding of raffles and social events like dances and concerts. It seems the IRB was mooted as a possible source of finance, as was the Sinn Fein party, but the problem there lay in the fact that some of the members were not in favour of using physical force to achieve independence. It was felt they could possibly baulk at giving financial help to the IRA. In the end it was agreed the IRB should be approached for funding and Collins let it be known he knew sources through which the IRB could be approached and influenced to advance the necessary monies.

The procurement of arms, especially in the short to medium term, became a main focus of the organisation's attention throughout 1918. An order was issued by the National Executive to Volunteers across the country to collect all arms and shotguns and also to raid any gun shops in their areas. Over the course of the year there were many reports of IRA companies across the country engaging in various actions and schemes to procure arms and ammunition wherever they could. In his witness statement, Nicholas Laffan, who was Captain of 'G' Company, 1st Battalion of the Dublin Brigade, recalled how at one point he and three of his comrades were instructed to collect rifles from a house in Lower Baggot Street after prior arrangements had been made with the 3rd Battalion, in whose area the house was located. He went on to say:

> When the rifles were being collected, the house was surrounded by 15 DMP men and 2 detectives, but the men selected for the collection of the rifles had entered the house by the back. In order to get the rifles safely away, it was decided that Dodd and Burke would put the rifles in two sacks while the other two men would leave by the rear and walk into the main thoroughfare, thereby attracting the attention of the police.
>
> The ruse succeeded. Burke and Dodd walked out with the rifles, the other men keeping between the police and the men carrying the weapons. The two detectives followed as far as Michael's Lane, off Winetavern Street, where they stopped. As the lane was so narrow, the men with the rifles were too far ahead for the police to get near them and they succeeded in taking them to Tom Burke's house in Mountrath Street, off Chancery Place.[58]

Laffan also recalled how, in April 1918, his company succeeded in acquiring four rifles and about 150 rounds of ammunition from Islandbridge Barracks, which accommodated British soldiers. The rifles were smuggled out in a military car leaving the barracks and Laffan paid the driver £3 for his trouble. He also recalled receiving a note from Peadar Clancy, Vice-Brigadier of the Dublin Brigade, asking that he meet him at Kingsbridge railway station and to bring a sandwich with him, meaning a gun. Laffan duly met Clancy, who had his car with him. He went on to recount what then happened:

> We went into the railway station and met a British Army Captain who had two large suitcases which he put in the car. He accompanied us to Islandbridge Barracks, where we were stopped at the gate. The captain produced some papers and we were admitted. He went to the stores, where he took the cases. We remained in the car. The captain then appeared with a soldier carrying his two cases and put them into the car. On arrival at the gate the same military policeman came over and, looking into our car, remarked, 'These are yours, Captain?' The captain said 'Yes.' The military policeman then said, 'Pass on!', and off we went. We drove to the Grosvenor Hotel, Westland Row, where we parted with the officer.
>
> We took the two cases to our dump in Rutland Place. The cases contained revolvers and ammunition of the .38 calibre.[59]

Laffan also recalled in his statement how he and his men were involved in various very innovative attempts to procure arms and recounted one incident when a deserter from the British Army indicated soldiers in Portobello Barracks were willing to sell rifles through the railings at night. Over time, Laffan and his comrades procured fifteen Lee Enfield rifles, six revolvers and about 1,000 rounds of ammunition. They did so by wearing large overcoats with slit pockets so that they could get a grip on the rifles when carrying them away. Laffan also recalled how he had a bicycle with two 6ft lengths of timber tied to it and he put the rifles between the timbers so they were not seen.

Within the ranks of the Volunteers across the country, the enthusiasm of the men and their determination to succeed knew no bounds and was displayed in abundance during the many arms raids carried out during 1918. In his witness statement, Patrick Joseph McElligott, a battalion commanding officer of the Irish Volunteers in Listowel, recalled his own role in a raid for arms in his home town:

> I, with other men of the company, took part in a raid on all hardware shops in the town for shotguns, dynamite and ammunition. We succeeded in obtaining approximately 19 shotguns with ammunition for same, some small revolvers and a quantity of dynamite. A man named Jack McKenna, a shopkeeper who owned about 10 or 12 of the seized shotguns as well as the dynamite, when questioned by the RIC would not give them an account of the guns seized from him. He was

> arrested, tried and sentenced to twelve months' imprisonment in Belfast Jail. Just after the arrest of McKenna, my brother, Robert, and I received from a British ex-soldier a Lee Enfield rifle and 100 rounds of .303 ammunition.[60]

In Cork city and county, the Volunteers were particularly active when it came to procuring arms. In his statement, Matthew O'Callaghan, 1st Lieutenant 'G' Company, 1st Battalion, Cork No. 1 Brigade, recounted numerous raids carried out by him and his comrades. He recalled:

> There was a raid at Jennings, College Road, when a small rifle and ammunition was secured. There was raid at Dale's Sunday's Well, and a revolver secured. A raid on Bradley's, Kyrl St, resulted in a shot gun and cartridges being secured. A raid at Coachford, Co Cork, brought two shot guns and one rifle … A raid at Captain's Clarke's house at Farran, Co Cork, resulted in two shot-guns, two revolvers and ammunition being taken. The captain resisted and was wounded by revolver fire. A raid at Wellington Bridge brought in a shot-gun, while a revolver was got in a raid at Victoria Cross.[61]

The Volunteers took every opportunity to bring arms into areas where it was believed they would be needed in the event of a major conflict with the British. This was never more evident than in a witness statement provided by George Fitzgerald, a member of the Volunteers Dublin Brigade. He recalled a directive from Michael Staines, the Brigade's Quartermaster General, ordering the Volunteers to clear a supply of ammunition delivered to Dodd's Grain Merchants premises in Dublin's Smithfield. He recounted how:

> A small party of Volunteers from my Company were rounded up and ordered to Smithfield. When we got there, we started emptying sacks of oats and retrieving small sacks of ammunition from them. Though we worked late into the night, we weren't able to empty all the sacks and only a portion of the ammunition was cleared.
>
> As the ammunition came from the sacks it was laid to one side, then taken by some of the Volunteers to a nearby yard. This entailed a lot of work and, on account of the small number of Volunteers engaged, the job remained unfinished that night.

> On the following day the Police and the Military raided the place and evidently took the rest of the stuff.
>
> I cannot say how many rounds of ammunition we took over but I believe that a considerable amount was seized by the police. A few days later we returned to McEvoy's yard, packed the ammunition there and left it ready for distribution by Michael Staines, who was then Quartermaster general.[62]

In Galway, the Volunteers were also busy and in his witness statement Michael Healy, captain of the Bullaun Company, recalled how he and his comrades collected arms in their local area:

> In the year 1918 our Company collected all the arms in the company area which corresponded in area with the parish of Bullaun. The RIC failed to get any although they searched for them. We collected ten shot guns, five single and five double-barrelled and a small number of cartridges. The owners of the guns were all friendly and handed them to us quite willingly. The time would be about July 1918.[63]

In October 1918 Healy took part in a raid on four houses in a neighbouring townland of Kilrickle together with a comrade, Lieutenant Timothy Nevin. They were met by four Volunteers from the Kilrickle Company including Michael Hogan, who later went on to attain the rank of colonel, and, it soon transpired, the idea of inviting Healy and Nevin to carry out the raid was because they would not be recognised in the raided houses. Healy recounted how he and Nevin entered the houses, while Hogan and the three other Volunteers remained outside. He recalled:

> We had no trouble in three of the houses getting three shot guns and some cartridges. These three families were quite friendly. The owner of the fourth house was a man named Hardy and was hostile. He and his son told us they had already given their gun to the Volunteers. We knew this was untrue and after a lengthy argument and some persuasion they produced a double-barrelled shot gun and handed it over to us.[64]

During 1918 the Volunteers also attempted to manufacture their own weapons and, as they had access to a good supply of gelignite left over from the Easter Rising, they used it to make grenades. They displayed a good deal of ingenuity and no small amount of nerve as they carried out what was in essence very dangerous work. In his witness statement, Martin Fahy, a member of the University Company of Volunteers in Galway and who later went on to become Brigade Engineer in South-West Galway, recounted how home-made mines were manufactured. He recalled learning how to fill the mines and make them ready for use by attaching detonators and fuses:

> The mine was made from the box of a horse-cart, that is, the metal portion of the box at the centre of the wheel in which the axle revolves when the cart is set in motion.
>
> It was roughly twelve inches long. Inside diameter was about three inches at its wider end and about two inches at the narrower end. The caps were held in place by means of a bolt going right through the centre of the cylinder with a nut at one end to tighten the caps. Later, the practice of having the bolt running through the centre of the cylinder was discarded in favour of a bolt running along the outside. This made it easier to fill with explosives.[65]

Fahy recalled the work was mostly carried out in the College Club under the pretence of holding a GAA meeting. More often than not, the explosives used in the mine was gelignite packed as tightly as possible. Once the mines were made, they were spirited out of the College for distribution around the Galway area.

In late 1917 two Volunteers, Joseph Lawless and Archie Herron, set up a household items repair business together in Dublin at a vacant premises, 198 Parnell Street. Lawless was an officer in the Volunteers and later became a colonel in the National Army and a member of the Investigating Staff in the Bureau of Military History. Herron was a native of Belfast and an active Volunteer even before the Easter Rising and a friend of James Connolly. Around July 1918, Heron engaged Lawless in a discussion about converting part of their premises into a bomb-making factory after a conversation he had with Mick Lynch, the Fingal Brigade Commandant. In his witness statement, Lawless recalled part of that conversation he had with Lynch, saying:

> He told me he had been appointed Director of Munitions on the GHQ Staff and that he was anxious to get going at once in turning

> out a type of bomb that would need no expensive plant or highly skilled staff to produce, and he wanted these in large quantities.[66]

The difficulty, as Lynch saw it, was locating a suitable workshop where regular supplies of material could be delivered without causing suspicion. As it transpired, the premises at 198 Parnell Street had been used in previous years as a small brass foundry, manufacturing plumbing fittings. The foundry was located in the basement under the repair shop. Unfortunately, since there was no back door to the premises it was necessary to enter the foundry through the shop and down a stairway. When Heron and Lawless agreed to the proposal to use their premises, a man called Matthew Gahan was chosen to undertake the bomb-making work. Lawless recounted how:

> He quickly began work sawing off four-inch lengths of one and a half-inch steel piping, notching them longitudinally and circumferentially with a hacksaw and enclosing each end with a screwed plug and drilling one of the plugs to take a fuse.[67]

Lawless recalled the bomb as being of a crude form and believed at the time a better and more efficient version could be made. Lynch believed Lawless's idea was too elaborate but he mentioned it to Dick McKee, Commanding Officer of the Dublin Brigade, who was very interested in it. Lawless provided an estimate of the cost to refurbish the foundry and McKee undertook to secure the best and most reliable staff to help out with the work. With the approval of Rory O'Connor, the Volunteers Director of Engineering, Matt Furlong, a native of Wexford, was appointed to oversee the work and teamed up with Lawless. Two other men, Tom Young and Sean O'Sullivan, joined them and the work got under way with the blessing of Michael Collins, who was very enthusiastic about the whole enterprise. The quality of the bombs, which followed the design of the famous 'Mills' bomb, was very acceptable, considering the limitations of the plant and the fact that the only high explosive available to the Volunteers was gelignite.

While the bomb cases and fittings were made at 198 Parnell Street, they were loaded elsewhere. The assembled bombs without the explosive were removed initially from Parnell Street every evening by staff members, who hung them about their persons on a harness covered by a greatcoat. However, as production increased a new way was found to spirit the bombs out of the foundry and a man called Chris Healy was hired to undertake the task. He had a horse and cart that he hired out for legitimate work and as well as carting the bombs away from Parnell Street, he also brought the raw materials and foundry coke to the premises. The bomb-making venture proved the Volunteers organisation not only comprised of fighting men but also of men who possessed a very fine sense of ingenuity. Against all the odds, they managed to set up and operate a very productive bomb-making factory in the centre of Dublin while all of the time managing to conceal it from the authorities.

While the Volunteers continued with their efforts to procure arms and ammunition throughout 1917 and 1918 especially, they also placed a growing emphasis on intelligence gathering, believing it was essential to monitor the movements of the Crown forces closely. The Volunteers also kept a close eye on individuals whom they believed were engaged in passing information on to the authorities. During the latter half of 1918 a fully functioning Intelligence Unit was set up under the control of Michael Collins and a certain cohort of suitable Volunteers were chosen to carry out its work. One such individual was Joseph Kinsella, the Intelligence Officer for the Dublin Brigade's 4th Battalion. He recalled in his witness statement how he was instructed to visit various companies and select a section of eight men and a sergeant from each whom he deemed suitable for the intelligence unit, taking into account the nature of their daily work and places of employment. Kinsella recalled how he carried out his work:

> Men were selected from Guinness's Brewery, from the various banks in the city, from the post offices and the railway. We had men who were employed on boats at the Quays, and we had shop-keepers. We had quite a number of men from the water works and various other places in the Corporation. We had one employed in the Kildare Street club, and we had tram conductors and drivers. We had men who were employed as civilian clerks in different barracks in the city.[68]

Kinsella recalled how the agents working in banks were very useful as they were in a position to exchange notes for gold, which was hidden away intended to be used by a future provisional government. He also recounted how he often exchanged up to £20 for gold in one week and handed it over to the Brigade's Intelligence Officer. Kinsella also made use of his agents in the post office, instructing them to intercept letters sent by members of the public to the authorities in which they offered up information about the Volunteers. The informants, he recalled, were often dealt with very severely.

Throughout 1917 and 1918, Irish republicans were clearly very busy preparing for a future conflict with the British. While 1918 in particular was a notable year for political upheaval in Ireland, there was a view, held by much of the republican leadership, that politics alone was not going to secure independence and a more violent approach would soon be required. Within a matter of weeks of 1918 coming to an end, a new campaign of violence against British rule in Ireland got under way. On 21 January 1919 the first shots of the War of Independence were fired at Soloheadbeg in County Tipperary, marking the beginning of a bloody conflict that dragged on to the summer of 1921. The fact it was sustained for so long was due in no small way to the preparations put in place by the Volunteers during the two years following the Easter Rising. Their dedication to drilling, parading and engaging in tough physical training allowed them to take the fight to the enemy, aided and abetted by the impressive arsenal of weaponry they managed to procure despite the best efforts of those in authority to prevent them from doing so.

PART THREE

The War of Independence

Conflict with the British

CHAPTER TEN

The War of Independence

1919

On 21 January 1919 at Soloheadbeg, deep in rural Tipperary, the first shots of the independence conflict were fired and the consequences of a local skirmish were to be felt across the country over the next two and a half years as the IRA took on the might of the British Army. It was a conflict that claimed many lives on both sides and eventually ended with the British government coming to the realisation that the future of Ireland needed to be negotiated rather than fashioned by subjugation and violence. That day was a red-letter day for another reason as it saw the first meeting of Dail Eireann in Dublin's Mansion House. The event at Soloheadbeg was not only coincidental but it did not have the blessing of the republican politicians meeting that day to plot the course of Ireland's future. The men involved in the ambush came from townlands and villages such as Donohill, Solohead and Hollyford, all near Tipperary Town, and the action they engaged in became the benchmark for many Volunteers units around the country.

It seems that just before Christmas in 1918, local Volunteers leaders Séumas Robinson, Sean Treacy and Dan Breen learned from intelligence reports that a substantial amount of gelignite was about to be delivered to Tipperary Town. Together, with other members of 'C' and 'E' companies of the Third Tipperary Brigade, they made plans to ambush a planned convoy transporting the gelignite from the town to a nearby quarry, believing it would come in useful once the long-anticipated conflict with the British began. The news of the impending arrival of the gelignite in the locality was seen as a godsend by the IRA men, many of whom were already hardened fighters determined to see an end to British rule in Ireland. Séumas Robinson, the accepted republican leader in the area, was a veteran of the

Easter Rising and a very good organiser of men. Sean Treacy had already spent two periods in jail for republican activities, including participating in a guard of honour for Éamon de Valera when he visited Tipperary Town. He had also spent some time on hunger strike in Mountjoy Jail and was well regarded among his republican comrades.

The general election in 1918 occupied the minds of republican activists for some months and by early 1919 the more belligerent of them had become increasingly uneasy and demanded a more violence-orientated approach to removing the British from Ireland. They were of the opinion the Volunteers organisation was too closely associated with the Sinn Fein Party, which embraced dual-monarchists like Arthur Griffith, constitutional republicans and others who still had their roots in the concept of home rule. The Tipperary men were by this stage very unhappy with the perceived lack of action from Volunteers Headquarters in Dublin. With that in mind, they decided the time had come to go beyond the talking of those in headquarters and take matters into their own hands by engaging face to face with the forces of the Crown.

The exact date of the expected shipment of gelignite was uncertain but the IRA knew it was intended for a local quarry. Lar Breen, brother of Dan, took a job at the quarry and maintained a close eye on all that was happening there. Meanwhile, Robinson and his men made plans to commandeer the gelignite and discussed how best it might be achieved. Intelligence suggested the convoy would have a police guard of between four and twelve men, which meant the Volunteers had to plan for many eventualities. Their initial plan involved an attempt to disarm, bound and gag the policemen and one of the Volunteers, Tadgh Crowe, was designated to lead them down the road after the seizure of the gelignite. He was to maintain a watch over them until his comrades escaped the scene of the ambush and then make his own getaway. The big unknown, of course, was just how many policemen would be in the convoy and how well armed they might be.

Eventually, Lar Breen discovered the gelignite was due to arrive around 16 January but he was still unsure of the exact date as well as the route to be taken to the quarry. This forced the Volunteers taking part in the ambush to wait around for a few days before they received confirmation of the exact arrival time. On 21 January, Paddy O'Dwyer from Hollyford, Captain of 'C' Company, 3rd Battalion, Tipperary Volunteers, was posted as a lookout in Tipperary Town and he watched as 160lb of gelignite was loaded on to a cart outside the military barracks. He also noted two policemen and two council workers were designated to escort the convoy to the quarry. O' Dwyer then cycled ahead of the convoy and watched as it reached the crossroads near the bottom of Kingswell Hill just outside the town. He waited in the vicinity to see which of the two possible routes the convoy took to the quarry, which turned out to be the longer route via Bohertrime. That decision allowed O'Dwyer to take the shorter route and he sped away on his bicycle to deliver the news to Robinson and Treacy. They positioned the men under their command behind the hedges of Cranitch's field situated close to the quarry. There was nothing left for them to do but wait.

It was almost an hour before the horse and cart carrying the gelignite and guided by the two workmen arrived. The two police constables, McDonnell and O'Connell, walked behind the cart and both had rifles slung across their shoulders. In his witness statement, O'Dwyer described what happened next:

> A screen of whitethorn bushes and briars provided reasonable cover from the view of anyone passing along the by-road. This position, which was about 250 yards from the entrance to the quarry, was on the right-hand side of the road as one approaches Solohead village from the Tipperary–Dundrum Road. Séumas Robinson and I were together on the extreme left-hand side of the position, about 25 or 30 yards from what I will call the main party of six, and the arrangements were that Robinson and I were to get out on the road when we heard the others call on the men with the cart and the escort to halt and put up their hands, the idea being that if they did not halt, Robinson and I would be in a position to stop the horse and cart. At least seven of the eight men were armed with revolvers, the exception being Sean Treacy. He, too, may have had a revolver, but at that time he was very fond of a small automatic rifle which he possessed, and I am almost certain that he had it with him on that day.
>
> Hearing Dan Breen and Sean Treacy shout, 'Halt, put up your hands', Robinson immediately started to get out on to the road, and almost simultaneously either one or two shots rang out. I distinctly remember seeing one of the two RIC men bringing his carbine up to the aiming position and working the bolt, and the impression I got was that he was aiming at either Robinson or myself. Then a volley rang out and that

> constable fell dead at the roadside. I am not certain whether it was that volley or the previous shot, or shots, which killed his companion. After the long wait, the whole thing happened very suddenly, in less, perhaps, than half a minute, and in much less time than it takes to relate.
>
> The driver of the cart and the County Council ganger were, naturally, very frightened. Dan Breen spoke to them and assured them that nothing was going to happen to them. One of these men, Godfrey, knew both Breen and Treacy well, and I imagine Flynn must have known them too. On Breen's instructions, Tadhg Crowe and I collected the two carbines belonging to the dead constables. Breen, Treacy and Hogan then drove away the horse and cart with the gelignite. Michael Ryan and Paddy McCormack remained on the road with Séumas Robinson guarding Godfrey and Flynn until such time as the gelignite was a safe distance away. Tadhg Crowe and I took the two carbines with us and hid them at a spot on the railway line about a half a mile from the scene of the ambush and where it was convenient for Tadhg to collect them later. We then parted and I went home to Hollyford on foot.[69]

The incident caused shock and outrage in the local area as two innocent and very well thought of family men had died violently carrying out their duties as policemen. The reaction to the ambush and the killings was predictable, with the local *Nationalist* newspaper decrying the incident as 'a very deplorable affair'. The news reached London and *The Times* ran the headline, 'Policemen Shot Dead in Tipperary' with the by-line reporting how a cartload of explosives had been captured. The authorities declared Tipperary to be 'a special military area' and banned the holding of fairs and markets. During the following weeks there was a massive military and police presence in the area and an aircraft was used for the first time in Ireland by the authorities for surveillance purposes. A reward was placed for the capture of Dan Breen, which eventually rose to £10,000 but it was never claimed.

The men of the Third Tipperary Brigade who took it upon themselves that day to ambush the convoy probably did not expect their decision to be the momentous one it turned out to be. Most likely there was never any intention on the part of the Volunteers to take the lives of the two unfortunate police constables. The violent confrontation at Soloheadbeg turned out to be a precursor to many similar events that took place over the following two years, leaving many dead and injured on both sides of the conflict.

The ambush at Soloheadbeg was essentially carried out without the permission of the Volunteers leadership in Dublin. As it transpired, over the following two and half years many similar actions across the country were sanctioned by local officers rather than national officers. As a result, the independence conflict comprised of what seemed like a never-ending series of unco-ordinated local ambushes of and, attacks on, the forces of the Crown. Despite the lack of headquarters oversight, local commanders and their men managed to chalk up impressive results, often leaving the enemy both bewildered and disorientated, forcing them to retreat to their police stations and military barracks. With the first shots fired and the first deaths recorded, the independence conflict was up and running and the view of republicans was it would have to be pursued to its conclusion.

On 3 February 1919 the accepted leader of Irish republicanism, Éamon de Valera, who had been imprisoned as part of the infamous 'German Plot' in 1918, escaped from Lincoln Jail together with two other inmates, Sean McGarry and Sean Milroy. Their escape was facilitated by a plan put in place by Michael Collins and Harry Boland and it made the news across the world. The whole episode embarrassed the prison authorities and the government in London, while the incident proved to be a real morale boost for the republican movement and went some way to increasing its support across the country. On his escape, de Valera decided the cause of Ireland's independence should be brought to a wider audience and he sent a delegation to the Paris Peace Conference, led by Sean T. O'Kelly. The delegation's remit was to plead the cause of Ireland's right to self-determination but the mission was a failure mainly because of interference from the British. De Valera left Ireland in June 1919 on a visit to America to promote Ireland's republican agenda and he was to remain there for around eighteen months. Unfortunately, while there he found himself embroiled in an internal Irish-American political row but he did manage to raise impressive sums of money for the republican movement at home. In his absence, Michael Collins and Arthur Griffith, among others, continued to forge ahead with republican policies and took every opportunity to make life difficult for the authorities in Dublin Castle.

On 23 February 1919 a meeting of the Third Tipperary Brigade drafted a proclamation signed by Séumas Robinson ordering all British military and police out of South Tipperary. The proclamation went on to warn those who opted to stay in the area they would be held to have 'forfeited their lives'.

As it happened, the Volunteers leadership in Dublin refused to endorse the proclamation and demanded it not be displayed publicly. The demand was ignored and the proclamation was displayed in a number places across Tipperary. Republican activity was gathering pace and, on 19 March, an IRA unit raided Collinstown Airfield, now Dublin Airport, and captured a total of seventy-five rifles and thousands of rounds of ammunition. In his witness statement, Patrick McCrea of 'B' Company, 3nd Battalion, Dublin Brigade, recalled the raid in great detail, saying:

> I think the first action of importance that I took part in was the raid on Collinstown Aerodrome in March 1919. I was called in on it as being attached to the Brigade Transport … On the night of the raid we mobilised in Parnell Square – about 25 strong.
>
> The men were to travel in five cars and three cars were to take them back on completion of the job. Two cars were deputed to take the rifles and ammunition.
>
> It was a bright moonlit night. The reason they selected a certain hour was because they knew when the guard would be changed and there would be no further change for four hours. There were two British soldiers on sentry duty and our men got close to them and held them up. They could not give any alarm. After that they rushed the guardroom, where, I think, 12 or 14 were taken by surprise before they could reach for the guns. They were tied up and, as far as I know, they gave no trouble, with one exception, and he got tied up by the heels to the rafters. I think we were two hours altogether in Collinstown. Seventy-five rifles and about fifteen or sixteen thousand rounds of ammunition we got there.[70]

Some ten days later the IRA took action in Westport, County Mayo, when it assassinated a resident magistrate by the name of John Charles Milling because he sent a number of men to prison for unlawfully assembling and drilling. Further unrest emerged in April 1919 when, for twelve days, the people of Limerick defied the British Army's decision to declare the city and parts of the county a 'special Military Area' under the guise of the Defence of the Realm Act. The British made the decision after the IRA attempted, on 6 April, to rescue one of their own men, Robert Byrne, from a local hospital where he was being treated for the effects of a hunger strike.

In the rescue attempt, Constable Martin O'Brien was killed and another policeman was wounded. In the shootout, Byrne took a bullet to his lung and, though he was spirited away from the hospital, he died later that night in the home of sympathetic local people. The military declaration required anyone wishing to leave or enter Limerick city to have a permit to do so, while troops and armoured cars were deployed on the streets. In response, the citizens set up a committee or 'soviet' to run the city, which was in place from 15 to 27 April, during which it printed its own money and newspaper while at the same time organising a food supply. The protest ended with the intervention of the Lord Mayor of Limerick and its Catholic bishop but the act of defiance underlined the growing sense of displeasure among the Irish people over British involvement in their country.

Around that time, the War of Independence came to County Cork when an RIC patrol was ambushed at Eyeries. Three officers were shot and wounded. On 10 April a meeting of Dail Eireann passed a motion calling on all Irish people to ostracise the RIC, while the British declared the counties Limerick, Tipperary, Cork, Kerry and Roscommon to be in a state of disturbance. In May, the IRA carried out the daring rescue of Sean Hogan of the 3rd Tipperary Brigade at Knocklong railway station in County Limerick. Hogan, who had participated in the Soloheadbeg ambush, was later captured by Crown forces and was being transferred to jail in Cork city. His comrades, Dan Breen, Séumas Robinson and Sean Treacy, planned and carried out the rescue aided by members of the Galtee Battalion of the East Limerick Brigade. The ambush of the train resulted in the deaths of two RIC men, Sergeant Peter Wallace and Constable Michael Enright, both of whom were escorting Hogan, while a number of IRA men sustained wounds. Travelling on the train that day was Dr Joseph Kearney, who was at the time a medical student in University College Cork and a member of 'A' Company, 2nd Battalion, Cork No. 1 Brigade. He was in the company of six other students. In his witness statement he gave a fine account of what took place at Knocklong station:

> When the train drew up at Knocklong we heard some commotion in the corridor. On opening the door into the corridor and looking down, I saw at least four men, who appeared to be armed, endeavouring to enter the second next compartment to ours.
>
> At first, I thought it was some kind of game but, on hearing shots, we quickly realised that there was something serious

Above: Thomas Clarke. Signatory of the Proclamation of the Irish Republic.

Right: James Connolly. Signatory of the Proclamation of the Irish Republic.

Patrick Pearse. Signatory of the Proclamation of the Irish Republic.

Thomas MacDonagh. Signatory of the Proclamation of the Irish Republic.

Eamonn Ceannt. Signatory of the Proclamation of the Irish Republic.

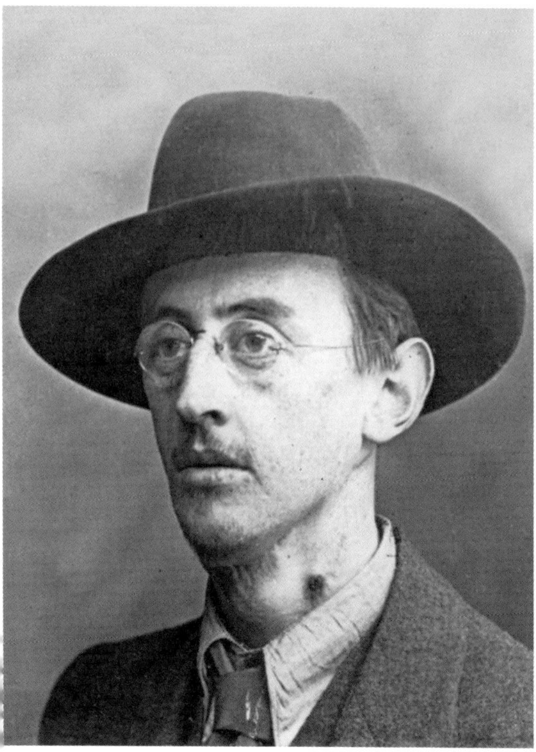

Joseph Plunkett. Signatory of the Proclamation of the Irish Republic.

Sean MacDiarmada. Signatory of the Proclamation of the Irish Republic.

Roger Casement. Hanged for Treason and for importing guns and ammunition into Ireland in 1914.

Erskine Childers. Delivered guns and ammunition from Germany into Howth Harbour on his yacht, Asgard, for the Irish Volunteers in 1914.

Bulmer Hobson. Member of the IRB Supreme Council and organised the landing and distribution of guns and ammunition at Howth for the Irish Volunteers in 1914. He went on to oppose the Easter Rising.

A group of Royal Irish Constabulary officers with Inspector Hetreed in 1917.

Above left: Winifred Carney. Personal secretary to James Connolly. Carney remained by Connolly's side throughout the Easter Rising.

Above right: Countess Markievicz. Sentenced to death for her part in the Easter Rising. Her sentence was commuted on account of her gender.

The coffin of Michael Collins being carried from the Pro-Cathedral in Dublin by some of his comrades in August 1922.

The aftermath of the burning of Cork City by the British on the night of 11/12 December 1920.

Crowds gather at Westland Row, Dublin, to welcome home republican prisoners from English prisons in 1916.

> afoot. I looked down the corridor again and there appeared to be a good deal of commotion and a policeman was being pushed out through the door on to the platform, with blood streaming from his head. We wondered what we should do. Apparently, some members of our party suggested we should get out of the line of fire. Before we left the carriage, I looked down the corridor once more and saw a policeman (later identified as Constable O'Reilly) with a carbine to his shoulder and he was firing at the rescuers of the prisoner at point-blank range as they were getting on to the platform from the corridor.
>
> Our party got onto the railway line and stood there for a few moments trying to decide our next move … Suddenly, Constable O'Reilly appeared from around the back of the train.
>
> On seeing us, he immediately took up his carbine and fired at us. We raced up the line in the direction of Kilmallock … Another man then followed and joined us for a moment. He had a bullet in his neck from which he was bleeding profusely. We advised him to go back and get his wound dressed, as we were unable to do anything for him because we had nothing with us. He said he was alright and jumped over the fence and went off across country. Later we learned he was none other than Sean Treacy himself.[71]

With the gunfire continuing, the medical students dispersed in many directions and eventually Kearney managed to re-join the train as it was pulling out of the station. He went on to recall:

> On the train also was Constable O'Reilly and he was profuse in his apologies for firing on the students … There was one policeman dead in the carriage. Another was dying. A third had escaped through the window when the shooting started and was discovered the following morning some distance away on the line, with nothing but his shirt and trousers on him and Rosary beads around his neck. The train went on then to Kilmallock, where the dead policeman and the dying man were taken from the train with Constable O'Reilly. The train then proceeded to Cork.[72]

While Hogan was rescued, a tough price was extracted as two IRA men, Ed Foley and Patrick Maher, were arrested soon after the Knocklong incident.

Maher had played no part in the rescue of Hogan but both men were put on trial in civilian and military courts before being found guilty. They were both hanged in Mountjoy Jail on 7 June 1921 despite many pleas for clemency.

June 1919 saw de Valera highlighting the cause of an Irish republic in the United States as he sought official recognition from the government in Washington and the support of the American people. On 6 June, the Senate in Washington passed a resolution requesting the delegation appointed by Dail Eireann be offered a hearing at the Paris Peace Conference. The resolution also supported the 'aspirations of the Irish people for a government of their own choice'. Meanwhile, the violence continued to be ratcheted up and, on 16 June, an IRA unit of around fourteen men armed with just hurleys and sticks ambushed a six-man British Army and RIC patrol at Rathclarin, just south-east of Bandon in County Cork. Five rifles, one revolver and some ammunition were seized, while a Volunteer and a soldier were injured in the encounter.

On 18 June Dail Eireann officially established the Dail Courts, which became known as the National Arbitration Courts and were to operate across the country. This was a radical change to the country's justice system, which, very notably, allowed women to act as judges. The new system was designed to circumvent and sideline the British courts system and was set up on the basis of parishes and districts. The new courts were to be arbitrated by local IRA commanders, parish priests and Sinn Fein personnel. Eventually, people referred to them as 'Sinn Fein Courts' and they worked surprisingly well during the independence conflict, becoming the accepted courts of arbitration across the country. On 19 June the first Dail Loan was approved for an amount of £500,000, half of it to be raised in Ireland and the other half in the United States. The money was held in bank accounts in Ireland and in the United States under the stewardship of three trustees, de Valera, Bishop Fogarty of Killaloe and James O' Mara, one of the few to serve in the House of Commons and Dail Eireann. Both loans were over-subscribed and the limit in America was increased substantially in August 1919.

July 1919 saw the setting up of the infamous group known as the 'squad' by Michael Collins, consisting of hand-picked Dublin Volunteers attached to his IRA Intelligence Unit. The men were employed on a full-time basis and paid a weekly wage of £4 10 shillings. They targeted spies and other individuals suspected of working with the British authorities. In his witness statement, James Slattery, a member of 'F' Company, 2nd Battalion, Dublin Brigade, recalled how he became involved with the new group:

> About a fortnight before the shooting of Detective Smith (30 July 1919), I received instructions to proceed to a house in North Great George's Street, I think it was No. 35.
>
> On arriving there I found a fairly big number of Volunteers present. Dick McKee and Mick McDonnell were there, and they picked out a number of us and took us to an inner room. Dick McKee addressed those of us who had been selected and asked if we had any objection to shooting enemy agents … When I was asked the question I said I was prepared to follow orders. As far as I remember it was not indicated to us at the meeting that we were to become a unit to be known later as the Squad. We were merely told we were to be given special duties.[73]

The Squad's first assassination took place on 30 July 1919 when they shot Detective Sergeant Pat Smith of 'G' Division based in Dublin Castle. The assassination was carried out under the authority of Dail Eireann and it was the first of many carried out by the Squad during the independence conflict. Slattery and three of his comrades, Tom Keogh, Tom Ennis and Mick Kennedy, were given the task of shooting the detective. After following Smith to his home on Millmount Avenue on a number of evenings and failing to shoot him because of one reason or another, they finally managed to carry out the assassination. Slattery, in his witness statement, recalled the fateful moment:

> We came back again to the bridge and after about a week we shot Smith. We had .38 guns and they were too small. I thought that the minute we would fire at him he would fall, but after we hit him, he ran. The four of us fired at him. Keogh and myself ran after him right to his own door and I think he fell at the door, but he got into the house. He lived for about a fortnight afterwards.[74]

The month of August 1919 began with more violence when two RIC officers were shot dead by IRA men from the Mid-Clare Brigade while they were on patrol near Ennistymon in County Clare. Constable Murphy, who was just 19 years of age, was killed instantly, while Constable Riordan, who was aged 43, returned fire but died later of his wounds. On 20 August, the Dail passed a motion requiring all its members and officials to take an Oath of Allegiance to the Republic and this was then extended to all members of the Irish Volunteers. This, in essence, meant the Irish Volunteers officially became the Irish Republican Army.

The month of September began with more violence with an ambush by the IRA of an RIC bicycle patrol in Lorrha, County Tipperary. Sergeant Philip Brady, a father of six young children, was shot dead and a constable by the name of Foley was seriously wounded. Once again, the ambush was not a nationally sanctioned one and was carried out on the orders of the local IRA leadership. September also saw the first engagement of the War of Independence between the IRA and the British Army. It took place in Fermoy, County Cork, on the 7th, a Sunday, when an armed party of soldiers marched to a service at the local Wesleyan Church. They were ambushed by members of the IRA's Cork No. 2 Brigade led by Liam Lynch and the confrontation resulted in the death of one British soldier and the wounding of three others. In his witness statement, Patrick Ahern, a second lieutenant in the Fermoy Company and later Intelligence Officer for the Fermoy Battalion in the Cork No. 2 Brigade, recalled that fateful morning:

> The usual drill and activities continued until early September 1919 when the raid on the church party of the Shropshire Light Infantry took place at the Wesleyan Church on Sunday morning, September 7th 1919. This was one of a number of small parties of military which used to parade to the churches of various denominations in the town on each Sunday morning. The strength of the party was usually about twenty and marched to the Wesleyan Church at Walkers Row. The party as well as all the others on church parade always carried rifles. The movements of the Wesleyan Church party were kept under observation for about three months. The party usually marched in fours from their barracks via Barrack Hill, the Square and Patrick Street to Walkers Row, the site of the Wesleyan Church ... Every possible aspect of the movements of the particular enemy party was covered in the preliminary investigation. It was decided to ascertain whether, when the military party entered the Church, they stacked their rifles inside the door, or took them into their seats with them. This latter investigation was also allocated to me and after spending

> a few Sundays in the vicinity of the Wesleyan Church, I established that the rifles were taken into the seats. When all the reports from the various observers had been examined, Liam Lynch decided to attempt to overpower the party just as it reached the Wesleyan Church.[75]

With all arrangements agreed upon and the men selected to take part in the ambush in position, Ahern went on to describe what happened on the morning of the ambush:

> Several men from the Ballynoe and Araglin Companies in addition to the Mallow and Fermoy men were engaged in various activities in connection with this job.
>
> Some were strolling around reading papers and generally appearing to be killing time in the vicinity of the route taken by the Church party as they neared the Wesleyan Church. All had instructions to rush the enemy party when the order, 'hands up' was given by Lar Condon, who was in charge of the main attacking party.
>
> Liam Lynch was with the Mallow party in their car, which was parked east of the Wesleyan Church. As the enemy approached the Wesleyan Church, the Mallow car with its passengers moved slowly towards it … The driver swung his car across the road behind the military party, thus cutting off their line of retreat, while the occupants of his car jumped on the soldiers. The engagement was all over in less than five minutes and the rifles were loaded into the car.
>
> The main attacking party, of which I was a member, were ambling along within arm's length of the enemy party when the order 'hands up' was given. I immediately grabbed the rifle of the soldier nearest to me and with very little effort succeeded in wrestling it from him.
>
> All members of the party were engaged in a short sharp tussle before the enemy party was overpowered. A few shots were fired during the scrap and Private Jones was shot dead, while I think three or four were wounded.[76]

The rifles, fifteen in number, captured by the IRA were spirited out of town by means of a relay of men to very remote districts. This was achieved despite the presence of hundreds of soldiers and police in the immediate area of Fermoy, who were tasked with searching for the cache. The success of the ambush provided a major morale boost for the IRA and proved to many of its members they had the capability to take on and, defeat the enemy. Over the following months, IRA units in Cork familiarised themselves with the rifles while all the time learning to use them properly, often with the help of ex-British soldiers who had thrown in their lot with republicans. Unfortunately, there was an immediate price to pay for the ambush because on the following night, British soldiers ransacked Fermoy town as an act of revenge, during which they smashed shop windows and looted the contents of many businesses.

On 10 September the British government issued a proclamation outlawing the Dail, while two days later the IRA assassinated Detective Constable Daniel Hoey of the Dublin Metropolitan Police's 'G' Division. Hoey had been a leading member of a raiding party on the Sinn Fein headquarters in Harcourt Street that saw Michael Collins escape by the skin of his teeth. Because of that, Hoey became a target for the Squad and, in his witness statement, James Slattery, who took part in the killing together with Mick McDonnell and Tom Ennis, provided a detailed account of Hoey's assassination:

> Ennis, Mick McDonnell and I came down Townsend Street. Mick said he thought that Detective Hoey would be going off duty at about ten o'clock, and he did go off. Hoey crossed over from College Street towards the police headquarters in Brunswick Street.
>
> I asked Mick if he was sure that this man was Hoey and he said, 'I am not quite sure, but we will go after him.' We intended that if he went straight to the door of the building we would shoot him, but instead of going there he went down Townsend Street nearly as far as Tara Street. We passed by when he was looking at a window and Mick said, 'It is Hoey all right.' He went into a shop and we passed back up to the corner of Hawkins Street.
>
> When we saw him approaching again, we crossed over to his side of the street, which was at the back of the barracks, and we shot him at the door of the garage.[77]

At the end of September, Collins officially set up the IRA Intelligence Unit with Liam Tobin appointed as his Deputy Director of Intelligence and Tom

Cullen as Assistant Director. The Unit worked out of 3 Crow Street, off Dame Street in Dublin, under the guise of the Irish Products Company.

The violence continued during October 1919, when on the 19th of the month another DMP 'G' Division detective, Michael Downing, was assassinated on Dublin's High Street. It was reported he had inadvertently come across some IRA men moving explosives. On the last day of October an IRA unit attacked Ballivor RIC Barracks in County Meath. During that attack one RIC officer was killed while a revolver, five rifles and ammunition were captured by the raiders. On 17 November, ten men from the 5th Battalion, Cork No. 3 Brigade somehow managed to get on board a British naval ship anchored at Bantry, held up the crew and made off with ten rifles, ten revolvers and ammunition, which, of course, was a huge embarrassment to the navy. On 29 November, another 'G' Division detective, John Barton, was assassinated by the IRA in Dublin. Once again, James Slattery was involved in the assassination and he provided an account of the killing in his witness statement, saying:

> Tom Keogh, Joe Leonard, Vincie Byrne and myself were sent out to look for Barton. On arriving at College Street somebody said that he had passed and gone into College Street so we went down there. I heard a couple of shots and the next thing I saw was Barton on the ground. The peculiar thing about it was that I saw Barton standing up again and firing a shot after he had fallen. Barton was not shot by the section with which I was operating. I believe he was shot by Paddy Daly's section.[78]

On 12 December, the IRA shot and wounded four RIC officers outside Dungloe in County Donegal, while two days later an RIC officer, Constable Edward Bolger, was shot by the IRA at Kilbrittain in County Cork. It was claimed he was unarmed at the time of the attack and was shot because he was the principal witness at the trial of seven IRA men held in November. Bolger was the first RIC man to lose his life in Cork during the independence conflict.

The year ended with a major operation carried out by the IRA when it attempted to assassinate the Lord Lieutenant of Ireland, Field Marshall Viscount French. It was an attempt to strike at the heart of British authority in Ireland. It had become known that French was due to leave his train at Ashtown station and journey by car to his residence, the Vice-Regal Lodge in the Phoenix Park. The plan, however, went awry and French escaped in one of the official cars, despite a road block being put in place. A gunfight did ensue between French's security detail and the IRA men, during which one Volunteer, Martin Savage, was killed and Dan Breen was severely wounded. In his witness statement, Vincent (Vinny) Byrne, a member of the Squad, recalled the attempted ambush of French:

> I reported to Mick McDonnell. There was a group of men in the front room of his house and, as I went in, Mick said: 'Byrne, you had better go up to the dump and bring down any grenades that are there.' I did what I was told. I collected the grenades and brought them to the house. They were given out to some of the party … So off we sailed up along the N.C.R. and out along to Ashtown, all cycling. We halted at Kelly's pub. After a few minutes we all went into the pub. Minerals, as far as I remember, were ordered. When I finished my glass, Mick called me and told me to get my bike and cycle towards the station and see if there was any sign of the train, or if there were any military police there … I had only gone about two hundred yards when I heard the sound of motor cars coming behind me. A motor horn sounded and I pulled into the side to let them pass. There were four cars in all. I wheeled around, cycled back as hard as I could and reported to Mick McDonnell about the military passing me going to the station.
>
> In a very short space of time, we could hear a train arriving. Daly, Leonard, Treacy, Robinson and Hogan went into the back yard of the pub, and into a field, where they took up positions behind the hedge covering the road. Mick McDonnell, Dan Breen and Tom Keogh rushed into the yard and started to pull a big farm cart. They had pulled it out as far as the dip in the side of the road, where it got stuck. In the meantime, an Inspector and a policeman arrived, coming from the opposite side of the road. The policeman stood in the centre of the crossroads, as a traffic man. The Inspector disappeared … We could hear the approach of the cars coming from the station. We had only time to get into position when the cars were upon us.
>
> As the cars approached, the men behind the hedge opened fire with revolvers and grenades.
>
> The first car to come was a dark blue one. Sitting beside the driver was a man in civilian clothes who, we learned

> afterwards, was Detective Officer Halley. He was firing from a revolver. As the car came clear of the corner, I let fly my grenade, which hit the back of the car and exploded. The next thing I saw was the peeler being blown across the road. The second car was stopped right opposite our men behind the hedge. This car was a closed one.
>
> The third car was a box Ford type, with a canvas roof, which flew by with a continuous fire on it. The fourth car which came along was an open Sunbeam car, and in it were a soldier driver and a sergeant. The sergeant was lying across the back of the car, firing from a rifle.
>
> Where we were standing, we were an open target for him. In fact, you could hear the bullets whizzing by … As the car was disappearing around the wide bend of the road, I heard Martin Savage saying something, and it sounded like this: 'Oh, lads, I am hit.' The next thing, he was dead, lying on the road.
>
> I observed smoke coming out of the second car, which was stopped. Also, I saw a hand waving a handkerchief. Someone shouted to him to come out, with his hand up, which the soldier did. He was the driver of the car. Mick McDonnell asked him where was French, and the soldier replied: 'Blown to bits in the car.' No one took it upon himself to see whether he was telling the truth or not. As he was standing in front of us, someone suggested that he should be plugged. Someone else responded: 'Oh, it's not him we wanted.' So, he was let go in safety.
>
> All this time, Dan Breen, who had been hit in the leg, did not notice it. As we had only bicycles, we could not get Martin Savage's body away. The next thing we were told to get back into town and to travel in twos … I went back to my job at two o'clock.[79]

At the end of 1919 the British forces in Ireland were much more visible and the IRA volunteers felt an increasing sense of insecurity. They were constantly under a nervous strain and looking over their shoulders in case of an enemy attack. By then, it was clear the War of Independence was set to become even more expansive and deadly. So, as one year ended and a new one dawned, there was one obvious certainty for the people of Ireland. The country they loved seemed destined for an immediate future shrouded in the darkness of conflict.

CHAPTER ELEVEN

The War of Independence

1920

Irish people generally like to usher in any new year with a sense of optimism and, as 1920 dawned, there were many who hoped for a more peaceful twelve months free from the increasing violence that had blighted the previous year. They hoped a political solution might be found to the vexatious question of independence, yet there was, in truth, little evidence to suggest that hope would be fulfilled. It was clear both sides of the independence divide had become more and more entrenched in their views and showed little inclination to compromise. As it transpired, the year 1920 turned out to be a pivotal one in terms of the ongoing conflict and the country actually witnessed an alarming increase in attacks and ambushes, which cost many more lives and injuries. In fact, during those early days of 1920, the people of Ireland had no idea the worst of the violence was yet to come.

For the political faction of Irish republicanism, the year started very well when it won control of Dublin, Cork and Limerick Urban Councils in January local elections. The election successes clearly indicated how people were coming around to the notion that if independence was ever to be achieved it would require a combination of political activity and military action. On the other hand, the men of violence began the year with the first officially sanctioned attack on an RIC barracks in Carrigtwohill, County Cork, carried out by the Cork No. 1 Brigade. In his witness statement, Michael Leahy, who was Commandant of the Brigade's 4th Battalion, recalled how he fixed the night of 2 January for the attack and planned to use the Cobh, Middleton and Knockraha companies in the operation. Having contacted the leadership of all three companies, he put his plan into action, which involved some forty men. Prior to the attack, he had his men block roads surrounding the village by cutting down trees and erecting stone barriers. Leahy went on to recount the events of that night:

> For the actual attack I placed four or five men with rifles in houses across the street from the barracks. I, myself, took up a position with six riflemen, some with grenades, at the rear of the barracks. Two or three of these men were in a hayshed with me and about three others behind a wall about ten feet from the gable end of the barrack building … About 11 p.m., when I had satisfied myself that every man was in his allocated position, I gave orders to open the attack. Fire was begun by our riflemen in front and from those of us in the rear. Grenades were flung at the barracks windows, but because of the steel shutters, did no damage. The RIC replied with rifle fire and grenades. Verey lights were sent up by the garrison. This continued for about half an hour, when I concluded our fire was ineffective and had no chance of forcing a surrender of the RIC. I therefore ordered that the gable end of the barrack wall be dynamited with a view to obtaining entrance and taking the place by assault. A few men bored about five holes in the barrack wall while John Moore from Cobh inserted the sticks of gelignite. Constant fire was kept up on the RIC to cover the men engaged in this operation. About an hour elapsed before this was completed; meanwhile the garrison in the barracks kept up continuous fire with rifles and grenades. When the dynamite exploded, a large hole was blown in the gable end sufficient to admit two men at a time into what was the barrack dayroom.[80]

Earlier that evening three Volunteers had been arrested in the village and were being held in the barracks. Initially, Leahy had planned to burn down the barracks but the capture of the men caused him to change that course of action. He went on to say:

> About four of us got through the hole in the wall into the dayroom and found that the RIC had taken to rooms upstairs. We fired a few shots through the ceiling. I blew the whistle when we were in the day room; our lads ceased fire and I shouted to the police that we were inside the barracks and that

> they should surrender … They did so, coming downstairs with their hands up. The police were lined up, searched for papers and handcuffed. We marched them out to the village street. All the police carbines, a quantity of revolvers and some shotguns were captured together with a large quantity of ammunition and some grenades. The 'stuff' was put into a motor car and taken to Manley's place at Tubbereemire, about four miles distant. I formed all the lads up in the village street, congratulated them on the success of the job and, when they had sung a verse of the Soldier's Song, dismissed them.[81]

On 20 January, an RIC constable was shot dead in Thurles, Co Tipperary, and it led to RIC reprisals in the town, including the ransacking of many premises belonging to local republicans. In Dublin on the following day, the Squad assassinated District Inspector William Redmond of the RIC and, in his witness statement, Joseph Dolan, a member of GHQ Intelligence recalled the killing, saying:

> The first real Intelligence job I was on was the shooting of Assistant Commissioner Redmond, who had been sent here from Belfast to re-organise the 'G' Division, and had brought some of his own staff with him from Belfast … A detective in the Castle named McNamara, who was working with our Intelligence, gave us information about Redmond. We were after Redmond for about a fortnight, trying to get him on his way from the Castle to the Standard Hotel. We could have got him in the morning but Collins did not want any daylight shooting. I had his description and more or less knew him. He was a tall man and used to wear a hard hat and a black coat with a velvet collar. He had two overcoats, the second was a grey one. He was easily identified and could not be mistaken on the street.
>
> One evening I saw Redmond coming down from the Castle but he turned back and went in again. Paddy Daly, Tom Keogh, Vinny Byrne and myself were waiting and Redmond came out again. Tom Keogh turned to Vinny Byrne and myself and told us to cover them off. Redmond went straight up Dame Street, Grafton Street and Harcourt Street, and we followed him. Just as he came as far as Montague

> Street, Paddy Daly pulled out his revolver and shot him under the ear and Tom Keogh pulled out his revolver and shot him in the back. Daly and Keogh carried out the execution and Byrne and myself acted as a covering party for them. The area was full of British military but no attempt was made to follow us and we got away.[82]

By the end of January 1920, the cycle of violence that enveloped the country for the rest of the year was up and running. On 11 February the commander of the Wicklow Brigade, Seamus O'Brien, died in a shootout in Rathdrum. The following day saw Sean Hales and his unit attack the RIC barracks in Allihies in County Cork and one RIC man was killed in the engagement. After the attack, the RIC decided to abandon many of the small rural barracks across the country as they were seen to be vulnerable to IRA attacks. Also, in County Cork, the RIC barracks in Castlemartyr was attacked by an IRA unit led by Diarmuid Hurley on 14 February, and the following day Ernie O'Malley and Eoin O'Duffy led a unit that captured an RIC barracks near Castleblaney in County Monaghan. In both incidents the IRA made off with a quantity of arms and ammunition.

All this activity forced the authorities to proclaim counties Dublin, Wicklow, Louth, Longford, Westmeath, Sligo and Waterford, giving a clear indication they were worried about the increase in IRA attacks and ambushes. On 20 February a DMP Constable, John Walsh, was shot dead at the corner of Suffolk Street and Grafton Street in Dublin while his colleague, Sergeant James Dunleavy, was wounded in a shooting carried out by brothers Paddy and Gabriel McGrath. Paddy McGrath was wounded in the shootout and taken to Mercer's Hospital, where he was placed under armed guard. That evening, a party of Volunteers raided the hospital, overpowered the guard and spirited Paddy out of the building. On 24 February the death occurred of IRA Vice-Commandant Martin Devitt during an ambush of a four-man RIC bicycle patrol at Crowe's Bridge near Inagh in County Clare. Five days later, a group of Sherwood Foresters were ambushed and disarmed when transporting explosives outside Cobh in County Cork. One soldier was shot dead in the incident.

The month of March saw little let-up in the violence and, on the second day of the month, John Charles Byrne, a British intelligence agent, was assassinated by members of the Squad. Byrne, who went under the name John Jameson, turned up in Dublin posing as a commercial traveller in the jewellery trade. In his witness statement, Vincent (Vinny) Byrne described what happened to the agent, saying:

> He stayed at the Hammam Hotel in Upper O'Connell St. He was a CID man from Scotland Yard, and our Intelligence had this information. Jameson was got in touch with.
>
> He was very anxious to meet Michael Collins and stated he could supply him with all the arms he wanted. One evening, Jameson was met by one of the Squad who was to escort him to see the 'Big Fella'. They boarded the Glasnevin tram. Needless to remark, other squad men boarded the same tram. They arrived at the terminus and proceeded to walk along the Ballymun road for some distance, when he was shot dead.[83]

On 5 March, John Martin Heanue, an RIC officer, was shot dead when he called at his local village shop in Bouladuff in County Tipperary. It seems Heanue and another constable were in the shop when they were confronted by three members of the Tipperary No. 2 Brigade. A gunfight ensued and Heanue was mortally wounded. On 20 March the country was rocked by the death of Tomas MacCurtain, the Lord Mayor of Cork and commander of the Cork No. 1 Brigade. He was shot dead at his home in front of his wife by men with blackened faces, who were later observed entering a local police barracks. The murder of the well-liked and respected MacCurtain caused a wave of grief across the city as well as outrage and his funeral saw thousands of the city's citizens turn out to pay their respects to the committed republican:

> Within just a few hours of his death in the early hours of 20 March 1920, the coffin of Lord Mayor Tomas MacCurtain was carried by hearse from his home in Blackpool to Cork City Hall. Heartrending scenes were witnessed. Men and women knelt down in the street and wept. Such was the intensity of the crowds that sections of Volunteers had considerable difficulty in managing the crowds and local traffic. The streets around Blackpool became absolutely impassable. Contingents of Sinn Fein members, members of trade and labour bodies, members of Cork Corporation and many more crammed into the area. A piper's band played the Dead March en route to the City Hall, and the procession

> of mourners, extending over two miles in length, included a large number of clergy and public men. The police were withdrawn from the streets of the city. Everyone wore the tricolour draped in black, and all the window blinds in the city were drawn as a mark of respect. The 1st Battalion of the Cork Volunteers acted as bodyguard, and at City Hall a party of men remained to watch over the coffin throughout the night. The business of City Hall was suspended for the removal and the funeral the following day. The Republican Flag was at half-mast above the municipal civic emblem, and on the door of the entrance hall appeared a card bearing the inscription, 'Closed in consequence of the murder of Tomas MacCurtain, first Republican Lord Mayor of Cork' …
>
> After the high noon mass, the funeral procession started to St Finbarr's Cemetery. The coffin was shouldered by six Volunteers in uniform. The bishop in his carriage came next. The clergy, numbering about one hundred; Christian Brothers and Presentation Brothers followed, who wore Sinn Fein mourning rosettes. Then came Volunteers Pipers playing 'Wrap the Green Flag Round Me'. Behind was Father Dominic, who was the Lord Mayor's chaplain, who was accompanied by Mr Terence McSwiney and other officers of the Volunteers … The chief mourners walked behind, and after were members of the Corporation, Harbour Board, and public bodies and organisations. However, the general public comprised over 10,000 people. It took one hour and a half to pass any given point … At the cemetery, Bishop Cohalan blessed the grave. When it was covered, the Last Post was sounded and three volleys of shots were fired.[84]

Five days later one of the most significant events of the War of Independence took place with the arrival of the Black and Tans into the country. Little did the people of Ireland realise how this force of dubious characters would go on to cause so much havoc during their infamous stay and how detested they would become among the general public.

Throughout March, the killings continued, with RIC men losing their lives in incidents in Kilkenny, Limerick, Cork and in Tipperary, where two officers were shot dead as they left a church on St Patrick's Day. On 24 March the Squad assassinated a British Intelligence officer called

Molloy (who often used a number of different names) in Dublin. In his witness statement, Vincent (Vinny) Byrne recalled the incident:

> This sergeant was in touch with our Intelligence and was anxious to meet Liam Tobin.
>
> On the evening 23rd March 1920, he met Frank Saurin, one of our Intelligence Officers, who took him into the Café Cairo in Grafton St for tea. I was detailed to follow them for the purpose of being able to identify Molloy. I took a chair at the next table. Frank Saurin turned to me and said: 'Hello, so-and-so'. Then, turning to Molloy, he had a few words with him and he invited me to join them, which I did. I was introduced to Molloy. After a little while, Frank said: 'Our friend is very anxious to meet Liam Tobin and I am sure you could arrange it'. I said: 'I will see', and then agreed … After having tea, I made arrangements to meet him the following evening at 5.30 p.m. at the corner of South King St and Grafton St … On the evening that I was to meet Molloy, the Squad and myself proceeded to the appointed place and, there we saw our, man waiting. He waited about three-quarters of an hour, and then moved off down Grafton Street. We made several attempts to get him, but, owing to the large number of people in the Street, it was very difficult. He turned into Wicklow St and proceeded as far as the corner of South William St. Here we opened fire and he fell dead.[85]

On 26 March 1920 one of the more high-profile assassinations of the independence conflict took place in Dublin. Alan Bell, a resident magistrate, had been given the task of tracking down Sinn Fein finances and was having some success. He had confiscated around £70,000 from Sinn Fein headquarters accounts and was on the trail of more funds across the country. Despite being warned to desist from his work, he ignored the threat and was pulled from a tram by some Squad members and executed in broad daylight. In his witness statement, Squad member James Slattery recalled the operation, saying:

> We were informed that a British financial agent by the name of Alan Bell was over here on behalf of the British government trying to locate republican and Dail funds and in

> our own interests he should be disposed of. I think he lived in Monkstown. A few days after the shooting of Molloy, Mick McDonnell detailed myself and several others to meet the tram taking Bell into his office one morning. Tom Keogh was sent out to Bell's house on a bicycle and was to cycle in ahead of the tram on which Bell was travelling. My party were waiting in the vicinity of the showgrounds in Ballsbridge and Tom Keogh came cycling along and signalled to us that the wanted agent was on the next tram. We stopped the tram at, I think, Anglesea Road, boarded it and Bell was taken off and executed. I was on the top of the tram and, when I was coming down the steps, I heard the shooting and saw Bell falling on the side of the road.[86]

The violence across the country continued at a pace and during the night of 3–4 April the IRA attacked and destroyed over 300 RIC barracks in rural areas as well as around 100 Income Tax offices. On the night of 5–6 April, a further 150 rural barracks were destroyed and they were all abandoned in favour of the more secure barracks in the larger urban areas. On 5 April a number of IRA prisoners, led by Peadar Clancy, began a hunger strike in Mountjoy Jail and demanded to be treated as prisoners of war. A general strike and a large demonstration on 14 April led to the prisoners being released. In the County Clare town of Miltown Malbay, the RIC and British Army fired indiscriminately into a crowd of local people celebrating the prisoners' release. Unfortunately, three people (one of which, John O'Loughlin, was an IRA member) were killed, while six others were wounded.

During the latter part of April an RIC officer and an IRA man died in an engagement outside the church in Kilmihil, County Clare. The IRA also ambushed and killed RIC men Sergeant Cornelius Crean and Constable Patrick McGoldrick near Ballinspittle in County Cork. Sergeant Crean was a brother of the great explorer, Tom Crean, who was part of Shackleton's expedition to the South Pole in 1909. On 27 April, sixty men of the IRA East Limerick Brigade, led by Vice-Commandant Thomas Malone, attacked the RIC barracks at Ballylanders in County Limerick, which was defended by five RIC men. In his witness statement, Malone provided a fine account of the attack, saying:

> In the attack on Ballylanders Barracks, we put Hannigan in charge of a section occupying one of the houses there opposite

> the Barracks. Crowley's house was occupied and several other houses. I picked seven or eight fellows to come with me into a house adjoining the Barracks. We burst through the slates of the house in which we were and got out on to the roof of the Barracks. We burst through the slates of the roof of the Barracks … the other sections opened first on the windows of the Barracks. We broke in the roof of the Barracks anyway and threw in a few bombs and called on the RIC to surrender. They began some kind of discussion with us … While the discussion was going on, one of the policemen stole in through the door of the room underneath and fired upwards. He very nearly got me … I replied to the fire. I believe I hit him alright. One of the RIC men was wounded in the thigh. I signalled to our lads to open fire again, and then we flung in paraffin and petrol through the hole in the roof and ignited it. After ten or fifteen minutes, we called on the RIC again to surrender. We could hear them shouting, 'We surrender.' At some stage, Meade, one of our men, was wounded in the lung. He was on the opposite side of the street in one of the houses. When the RIC surrendered, I told them that nothing would happen if they came out and brought all their stuff out. They did bring out all of their stuff except a box of bombs. The Sergeant told me it was under the bed in one of the bedrooms and that the place was on fire, but we got in through the fire and got it out. I think we got everything that was in the barracks, rifles ammunition, revolvers and this box of bombs.[87]

The month of May arrived, bringing with it an increase in violence and on the 8th the IRA captured Cloyne barracks in County Cork. The following day some 200 IRA men under the command of Frank Aiken attacked the RIC barracks in Newtownhamilton in County Armagh. A two-hour firefight ensued, with the IRA eventually breaching the barracks wall with explosives before storming the building. The barracks was then set alight with petrol sprayed on it with a potato spraying machine. On 10 May three RIC officers were killed in an ambush at Ahawadda Cross near Timoleague, carried out by members of the Bandon Battalion led by their vice-commanding officer, Charlie Hurley.

On 19 May the IRA shot dead two RIC sergeants on Upper Mallow Street in Limerick. The RIC ran amok in the city, firing shots indiscriminately at civilians, one of whom was fatally wounded. The month of May also saw Dublin dock workers refuse to handle British military supplies and they were joined by members of Irish Transport and General Workers Union. The railway drivers refused to drive the trains carrying British troops and that action continued until the following December. On 28 May the IRA attacked the RIC barracks in Kilmallock, County Limerick, which was being held by around thirty policemen at that time. In his witness statement, John O'Brien, Vice-Commandant of the 6th Battalion, East Limerick Brigade, recalled the attack:

> Before the attack commenced, a lot of trees were felled across the roads for a radius of twenty miles from Kilmallock, and the railway was torn up not far from Emly. We assembled in a field just behind the town and we were allotted our positions by Sean Forde. Our position was right opposite the barracks, in Cleary's Hotel ... We went in and took up our positions. We made a barricade at the windows with pillows and cushions and waited for the signal, which was to come at midnight. When it came ... all the lights in the street were put out and the shooting started. The local Volunteers had procured a horse-drawn tanker of oil belonging to petrol companies. It was brought to a point near the barracks from where the oil was pumped on to the barracks, the roof of which had been well broken by our men who had occupied the house next door. At different times during the night, we sang 'The Soldiers Song'. It was taken up from house to house, all singing in loud voices. Sean Forde would ask us to stop singing every now and again and he would then shout out to the police to surrender. This continued until 3 or 4 o'clock in the morning, when two or three of us left the hotel by the front door and made our way to another house. Liam Scully was killed about that time. He was a Kerry man and a teacher of Irish. Day was breaking and it was getting very bright when the attack was called off. The barracks and the lean-to building were practically burned out. Forde thought it was too dangerous to keep the men there any longer as military reinforcements for the garrison might come, so we withdrew. Two of the RIC men were killed and a share of them were wounded.[88]

During the early days of June, the RIC barracks in Blarney and in Carrigadrohid (both in County Cork), Fenit in County Kerry and Drangan in County Tipperary were attacked. In the middle of the month, Sinn Fein won control of all but four of the county councils in elections as well as 172 of the 206 rural district councils, and all the republican-controlled councils gave their allegiance to the Irish Republic.

On 15 June, RIC District Inspector Percival Lea-Wilson was shot dead in Gorey, County Wexford, on the orders of Michael Collins. Lea-Wilson was reputed to have ordered the execution of Sean McDermott in 1916 and, as a consequence, he became a target of the IRA. During June three IRA men, Dave Brennan, Patrick Buckley and Liam Danaher, were badly burned as they attempted to burn down Drumcollogher Court House. All three men later died having succumbed to their injuries. Over the course of the month the IRA staged a number of local raids across the country and managed to secure an impressive cache of arms and ammunition, which were used over the course of the conflict.

On 26 June the high-profile British General Cuthbert Lucas was captured by the IRA while he was in a fishing lodge near Fermoy in County Cork. He was the highest-ranking British officer to be captured during the independence conflict. His capture, which was sanctioned by Liam Lynch, the Commandant of the Cork No. 2 Brigade, was carried out in the hope he could be swapped for IRA prisoners being held at that time by the British. As it transpired, the British eventually gave up looking for Lucas, who was held for weeks by the East Clare Brigade. There was no swap of prisoners and Lucas, who proved to be the very essence of a gentleman while being held captive, eventually escaped, somewhat easily, in late July, most likely because it became inconvenient for the IRA to continue holding him.

June 1920 also saw the collapse of the British courts system in Ireland as potential jurors refused to participate in trials. The Chief Secretary for Ireland, Hamar Greenwood, reflecting on the situation, claimed that 'the administrative machinery of the courts has been brought to a standstill'. The Dail Courts that emerged at the end of 1918 and during the early days of 1919 were, in effect, the recognised courts of the Republic that had been declared after the 1918 general election. The Dail Courts were quickly accepted by the people as the courts of the land and, as a result, the British court system was shunned. In May 1920 the Dail Courts were formally adopted by the Republic and initially put under the authority of the Department of Agriculture, which was a nod to their initial function of resolving agrarian disputes. In June the authority over the Courts was transferred to the Department of Home Affairs under the leadership of Austin Stack.

The Dail Courts, which were formally established by a decree of Dail Eireann on 29 June 1920, were expected to act as criminal and civil courts and were given the right to administer the laws of the land instead of the British courts system. The new courts system had three levels: the Parish Court at the bottom of the scale, the District Court in the middle and the Supreme Court at the top of the scale. The Parish Courts dealt with small civil claims under £10 in value and petty criminal offences. The District Courts dealt with appeals from the Parish Courts, criminal trials, civil claims from £10 to £100 in value and land title claims exceeding £100 in value. The Supreme Court had what was termed as 'unlimited jurisdiction over all civil and criminal cases and, also heard appeals from the Circuit sittings of the Districts Courts'. In essence, during the early summer of 1920, the republicans took the matter of law and order across the country into their own hands and could rightly claim their justice system was not only successful but was quickly accepted and embraced by the majority of the population.

The second half of 1920 showed little sign of the violence easing and, in fact, there was every indication it was being ramped up as each day passed. From the outset of July, the IRA continued to be active right across the country. During the first week of that month numerous attacks and incidents took place that, unfortunately, cost the lives of IRA men and a number of civilians. On 11 July, Alexander Will from Scotland became the first Black and Tan to lose his life in the conflict. He died in an IRA attack on the RIC barracks in Rathmore, County Kerry. That same day an IRA force of about fifty men led by Ernie O'Malley attacked the RIC barracks at Rearcross in County Tipperary. One RIC man was shot dead during the attack, while three IRA men, including O'Malley, were wounded. On 13 July an IRA unit, under the command of Tadgh Brosnan, attacked an RIC supply patrol near Dingle in County Kerry. During the attack two RIC men were shot dead, while two of their colleagues were wounded. Four days later, Colonel Gerald Smyth, the Divisional Commissioner of the RIC, was assassinated in Cork city. Smyth had previously urged RIC officers in the city to shoot civilians who disobeyed their orders. In his witness statement, Daniel Healy, a member of the IRA Active Service Unit in Cork, described in detail the killing of Smyth:

> On 17th July 1920, I was told by 'Pa' Murray to report to the Sinn Fein Hall, North Main Street, and to bring a revolver.

The purpose was to shoot Colonel Smyth, Divisional Commissioner of the RIC. Smyth had previously served in the British Army and had lost an arm in the First World War. He was appointed to the RIC early in June 1920 and in the course of a tour of certain RIC barracks in County Kerry had incited the police to shoot at sight persons suspected of having Sinn Fein sympathies. At Listowel on 17th June 1920 he ordered the RIC to hand over their barracks to the military and to transfer to different stations in the district. He then addressed the police, instructing them to 'shoot and shoot with effect' any civilians who might not immediately obey a 'hands up' order. As a result, of Smyth's inflammatory remarks, five RIC constables resigned in Listowel.

Elsewhere in Kerry, Smyth repeated his incitements to murder and when he came to reside for a while in the County Club on the South Mall, Cork, early in July, 1920, the Brigade decided that an attempt should be made to shoot him. The County Club, the resort of landed families and high military officers, had a loyal staff. Consequently our Intelligence department had difficulty in making contact with any member of the staff until, at last, a young waiter in the Club agreed to co-operate. Thereafter, the names of British officers, military and police, who stayed there were known to our Intelligence Service. Colonel Smyth was staying there during the first fortnight of July 1920.

This information was conveyed to the Brigade and it was decided to shoot him on Tuesday morning, 13th July. However, he packed his bags that day and announced his intention of going away for the week, so that arrangements for shooting him fell through.

He returned unexpectedly the following Saturday evening and, on receipt of this Information … members of the 1st Battalion were hastily mobilised on … the night of 17th July 1920. About 10 p.m. on the night in question, the six of us went into the County Club and down a passage to the lounge, which we entered with drawn revolvers. Smyth was seated with another man, County Inspector Craig of the RIC, in a corner of the lounge in which there were about twelve other people. We immediately opened fire, killing Smyth and wounding Craig.

> Smyth tried to draw his revolver when he saw us entering the lounge but without avail. We then left the premises and got safely away.[89]

On 19 July, an IRA ambush near Tuam in County Galway saw two RIC men lose their lives. After an unsuccessful search to find the killers, the RIC burned down the Town Hall and another hall used by Sinn Fein before firing shots and throwing hand grenades at local people attempting to put the fires out. The last week of the month saw an escalation of the violence across the country, especially in Munster. There numerous members of the RIC and other Crown forces died or were wounded in almost daily incidents, most notably in Bandon and Clonakilty in County Cork and in Oola and Bruree in County Limerick.

In Dublin the Squad was given orders by Michael Collins to assassinate a man called Frank Brooke, who was a Director of the Great Southern and Eastern Railways and a member of Lord French's Advisory Council. It was his association with French that brought Brooke to the attention of Collins and his Intelligence Unit. Brooke had also made clear his detestation of the republican movement and it was inevitable he would end up on the IRA hit list. His killing was, in essence, a political assassination, and the only one of its kind during the conflict. In his witness statement, James Slattery provided a detailed account of the assassination:

> In the forenoon of a day towards the end of July, 1920, Paddy Daly, Tom Keogh and myself proceeded to the offices of the railway company on Westland Row. Brooke was sitting at his table when we entered his office. We immediately opened fire on him and he fell. As we were going down the stairs again Daly said to me, 'Are you sure we got him?' I said I was not sure, and Daly said, 'What about going back and making sure?'
>
> Keogh and myself went back. When I went into the room, I saw a man standing at the left of the door and I fired a shot in his direction, at the same time looking over at Brooke on the floor. I fired a couple of shots at Brooke and satisfied myself that he was dead.
>
> Although I did not wound the other man, who was in the room, I was informed afterwards that it would have been a good job if he had been shot, as he too was making himself a nuisance.[90]

It transpired the other man was T.A. Cotton, a fellow director and, the Irish Traffic Manager of the London and North Western Railway Company, and he was a man who held the same views as Brooke in relation to the republican movement.

The violence not only continued through August 1920 but actually became much more intense and hardly a day passed without a report of an ambush or an attack, most of which resulted in death or injuries. On 7 August the IRA's East Limerick Flying Column, under the command of Donnacha O'Hannigan and George Lennon, in tandem with a Cork column under the command of Tom Barry, ambushed an eight-man RIC foot patrol near Kildorrery in County Cork. All the RIC men were wounded in the firefight, while the IRA made off with six revolvers and 250 rounds of ammunition. On 12 August, Terence McSwiney, Lord Mayor of Cork, was arrested and he immediately began a hunger strike that was to take his life the following October.

On Saturday 14 August, a British aeroplane made a forced landing at Drominagh in County Cork. British soldiers were detailed to protect the aircraft until repairs were carried out on it. The following day, a poorly armed local IRA unit, led by Jack O'Connell, launched an attack on the soldiers, during which a sentry was shot dead. A couple of hours of gunfire ensued, which brought more British military into the area and forced the IRA to retreat. O'Connell and Paddy Clancy, who had just been appointed Commandant of the North Cork Flying Column and who was a personal friend and comrade of Sean Moylan, retired to O'Connell's home in Derrygallon some 3 miles outside Kanturk in the hope of evading the British. They were seen by an informer, who passed on the information to the police in Kanturk. Both men were sleeping when the house was surrounded by soldiers and police. They attempted to fight their way out but were eventually shot dead some distance from the house. Both men defended themselves heroically until they had expended all their ammunition. Moylan, who was at the time clearly distraught at the death of his comrades, recalled:

> They were both shot dead, one good courageous officer, the other outstanding in courage, character and capacity, the possessor of all those manly graces which endeared him to all who knew him and which keep his memory still fragrant in their hearts.[91]

Such was the bond between the fighting men of the IRA by that stage of the independence conflict they all took every opportunity to display their respect and admiration for each other. In Moylan's case it was no different and he went on to poignantly recall how he:

> Carried his (Clancy's) body over hill and dale and murmuring stream to bury him beneath the haunted mountain on which his eyes first opened.[92]

That same day, the IRA assassinated an RIC District Inspector, William Wilson, in Templemore, County Tipperary. The police and some military burned several businesses in the town as well as the Town Hall in reprisal. Two British officers from the Northampton Regiment died accidently in the burnings. On 17 August Terence McSwiney was transferred from Cork Prison to Brixton Prison in England. Between 17 and 21 August the IRA carried out attacks on Crown forces in counties Donegal, Kerry, Clare/ Galway, Kildare, Louth and Longford, during which a number of the enemy were killed or wounded and quantities of arms and ammunition were captured. On 22 August one IRA man, Michael Galvin, a member of the Kilmurray Company, was killed in action during the ambush of a British Army unit at Lissarda in County Cork.

Over the last week in August 1920 the RIC lost men in counties Roscommon, Limerick and Longford, while the British Army lost a soldier in an engagement with the IRA in Midleton in County Cork. On the last day of the month, the IRA suffered the loss of four men, all members of the Monaghan Brigade, under the command of Eoin O'Duffy, when it carried out raids for guns and ammunition at the homes of several prominent unionist families in the county. On the political front, the month of August saw the Restoration of Order in Ireland Act become law and the British government was given power to govern Ireland by regulation. Courts martial replaced the criminal courts and coroner's inquests were replaced with military courts of inquiry.

The first couple of weeks in September saw more Crown forces deaths at the hands of the IRA who also lost a number of men. There was a particularly sad incident on 14 September in Kinlough, County Leitrim, when a man called James Connolly was shot dead by some Black and Tans when they called at his house to arrest his son. Unfortunately, a deaf Connolly did not hear the order to put his hands up and he was shot dead on the spot. On 20 September the conflict came to Dublin in a big way when the IRA ambushed a British troops ration party outside Monk's Bakery on Church Street. The attack claimed the lives of three soldiers, while others were wounded. One of the IRA men, 18-year-old medical student Kevin Barry, was arrested at the scene and subsequently charged with murder. He was later convicted of the charge and hanged despite much international outrage. On the same day of the Church Street attack, RIC Head Constable Peter Burke and his brother, Sergeant Michael Burke, were shot dead in Ballbriggan, County Dublin. Crown forces retaliated by burning and looting houses and businesses in the town. They killed two IRA suspects, James Lawless and John Gibbons, and there was widespread condemnation of the sacking of the town.

There seemed to be no end to the cycle of violence and two days later six RIC officers were all killed in an IRA ambush at Rineen in County Clare. The ambushers then successfully fended off an attack by British soldiers sent as reinforcements. Later that day a local magistrate, Alan Lendrum, was shot dead as some IRA men attempted to take his car. In retaliation, three villages in the immediate area were ransacked by Crown forces. On 28 September an IRA unit led by Liam Lynch and Ernie O'Malley attacked the British Army barracks in Mallow, County Cork. They seized weapons and freed some republican prisoners, while a British Army sergeant was shot dead during the raid. It turned out to be the only army barracks to be captured by the IRA during the War of Independence. The attack on the Barracks in Mallow involved around twenty men, with others covering them and was planned down to the last detail. The attack was based on information brought to Lynch by a Volunteer called Dick Willis, who was working on a building contract in the Mallow barracks and the information he brought suggested it could be captured. Sean Moylan was among the leaders involved in the planning of the attack and though he and his active service unit did not take part in it, having been sent by Liam Lynch on another mission, he later provided a fine commentary on what took place. He recounted:

> Willis had carefully noted the movements of the guards and sentries, and the manner in which visitors to the barracks were received. Willis proposed that he and another Volunteer, Jack Bolster, should be armed with revolvers. They would introduce a third man, also armed, posing as a foreman there to check on the work being done. On a given signal, they would hold up the guard and sentries, giving the Active Service Unit an opportunity to rush the gate from outside. The question of getting the gate open, said Moylan, was a tricky

> one. A proposal was made that a member of the Active Service Unit should approach the guard with a letter for the officer in charge. Once the guard had been engaged in conversation, the ASU would charge the gate. Moylan recalled there was no lack of Volunteers for the operation and that O'Malley more or less nominated himself to carry the letter … Paddy McCarthy, a great personal friend of Moylan, was chosen to pose as the site foreman, even though he knew next to nothing of the building trade.[93]

Moylan went on to extoll all of McCarthy's virtues and it was obvious he rated his friend and comrade as man of great character and integrity, saying:

> He was of that sparse but richly endowed brotherhood, the men who knew no fear. For an hour, we worked over a draft of a repair specification which I made. I explained to him the meaning of the terms, the methods by which he could at least minimise the danger of showing his complete ignorance of the building trade, and felt at the end that he was at least sufficiently lessoned to pass muster among a group of men who were doubtless no better informed than he was.[94]

Moylan and his ASU left Mallow before the raid on the barracks to carry out a different mission but he later gave a good account of what transpired:

> Dick Willis confirmed that the British officer in charge of the barracks in Mallow was concerned about the inadequacy of the water supply and had spoken to him about it.
>
> Willis assured him that he would speak to the Town Clerk and arrange for a water Inspector to call to the barracks on the Tuesday morning to see if a better supply could be tapped into the barracks. The arrangement fitted perfectly with the attack plan and it was decided that Ernie O'Malley should play the role of the Council water inspector.
>
> On the morning of the attack, Paddy McCarthy, posing as a foreman, arrived at the barracks and had a discussion with Willis about the work being done. Bolster, meanwhile, was working outside the window of a room where off-duty soldiers were taking their ease. Ernie O'Malley appeared at the gate,

> brandishing a letter for the barracks commander. He was admitted on the premises and immediately grabbed the sentry's rifle, which was the signal for the others to move. Bolster then threw open the window where he was working, drew his revolver and yelled at the troops to stay where they were. Willis and McCarthy now rushed to the guardroom door with their guns drawn and jumped between the soldiers and the rack where the rifles were stored. A British sergeant charged at Willis, who had no option but to shoot him dead. Simultaneously, a number of IRA men poured into the barracks, encountering no resistance. The raiding party seized every weapon and every round of ammunition in the barracks before leaving.[95]

There was a price to pay for the attack as enraged soldiers carried out a reprisal that night in Mallow when they burned many houses and businesses in the town. The month of September 1920 ended just as it started, violently, as the day after the Mallow barracks attack two RIC officers died in an IRA ambush just outside Borrisoleigh in County Tipperary. On the same day, two other RIC officers were shot dead in Ryan's pub in O'Brien's Bridge in County Clare. On the last day of the month, an IRA ambush of an RIC lorry near Tubbercurry in County Sligo saw a District Inspector lose his life while several of his colleagues were wounded. In reprisal, the RIC and Black and Tans burned many homes and businesses in the area.

October saw an escalation of the violence and there was a shoot-out in Dublin's Drumcondra district as Crown forces staked out an IRA safe house where Dan Breen and Sean Treacy were staying. Breen was severely wounded as both men made their escape, while two British intelligence officers, Major E. Smyth and Captain A.P. White, were killed. The following day, four RIC constables died in an IRA ambush in County Roscommon and five IRA men died and nine others were injured when they accidently detonated explosives in County Wexford. A couple of days later the British eventually caught up with Treacy, one of the IRA's most wanted men. British soldiers and undercover agents raided a safe house on Talbot Street in which he was staying. A gunfight ensued on the street during which Treacy was killed but not before he managed to kill one of the agents, Lieutenant Price. Unfortunately, two civilian bystanders were killed by British machine gun fire.

On 22 October, two British soldiers of the Essex Regiment lost their lives in an ambush of a transport lorry carried out by members of the 3rd Cork Brigade at Toureen on the Cork to Bandon Road. Five other soldiers were wounded, one of whom died from his wounds some days later. The IRA men made off with fourteen rifles, two revolvers, bayonets, Mills bombs and around 1,400 rounds of ammunition. Three days later, Terence MacSwiney succumbed to the hunger strike he started back in August and died in Brixton Prison. Two of the ten men who joined him on the strike, Michael Fitzgerald and Joseph Murray, also died before Arthur Griffith ordered an end to the protest. MacSwiney's death was another blow to the republican leadership both nationally and in Cork, and tributes poured in from all corners of the world as his body was laid to rest. There was a great deal of media coverage of his death and the subsequent conveying of his body from London back to his native Cork. Based on various media reports from that time, *Century Ireland* reconstructed a very fine account of MacSwiney's final journey home:

> The journey of his remains through London on 28 October was a magnificent but sombre spectacle. Following a Requiem Mass in St George's Cathedral, at which, Archbishop Mannix was among the officiating priests, thousands of sympathisers lined the route to Euston Station to where the large procession made its slow progress. The bulk of those who made up the cortège came from branches of the Irish-Self Determination League in London, Liverpool and other centres across Britain. MacSwiney's remains were then taken to Holyhead and onto Cork, where they arrived the following day.[96]

The original plan was to take MacSwiney's body back to Dublin but the British authorities put a stop to that, fearing its arrival in the capital might spark a large-scale political demonstration. So, against the wishes of MacSwiney's family, the body was placed on board the *Rathmore*, a chartered ship, and sent to Cork accompanied by 200 armed British soldiers. At that time the *Irish Independent* reported the scenes at Holyhead as the 'desecration of the martyred dead'. MacSwiney's body lay in state in Cork City Hall for one night and was then brought to St Mary and St Anne Cathedral, where Requiem Mass was celebrated. The funeral cortège then made its way to St Finbarr's Cemetery where MacSwiney was laid to rest in the republican plot and just a few feet from his great friend and fellow republican, Tomas MacCurtain. Arthur Griffith delivered the graveside oration, saying MacSwiney had:

> endured all that the power of England could inflict upon him and in enduring, triumphed over that power. His body lies here,

> his soul goes marching through all the ages. He is not dead. He is living forever in the hearts and conscience of Ireland.[97]

On 28 October members of the 3rd Tipperary Brigade ambushed a British Army lorry near Golden. Three soldiers were killed in the engagement, while six others were wounded. The last day of the month saw the shooting dead of an RIC Inspector by the IRA at the Grenville Arms hotel in Granard, County Longford. His killing led to businesses and houses being burned in the town by the RIC and British military. That same day was a terrible one across County Kerry when ten people in total died. Two RIC constables were killed in Abbeydorney, while two more died in Ballyduff. In retaliation the Black and Tans burned the creamery in Ballyduff and killed a local civilian. Two Black and Tans were shot dead in Kilorglin and their comrades ransacked the town in retaliation and shot a local civilian. Also, that day, an RIC constable and a British Auxiliary were shot and killed in Tralee, which sparked days of terror and mayhem in the town.

November 1920 turned out to be one of the bloodiest of the War of Independence when chaos and mayhem abounded across the country. From the very first day the scene was set for a period of unprecedented violence. The town of Tralee was attacked by the Black and Tans and they destroyed the Town Hall and several shops. They fired indiscriminately in the streets and one civilian was shot dead. Another man, an ex-service man, was beaten and shot and died of his wounds some days later. That same day, Kevin Barry was hanged in Dublin for his part in the Church Street attack in September 1920, during which three British soldiers died. The RIC also lost a man that day when Constable Peter Cooney was shot dead near Ballinalee, County Longford. It seems he was suspected of being a spy and his execution may well have been ordered by Michael Collins. It was alleged at the time of his death that Cooney had on his person coded dispatches with the names of Longford IRA men.

The Black and Tans shot a pregnant woman called Eileen Quinn at Kiltartan in County Galway as she sat outside her house in the company of a young child. They shot her from a passing lorry and were apparently drunk and had been firing randomly as they passed through the district. At a subsequent military court it was claimed no shots were fired and the court returned a verdict of 'death by misadventure' and the opinion that the victim was shot by a member of the police. Also, on 1 November, IRA men from West Waterford, led by George Lennon and Pax Whelan, ambushed an RIC and British Army patrol at Piltown. One soldier was killed in the ambush, while two others were wounded. Seventeen soldiers were captured and later released but not before they were relieved of their arms and ammunition consisting of eighteen rifles, carbines and revolvers plus grenades and ammunition.

On 2 November a North Longford IRA column, led by Sean MacEoin, defended the village of Ballinalee from an attack carried out by the British. The British arrived in eleven lorries carrying troops but were forced to retreat after a nearly three-hour gun fight. Between 3 November and 10 November, five members of the Crown forces, seven IRA men and one civilian, a young girl, all lost their lives in various attacks and ambushes across the country. On 14 November, Father Michael Griffin disappeared from his residence in Galway and it emerged he had been abducted and murdered by Auxiliaries at Barna just outside the city. The killings continued on the following day with the deaths of three British Army officers at Waterfall in County Cork. That same day, three IRA men and one civilian died at the hands of Auxiliaries in Killaloe, County Clare and, the killing frenzy continued with the deaths of two Auxiliaries at the hands of the IRA in Macroom, County Cork. Two days later, Cork city saw the assassination of an RIC sergeant and, hours later the RIC gained revenge when they shot dead three civilians in their homes. All in all, the country was looking into the abyss but worse was yet to come as the violence spiralled out of control during the second half of the month.

The month of November 1920 will always be remembered for two of the most notable incidents of the entire conflict. The first incident took place in Dublin on Sunday, 21 November and was forever more known as 'Bloody Sunday'. It was the day Michael Collins unleashed the young men who made up his Squad on the British Intelligence community in the capital. By that stage the British Intelligence service had established an extensive network of spies and informers around Dublin and Collins targeted a group of British Intelligence officers known as the 'Cairo Gang'. The gang took its name from the Cairo Café on Grafton Street that they frequented and from their service in the British military intelligence in Egypt and Palestine during the Great War. The republican leadership was aware of the gang's existence and Richard Mulcahy, the then IRA Chief of Staff, once described them as 'a very dangerous and cleverly placed spy organisation'.

Collins and his Intelligence Unit concluded the British intended to wipe out the republican leadership and, in anticipation of any such attack, he directed the Squad to strike first and eliminate the Cairo Gang. Consequently, Dick McKee was given charge of planning for the strike and the gathering of Intelligence. Over time, the Intelligence Unit cultivated a very sophisticated network of informants from many walks of life and had little trouble in compiling the addresses of the targeted British agents. Information came readily from many sources including housemaids, post office and railway workers as well as at least one police informant. Initially, Collins targeted around fifty British agents but that figure was revised to around thirty-five individuals because in many cases there was a lack of evidence to justify a killing.

On the morning of the attack, the Squad assembled at 8 a.m. outside St Andrew's Church on Westland Row before making their way to their various assigned locations. All of the killings took place around the South Dublin inner city, with the exception of a shooting in the Gresham Hotel. As it transpired, fifteen British agents died that morning at the hands of the Squad, supplemented by a number of men from the IRA's Dublin Brigade. The agents died in houses located on Upper and Lower Mount Streets, Baggot Street, Fitzwilliam Square, Morehampton Road and Earlsfort Terrace. The killings were all carried out with a ruthlessness that belied the young age of most of the assassins. Vincent (Vinny) Byrne, in his witness statement, recalled his involvement in the operation and the manner in which he went about his business was, it seems, typical of each member of the Squad that day. Byrne led the raid on 28 Upper Mount Street, where he and his group, comprising six of his comrades, were to deal with two British officers, Lieutenant Bennett and Lieutenant Aimes. With five men keeping guard, Byrne and Tom Ennis entered the house and they each located an officer in different bedrooms. Byrne went on to recount what happened next:

> I then marched my officer down to the back room where the other officer was. He was standing up in the bed, facing the wall. I ordered mine to do likewise. When the two of them were together, I said to myself: 'The Lord have mercy on your souls!' I then opened fire with my Peter. They both fell dead.[98]

Many of the planned assassinations did not take place because the targeted individuals were either not at home or, in some cases, the men looking for them got their tactics wrong. However, the raids did have the impact Collins and his people had hoped for on the British agents, many of whom sought refuge in Dublin Castle. Collins, it seems, was pleased with the results of his men's work and later declared:

> My one intention was the destruction of the undesirables who continued to make miserable the lives of the ordinary decent

> citizen. I have proof enough to assure myself of the atrocities which this gang of spies and informers have committed. I have paid them back in their own coin.[99]

The British responded that afternoon when they launched an attack on Croke Park, which was hosting a football match between Dublin and Tipperary before an estimated crowd of 5,000 people. The British concluded the men involved in that morning's assassination spree would attempt to evade the security forces by disappearing into the crowd. As the game got under way, Crown forces surrounded the ground. They had orders to guard the exits and search every man in the crowd in the hope of finding firearms. For reasons that are not still clear, shots were fired and chaos ensued. The police claimed they were fired on first but they were unable to prove that assertion. The *Freeman's Journal* later reported:

> The spectators were startled by a volley of shots fired from inside the turnstile entrances. Armed and uniformed men were seen entering the field and, immediately after the firing broke out, scenes of the wildest confusion took place. The spectators made a rush for the far side of Croke Park and shots were fired over their heads and into the crowd.[100]

The firing continued for about ninety seconds and some reports claimed the crowd was also fired on from the pitch and from outside the ground on Canal Bridge. It is estimated that 114 rifle rounds were fired as well as fifty machine gun rounds together with an unknown amount of revolver rounds. When the shooting was over, seven people had been shot dead and five more wounded so badly they later died from their injuries. Two other people were trampled to death in the stampede to get out of the ground. Two Tipperary players, Michael Hogan and Jim Egan, were shot while on the pitch. Hogan died and Egan recovered from his wounds. No firearms were found in the ground or around its vicinity.

The action taken by the Crown forces was not sanctioned by the Dublin Castle authorities, who were quick to blame the IRA assassins for the whole debacle. An official statement was released which claimed that:

> A number of men came to Dublin on Saturday under the guise of asking to attend a football match between Tipperary and Dublin. But their real intention was to take part in a series of

> murderous outrages which took place in Dublin that morning. Learning that a number of these gunmen were present in Croke Park, the Crown forces went to raid the field. It was the original intention that an officer would go to the centre of the field and, speaking from a megaphone, invite the assassins to come forward. But on their approach, armed pickets gave warning. Shots were fired to warn the wanted men, who caused a stampede and escaped in the confusion.[101]

That assertion was rejected in Ireland and even ridiculed by *The Times* in London as well as the British Labour Party. Later on 'Bloody Sunday', two high-ranking IRA men, Dick McKee and Peadar Clancy and another man, Conor Clune, were murdered in Dublin Castle. The authorities claimed the three men were shot as they tried to escape. Two military courts of inquiry were held into the Croke Park shootings and one found that, 'the fire of the RIC was carried out without orders and exceeded the demands of the situation'. The events of that dreadful day had a profound impact on the Irish people and turned public opinion further against the British. The murder of innocent men, women and children made international headlines and seriously damaged Britain's image abroad. In total, thirty-two people died in Dublin that day, marking the single worst day of violence in the War of Independence.

The violence continued right through to the end of the month with further killings of individuals on both sides. On 28 November, Tom Barry led an ambush at Kilmichael in County Cork, which resulted in the deaths of seventeen soldiers and three IRA Volunteers. The ambush has gone down in folklore as one of the iconic events of the conflict and it portrayed just how organised and ruthless the IRA flying columns around the country had become. So, who were the antagonists that day in the heart of rural mid-Cork? On one side was an active IRA Flying Column of thirty-six Volunteers under Barry's command. On the other side was a company of Auxiliary Division police under the command of Francis Clarke, all of whom had made themselves deeply unpopular in the area where they were based in Macroom.

The IRA men had assembled the previous Sunday in Ahilina around 2 a.m. and each man was given thirty-five rounds of rifle ammunition. The group also had in their possession some revolvers and a number of Mills bombs. One hour later, they were told they were about to launch an attack on the Auxiliaries and a local priest was on hand to hear the men's confessions. They all then set out on foot in heavy rain and reached the ambush site at 8.15 a.m. The site, as Barry recalled, was:

> in the centre of a bleak and barren countryside, a bogland interspersed with heather and rocks.[102]

The Volunteers took up their positions among the rocks on either side of the road, conscious there was no obvious escape route for them should the ambush go wrong. Jack Hennessy, in his witness statement, recalled how the ambush site:

> was on the road running through marshy land. There were no fences but back a little off the road there were fairly large clumps of rock. There was no line of retreat.[103]

The column settled in to wait for the arrival of the enemy and it proved to be long and uncomfortable on a cold and damp day. They were sustained only by a small amount of food and a large bucket of tea sent down by the people of the one nearby house. Eventually, the first lorry carrying the Auxiliaries arrived followed at a distance by a second vehicle. Barry moved out on to the road, dressed in an IRA officer tunic designed to confuse the enemy and ensured the lorry came to a stop. As it slowed, Barry gave the order to open fire before throwing a Mills bomb that exploded in the open cab. Soon, a close-quarter fight ensued, during which some of the Auxiliaries were killed by blows from rifle butts and from bayonetting. Barry later claimed the fight did not last long and it cost the lives of nine Auxiliaries.

When the second lorry arrived at the ambush scene it contained nine Auxiliaries, all of whom dismounted and exchanged fire with the Volunteers. Barry is reported to have ordered his men to open rapid fire and not to stop until all of the enemy were dead, ignoring their attempts to surrender. Hennessy recalled:

> At this time the second lorry was just opposite our position. The Auxies jumped out and tried to find cover. The lorry driver held his seat and attempted to back the lorry out of its position. I was engaging the Auxies on the road. I was wearing a tin hat. I had fired about ten rounds and had got five bullets through the hat when the sixth bullet wounded me in the scalp. Vice Comdt. McCarthy had got a bullet through the head and lay dead. I continued to load and fire but the blood dripping from my forehead fouled the breech of my rifle. I dropped my rifle and took Ml. McCarthy's. Many of the Auxies lay on the road dead or dying.

> Our orders were to fix bayonets and charge onto the road when we heard the three blasts of the O/C's whistle. I heard the three blasts and got up from my position, shouting, 'hands up'. At the same time one of the Auxies about five yards from me drew his revolver. He had thrown down his rifle. I pulled on him and shot him dead … Nearly all the Auxies had been wiped out. When I reached the road a wounded Auxie moved his hand towards his revolver. I put my bayonet through him under the ribs.[104]

By all accounts the aftermath of the fight was a grim scene with the dead and dying scattered across the area. Only two of the Auxiliaries survived the ambush, one of whom, H.F. Forde, was left for dead but was discovered the following day with a bullet to his head among other injuries. He is reputed to have lived the rest of his life with brain damage. The other surviving Auxiliary, Cecil Guthrie, managed to escape the scene though badly wounded. Later reports suggested he asked for help at a local house that, unfortunately for him, was occupied by two IRA men who promptly shot him dead with his own gun.

Three IRA men, Michael McCarty, Jim O'Sullivan and 16-year-old Pat Deasy, lost their lives in the ambush. Deasy, who had initially been eliminated from the column because of his age, followed it for miles before being eventually allowed to participate in the ambush. In his book, *Guerilla Days in Ireland*, Barry claimed the Auxiliaries called out, 'we surrender' and said he saw some of them drop their rifles. When three of his own men stood up, the Auxiliaries opened fire, killing O'Sullivan instantly and mortally wounding Deasy. The ambush was viewed by Barry and his comrades as a great military victory, while the British saw it as a 'brutal massacre'. In later years there was much controversy and disagreement over how Barry and his men dealt with the enemy and, most especially over Barry's claim of a 'false surrender'. Those controversies have not, however, diminished the place in Irish folklore the Kilmichael ambush now occupies.

In response to the Kilmichael Ambush, which Lloyd George claimed was 'of a different character' to other IRA operations, and the escalating level of violence, the government decided to proclaim martial law at the beginning of December in counties Cork, Kerry, Limerick and Tipperary. On 11 December, the IRA ambushed an Auxiliaries patrol near Dillon's Cross in Cork city. That night, the Crown forces retaliated by shooting dead two brothers, Cornelius and Jerimiah Delaney, in their home, both of whom were IRA Volunteers. They also proceeded to burn the commercial centre of the city, destroying around sixty shops, as well as Cork City Hall and the nearby Carnegie Library, causing many important documents to be lost. A report in the following day's *Irish Times* laid out the devastation caused by the burning:

> The scenes presented today were lamentable. From Merchant's Street, which is some little distance from Patrick's Bridge, on to Cork Street, on the left side of Patrick's Street, there is a devastated area which covers no less than five acres. It is all valuable property embracing some of the most flourishing establishments in Munster.[105]

The Government of Ireland Act became law on 23 December, setting up the state of Northern Ireland, but the requirement in the Act to establish a Dublin Home Rule parliament was ignored by republicans. The last week of December saw various incidents across the country, all of which claimed the lives of around twenty IRA men while a similar number of civilians and Crown forces personnel also died. Even Christmas Day saw the killing of two suspected IRA Volunteers in Tralee, County Kerry. Two days later, five IRA men and one Black and Tan were killed when Crown forces surrounded a disused mansion in rural Limerick being used by republicans for a fund-raising dance. On 29 December, the government in London sanctioned an 'official reprisals' policy across the country and the following day martial law was extended to counties Clare, Kilkenny, Waterford and Wexford. The final act of violence took place on 30 December when the IRA attacked an RIC patrol near Dundrum in County Dublin.

It is clear the year 1920 was the most violent of the War of Independence and the consequent suffering impacted many communities all across the country. The arrival of the Black and Tans and the Auxiliaries exacerbated the tensions that had been in existence for over a year. Their presence, allied to the intransigence of the government in London and their authorities in Dublin Castle, only served to fuel the determination of republicans to rid the country of British influence. As the year ended, the people of Ireland were resigned to one fact, that the fight for their country's independence was far from over and was about to continue into another year.

CHAPTER TWELVE

The War of Independence

1921

The dawning of a new year in January 1921 brought more questions as to what might be in store for Ireland during the following months. The War of Independence showed no sign of abating as it moved into its third calendar year and there was every indication the number of deaths and injuries on both sides of the conflict was set to increase. In fact, between January and the time a truce was called on 11 July, in excess of 1,000 people were destined to lose their lives. From the outset of 1921 the British Government under the leadership of Lloyd George took the view it was time to crush the IRA. If that aim was achieved the government in London felt it would be able to negotiate with Sinn Fein from a position of strength. On the other hand, the IRA evolved into a very sophisticated guerrilla army in 1921 and especially so in Munster. Over the first six months of the year it launched operations against the forces of the Crown that shook the British administration to its core, leaving it to conclude the victory it had expected to achieve was gradually slipping away.

At the beginning of the War of Independence, Lloyd George believed the IRA was nothing more than a criminal 'murder gang' and it would be defeated by the police in Ireland, namely the RIC. With that in mind, the government decided to supplement the police force with the Black and Tans and the Auxiliaries. This meant there was a lesser role for the British Army stationed in Ireland. However, at the end of 1920 the British authorities changed their approach to the conflict and took into account the threat being posed by the IRA's Active Service Units, often referred to as 'flying columns'. These units were particularly active in Munster and their actions forced the government in London to finally acknowledge that a state of war existed in Ireland. As a result, martial law was declared across Munster on

5 January 1921 and very quickly the British Army assumed a lead role in the conflict.

By January 1921 the IRA had around 5,000 men active in the field armed with in the region of 3,000 rifles. However, over the course of the year the British found more effective ways to counteract the IRA and the growing frequency of their military patrols forced republicans to limit their previously successful strategy of ambushes and attacks on barracks in favour of smaller-scale activities, such as the shooting of individuals or the destruction of communications infrastructure. It was clear by the early weeks of 1921 the IRA needed to stay in the fight as best it could while all the time hoping the British determination to maintain control of Ireland would eventually dissipate.

The scale and the intensity of the independence conflict continued apace during January, beginning on New Year's Day, when the IRA ambushed an RIC patrol in Ballybay, County Monaghan. One officer was killed and a civilian also lost his life. The RIC later carried out a reprisal in the area and twelve IRA men were arrested. In Middleton, County Cork, seven houses were burned down as part of a new government policy known as 'Official Reprisals'. The burnings were carried out by the RIC in response to the killing of three of their number a few days earlier. On 5 January martial law was extended to counties Clare, Waterford, Kilkenny and Wexford.

Two days later, in a shootout near Ballinalee, County Longford, the RIC raided a cottage looking for Sean MacEoin, Commander of the North Longford IRA. He fired shots from the cottage, killing District Inspector Thomas McGrath and wounding a constable before making his escape. On 5 January the IRA shot an alleged informer, Michael Cassidy, on a farm near Castlecomer in County Kilkenny, leaving his body with a placard pinned to it claiming he was a spy. In fact, the following six months would see many informers shot by the IRA and their bodies left by roadsides. On 8 January a British Army patrol was ambushed by an IRA unit at Pickardstown in County Waterford. However, the ambush went badly wrong as the British Army sent more reinforcements than was expected and two IRA men lost their lives in the engagement. Four days later, on 12 January, the IRA ambushed a British troop train carrying 150 soldiers at Barnesmore Gap in County Donegal. A number of soldiers were wounded in the attack despite returning fire with a Lewis gun mounted on the train.

That same day, acting on information received from an informer, the British Army raided a derelict house being used as an arms dump by the IRA at Clogheen in County Cork. They captured a large number of weapons including a Lewis gun as well as ammunition. A 16-year-old girl, Mary Bowles, and, four IRA men were arrested. A large amount of IRA correspondence was also found as the house was reputedly the headquarters of the Cork No. 1 Brigade. On the same day another IRA arms dump was discovered at Glanworth, also in County Cork. The discoveries of the arms dumps gave rise to the suspicion that the British were operating a network of informants throughout Cork.

The following day, British troops manning a checkpoint on Dublin's O'Connell Bridge opened fire on civilians, killing two people, Martha Nowlan and a young boy called James Brown. That same day an RIC lorry carrying eight men was ambushed in Cratloe, County Clare, and two policemen were killed in the engagement. In reprisal a number of houses in the area were burned down by the British Army in what was the first 'Official Reprisal' act in County Clare. On the political front, the British Labour Party launched a campaign for peace in Ireland at a meeting in Manchester and subsequent meetings were held in other British cities such as Cardiff, Glasgow and London. On 18 January, following an ambush by the IRA of Auxiliaries near Headford in County Galway, Crown forces went on a terror spree, killing four local men, all civilians and sons of local farmers, and injuring many others while also burning down buildings. At subsequent military courts of inquires the RIC and Auxiliaries claimed all the men were attempting to escape when shot, which was patently untrue. In his monthly report, the RIC Inspector for Galway West Riding, when commenting on the killing of the four men, said, 'This resolute action on the part of the Crown forces is having an excellent effect on the peace of the locality.' Two days later, on 20 January, an IRA unit in County Clare under the command of Michael Brennan ambushed an RIC lorry at Glenwood. Six constables were killed while two others escaped injured. In his witness statement to the Bureau of Military History, Michael Brennan provided a first-class account of what happened on that day, saying:

> On Jan 20th, we laid an ambush at Glenwood on the road between Sixmilebridge and Broadfort along which a lorry of Black and Tans was expected about 11 a.m. We took up positions before dawn just where a straight stretch of the road ran through a cutting up to a bend. The low flanking wall of a gateway just on the bend provided an excellent position for enfilading the roadway and I located myself there with five or six men, partly because I could use my 'one-handed rifle'

more effectively when I could rest it on the wall. A big convoy of lorries was always a possibility on this road, so a good and well covered line of retreat up through the woods into the mountains was available.

We waited all day but nothing appeared and about 4 p.m. I called in the outposts and we prepared to move off. Just then we heard the sound of a lorry and I sent the men back to their positions along the road. There was no time to get the outposts posted, but as it sounded like one lorry, it seemed a fair chance. Several civilian lorries had passed during the day so, in the absence of signals now, we would have to wait until they were literally on top of us before moving. Firing would be opened on a whistle blast from me. The lorry moved into position and I saw it was occupied by Black and Tans. The whistle brought a burst of fire from front and side. My party all aimed at the driver, but though they knocked off his cap and hit nearly everybody else on the lorry, he was unscathed.

His steering column was broken though and the lorry went out of control, rolling in against the wall where we were standing. The driver jumped clean over the bonnet and, bolted, pursued by one of our men. Very few shots were fired at us as most of the RIC men were down and the survivors threw away their rifles and ran for it. They were being pursued, but I recalled all our men as we had the rifles. A check-up showed that a District Inspector and five of his men were dead, four got away, but two of them were wounded.

One of our men was slightly wounded. We captured 10 rifles, 7 revolvers and a quantity of .303 and .45 ammunition. We burned the lorry and retreated back into the hills. Most of the men were from units within a radius of seven or eight miles and they went to their home districts. The rest of us got some food in the scattered houses and arranged to sleep in the usual barn. The British struck quickly and harshly at the country around Glenwood. Within a few hours of the ambush, we counted 36 burning houses from our position up on the mountains.[106]

That same day an RIC District Inspector was shot dead in Listowel, County Kerry, while in County Cork, near Bandon, an ex-British Army soldier was shot dead by members of the IRA's West Cork Brigade because he had been exposed as a spy. In Millstreet in the same county another man, Daniel Lucey, was executed by members of the Millstreet Battalion on the grounds of being an informer. In Dublin, the IRA ambush of an RIC lorry at Drumcondra Bridge went badly wrong when Auxiliaries arrived unexpectedly on the scene. One Volunteer, Michael Magee, was wounded and died later of his wounds, while five of his comrades, Patrick Doyle, Francis Flood, Thomas Bryan, Bernard Ryan and Dermot O'Sullivan, were captured. All, with the exception of O'Sullivan, were hanged in Mountjoy Prison on 14 March 1921.

On 22 January three off-duty RIC men were shot dead by the IRA near their barracks in County Monaghan. The following day a unit under the command of Tom Barry entered Bandon in County Cork and attacked the RIC and Military barracks. The attack was a failure and the unit lost one man, Dan O'Reilly from Kilbrittain. On 23 January the IRA executed Thomas Bradfield, a farmer from Carhue near Bandon, on the grounds he was an informer. In his witness statement to the Bureau of Military History, James ('Spud') Murphy, a member of Tom Barry's flying column, recalled how Bradfield was exposed as a spy and informer:

> We were in the Ahiohill district on the night of 31st January 1921 when the column O/C, asked Dan Corcoran and myself to accompany him to the house of Thomas Bradfield.
>
> We were driven there in a horse and trap by Tim Coffey … Tom Barry approached the house and asked the maid whether Mr Bradfield was at home. She said that he was out in the fields. Dan Corcoran accompanied the maid to the field to call Bradfield and to inform that the officer wanted him. We were all wearing Sam Browne belts outside our trench coats and Bradfield assumed we were members of the British forces. When Bradfield came in he welcomed us and invited us into the sitting room, where he gave us some refreshments. He sat down and began to talk to Tom Barry about the activities of the IRA in the area, giving a number of names of prominent officers. At this stage I had taken up position at the front door and Dan Corcoran was likewise at the back door.
>
> When Bradfield had given sufficient information, Tom Barry disclosed his identity and Bradfield was certainly shocked. We immediately placed himself under arrest and

> removed him on foot to the Ahiohill area. He was tried that night and when we were moving from Ahiohill to Burgatia House on the night of 1st February 1921, Bradfield was executed. His body was labelled as that of a spy and was left on the roadside.[107]

At the end of January 1921, the British Army in Dublin began to carry republican prisoners in their lorries while on patrol to stop grenades being thrown at them. The practice was discontinued when foreign journalists started to report it and the lorries were covered with a mesh to prevent grenades entering the vehicles. The IRA attempted to get around the barrier by attaching hooks to 'Mills bombs' in the hope they would become attached to the mesh.

The first day of February 1921 saw the first execution under martial law of an IRA man, Captain Cornelius Murphy from Millstreet. He was shot in Cork's Military Detention Barracks, having been convicted of carrying a revolver. That day members of the Drimoleague company in Cork ambushed four RIC men in the village, killing one constable and wounding one other. The following day an IRA flying column, under the command of Sean MacEoin, ambushed two lorries containing seventeen Auxiliaries at Clonfin in County Longford. A two-hour firefight ensued and four Auxiliaries and a driver were killed, while eight others were wounded. The IRA captured eighteen rifles, thirty revolvers and a Lewis gun.

On 3 February the IRA in Limerick ambushed an RIC and Black and Tan patrol at Dromkeen, during which eleven men lost their lives. The ambush was carried out by the East and Mid Limerick Brigades under the command of Donnchadh O'Hannigan. Some forty men were in place on the morning of the attack and the plan was to ambush the convoy on its return journey that day. Once the patrol had passed the ambush spot on its outward journey, road blocks were set up and nearby houses occupied. Around 2.30 p.m. the patrol approached the ambush site from the Caherconlish direction. When the barricades were reached, Inspector Adam Samson, occupying the front seat, ordered the driver, Constable John Cox, to slow down. However, when the first shots were fired, Cox immediately increased his speed.

Cox quickly realised their way forward was blocked and he swung the lorry around and drove to towards Drumkeen Church, all the time under heavy fire. The lorry overturned and the occupants were thrown from it. Two of the men in the back were killed instantly, while one of their comrades, by that stage under the lorry, began firing until he was shot dead.

Samson and Cox, dressed in civilian clothes, managed to escape because the IRA men on the road did not fire at them as they were unsure of their status. The second lorry with eight men aboard then came under intense fire. Its driver, Constable Stephen Millin, died almost immediately and the lorry came to a sudden stop, leaving those inside in a precarious situation. Constables Adams and Foody survived the onslaught but on being captured they were later shot dead.

Two badly wounded RIC men, Constables Pierce and Smith, were removed from the scene by the IRA men to a nearby house and were later brought to hospital in Limerick, where they died. In total, eleven men perished in the ambush and there were no IRA fatalities, while thirteen rifles and 400 rounds of ammunition were captured. A search of the bodies realised a total of nine pound notes. The IRA men added two more and the money was given to the local parish priest to offer up Masses for the dead men's souls.

On 7 February. British Army troops shot dead a teenage boy, Michael Kelleher, and wounded two other boys, brothers Michael and Donal Herlihy, as they were playing hurling in Knocknagree, County Cork. Both Herlihy boys went on to become prominent clergymen, with Donal becoming Bishop of the Diocese of Ferns. On 9 February two men, James Murphy and Patrick Kennedy, were arrested by Auxiliaries in Dublin and later found in Drumcondra having been shot. Kennedy was dead and Murphy was dying but, before he passed, he confirmed they had been shot by their captors. Two days later the IRA attacked a troop train near Millstreet in County Cork and one British soldier was killed. In his witness statement, Commandant Sean Moylan recounted what happened that night, saying:

> It was decided to lay an ambush one mile south of Millstreet Station at a point where a high embankment made it possible for riflemen lying on each side of the track to have a clear field of fire without endangering each other. The plan saw a number of armed men placed on the station at Millstreet and they were to watch for a train carrying British military. When that train left the station, they were to jump on the footplate and for the driver to bring the train to a stop where their comrades were waiting … the signal for action eventually came on 11 February. The train came to a standstill at the ambush point and, as it was night time, lit oil torches were thrown into the cutting beside the train, thereby illuminating

> the carriages containing the British soldiers. They were called on to surrender but they instead opened fire. The column replied with fire of their own and the soldiers all tumbled out of the carriages. After ten minutes of continuous firing from the column, some fourteen soldiers surrendered and one other lay dead. The column had started the attack with eight rifles and marched away with twenty-three and their ammunition reserve was increased by around a thousand rounds.[108]

On 15 February, an IRA unit led by Charlie Hurley, O/C 3rd Cork Brigade, staged one of the more notable attacks on a train at Upton station in County Cork. Around ten o'clock that morning fourteen armed men showed up at the station. They tied up the station master and took over the station house. The men had been hastily brought together by Hurley after he received some intelligence from IRA colleagues in Cork city that twenty British soldiers, all members of the Essex Regiment, were due to travel to Bandon that morning. The IRA men, though enthusiastic, were not members of the Brigade's flying column but were members of local IRA units and, as such, were probably not as well trained or as sharp as their more finely tuned full-time colleagues.

The men who assembled for the attack were armed with seven rifles and a number of handguns. However, according to Michael Hopkinson in his book *The Irish War of Independence, The Definitive Account of the Anglo-Irish War 1919–1921*, the number of British troops travelling on the train had changed, unbeknownst to Hurley. While twenty soldiers did indeed board the train at Cork, another fifty got on at Kinsale. Hurley had placed two scouts at Kinsale and, when they realised extra troops were boarding there, one of the men cycled to Upton to warn his commanding officer of that important development but arrived far too late with the information. When the train left Kinsale it had seventy soldiers travelling together with a fair number of civilians, some of whom were commercial travellers going about their daily work.

The doomed train pulled into Upton station and as soon as it did the IRA men opened fire on it, hitting soldiers and civilians. The *New York Times* later reported that 'a shower of bullets was rained on the train, practically every compartment was swept'. Richard Arthurs, the ticket collector, died instantly as well as two commercial travellers, James Byrne from Dublin and John Spiers from Cork. Another commercial traveller, Charles Penrose Johnston, who lived in Dublin, was hit in a leg and unfortunately bled to death. It wasn't long before the British troops reacted and returned fire in a battle that lasted around ten minutes. The inquest later learned that two IRA men were killed in the battle. The dead men, Lieutenant Sean Phelan and Section Commander Batt Falvey, had to be left at the scene by their comrades as they made a hasty retreat. The bodies were taken by the military to Cork and were later claimed by members of Cumann na mBan purporting to be relatives of the dead men. The retreating men helped a badly wounded Lieutenant Patrick O'Sullivan to a local farmhouse. Though he was eventually brought to a hospital in Cork by means of a pony and trap, he died of his injuries a few days later. Another man, Dan O'Mahony, was severely wounded in his hip but died some years later as a consequence of his wounds, while Charlie Hurley suffered a gunshot wound to his face.

Six civilians died in the attack while eight others were wounded, two of whom later died. Six British soldiers were wounded, three of them seriously according to the inquest. The *Irish Times* reported on 31 March 1921 that a Military Court of Inquiry found the civilians had been 'wilfully murdered by persons unknown'. However, in relation to the dead IRA men it found they had 'died from the wounds inflicted by the military in justifiable self-defence'. The simple fact is civilians were put in grave danger by both sides. The British claimed no civilians were travelling with the troops but that wasn't the case because C.P. Johnston died in a carriage occupied by soldiers, as did another railway employee, signalman John Sisk, a fact confirmed by the *Irish Times*. Other civilians who died that day in the attack were named as Thomas Perrott, William Finn and May Hall. The IRA were indeed negligent because they failed to take into account the possibility of civilians travelling in the same carriages as the troops. Their error was compounded, with disastrous effects, when they opened fire on the train. The Upton attack was, undoubtedly, a public relations failure for the IRA. The needless deaths of civilians in a hail of bullets confirmed the operation was one of their least successful of the independence conflict. No British soldiers died in an attack that cost the lives of three Volunteers. The plain truth is, compared with other attacks and ambushes, the Upton engagement fell far short of what was expected of the IRA fighting men at that time because innocent civilians died at their hands.

That same day an IRA ambush position at Mourne Abbey in County Cork was betrayed by an informer called Daniel Shiels, an unsavoury character who had served in the British Army and had ingratiated himself into the IRA's Kanturk Battalion, much against the wishes of Sean Moylan and other officers. Three IRA men, Patrick Flynn, Patrick Dorgan and Éamonn

Creedon were shot dead and a fourth man, Michael Looney, later died of his wounds. Eight other men were taken prisoner, two of whom, Thomas Mulcahy and Patrick Ronayne, were later court martialled and executed. Shiels was subsequently shot by the IRA for allegedly informing the British about the ambush party's position.

On 20 February 1921 an IRA Active Service Unit of the 4th Battalion, Cork No. 1 Brigade, comprising twenty-one men was surrounded in a farmhouse at Clonmult near Midleton by British troops and RIC men. In a firefight, twelve IRA men were killed, some, it was alleged, after they had surrendered. Two of the captured IRA men, Maurice Moore and Patrick O'Sullivan, were subsequently executed, while the death sentences on five others were later commuted. However, the survivors were adamant that, 'they surrendered in good faith and were gunned down as they emerged or else stood against a wall and executed', a claim that was denied by the British. In his witness statement to Bureau of Military History, Lieutenant Colonel John P. O'Connell, who was Captain of the Cobh Company, recounted that fateful day, saying:

> I led the sortie, carrying a rifle with fixed bayonet, and dashed through a hail of enemy bullets, across the yard to a gateway. I turned to the right and was fired on by two soldiers from the corner of a field bordering the western side of the haggard. I returned the fire wounding one, the other ran back. I turned around to look for my companions who had attempted the sortie with me, and discovered, to my astonishment, that I was alone. I went back down the boreen as far as the small isolated shed but could not find anybody ... As to what happened in the house after I had left it, the following account was given to me by ex-Lieutenant Diarmuid O'Leary, one of the two survivors of the column.
>
> 'When I left the house, four others followed me. The two men closest behind me were killed by enemy rifle fire immediately outside the door. The third man reached the entrance gate, crossed the boreen and went along an adjoining field, but was shot and killed, about a hundred yards away. The fourth man was called back by somebody in the house. He turned back and, luckily, got inside the house, unscathed ... Eventually the British set fire to the thatched roof of the house, and there was nothing left but to surrender ... The eleven

> members of the column then left the house, surrendered and were lined up, outside in the yard. Seven were shot in cold blood by Black and Tans, and the others would have met the same fate but for the intervention of a British military officer. The four survivors were taken away as prisoners, court martialled and sentenced to death. Two were executed, and the other two were saved from execution by the advent of the Truce in July 1921.'[109]

On 25 February members of the Cork No. 1 Brigade attacked a convoy of mixed military and police at Coolavokig near Ballyvourney in County Cork. One British officer was killed and several Auxiliaries and soldiers were wounded. On 28 February an IRA unit led by Sean Moylan ambushed an RIC patrol at Tureengarriffe in County Cork. James Cashman, a lieutenant in the Kiskeam company, was crouched in an exposed position behind rocks and stones on the south side of the road. In his witness statement to the Bureau of Military History he described what took place that day:

> The convoy, consisting of two cars, was allowed to drive into our position, where it was greeted by a burst of machine-gun fire and a call to surrender. The driver of the leading car accelerated out of the straight stretch of road round the bend at the eastern end, where he was held up by a trench. The second car halted and the occupants of both cars dashed for cover behind the roadside fences. As the enemy did not surrender at the opening burst all sections of the IRA party opened fire.[110]

The fighting continued for twenty-five minutes, during which the patrol was called on to surrender. Eventually, the RIC men laid down their weapons and, when Moylan and his men came down from their positions, they found Divisional Commander Holmes had been badly wounded while seven other RIC men had also taken bullets. One of their number, Constable Moyles, who was just 20 years old, was dead. Holmes died of his wounds the following day despite the attempts of two surgeons sent from Dublin to save him. On the day of the Tureengarriffe ambush, six IRA men, Sean Allen, Timothy McCarthy, Thomas O'Brien, Daniel O'Callaghan, John Lyons and Patrick O'Mahony, were executed in the Military Detention Barracks in Cork. All the men with the exception of Allen had been captured after an earlier botched IRA ambush at Dripsey in County Cork. Allen, a Tipperary man, was convicted of possessing a revolver. In retaliation for the executions, the IRA shot and killed seven off-duty British soldiers and wounded five others in separate incidents across Cork.

The month of March began with the capture and arrest of Sean MacEoin, the IRA North Longford Commander. He was charged with the murder of an RIC detective in early January. MacEoin famously gave an account of the killing during his subsequent trial that was not contested by any of the parties present. He went on to say:

> I was at the table writing when I was informed of the advance party. My account books were left in this house for safety. I was in partial uniform, wearing Sam Browne belt with two Mills No. 4 bombs in my pocket. Owing to some females in the house, I had to get out as I could not endanger them by putting up a defence in the house and, as this Officer and Police Force had already signified to my sister and mother their intention to shoot me on sight, I decided to give them a run for their money. I stepped out on the street, about three paces directly in front of the oncoming force, and opened fire with my revolver. The leading file fell and then the second file in the gateway brought their rifles to the ready. I then threw a bomb, and jumped back behind the porch to let it burst. When it had burst and the smoke had lifted, I saw the whole force had cleared away, save the officer who was dead or dying on the street.[111]

MacEoin was found guilty of the murder of District Inspector McGrath and sentenced to death. Michael Collins did attempt to organise MacEoin's rescue from Mountjoy Jail but it failed. MacEoin was eventually released after Collins threatened to break off the Treaty negotiations unless he was freed. On 5 March an IRA column led by Sean Moylan ambushed Crown forces at Clonbanin, County Cork. According to the British Army 6th Division Record, the engagement cost the lives of Colonel Commandant Cumming and another officer, Lieutenant Maligny, while eight other men were wounded. Republicans claimed the ambush cost the lives of thirteen British soldiers, while fifteen others were wounded. The ambush turned out to be a long drawn-out affair, which Moylan recalled in his witness statement, saying:

> The fight started around 2.30 p.m. It seemed to me that it had been in progress less than an hour when I looked at my watch. It was 5.30 p.m. My worry then was British reinforcements, Kanturk and Newmarket, where there were strong garrisons, were but a few miles distant. Buttevant, the main British garrison, only twenty-five miles away. The sound of firing could be heard (it actually was heard) in Newmarket and Kanturk. The reinforcements were overdue. Con Meany and Tom McEllistrim took a section to cover the road from the East. The fight went on and still no reinforcements arrived. I heard afterwards that a lorry with troops left Newmarket and, hitting a fence, overturned a mile from the town. The soldiers in Kanturk, in no way anxious to participate in the brawl, dug themselves into the various public houses in the town and were with difficulty collected. It was not until darkness was falling that the reinforcements arrived and when they came they came in strength. As darkness fell, we moved away, Millstreet and Kerry troops to the West. Those from Charleville and Newmarket retired north to Kiskeam.[112]

On 6 March in County Tipperary, a British Army patrol surprised a meeting of IRA officers. A firefight ensued and three IRA men, Martin Clancy, Patrick Hackett and Richard Fleming were killed. On 10 March a substantial British force carried out a large-scale sweep at Nadd, high in the Boggeragh Mountains in County Cork. A house in the area used as the Headquarters of the Cork No. 2 Brigade was surrounded but most of the HQ staff managed to escape while all the time keeping up rifle fire. Three IRA volunteers, David Herlihy, Edward Waters and Timothy Kiely, were killed in the firefight, while a number of others were wounded.

On 11 March the IRA executed two civilians, a Mrs Lindsay and her chauffer, James Clarke, and burned down her home at Leemount in County Cork. Mrs Lindsay had tipped off the British about an impending IRA ambush at Dripsey back in January 1921. Eight IRA men were captured as a result of her betrayal, while two volunteers were killed. Five of the captured men, Patrick O'Mahony, Timothy McCarthy, John Lyons, Daniel O'Callaghan and Thomas O'Brien, were executed at the end of February, while one other man, Captain Jim Barret, died of his wounds in prison in March. Also, on 11 March, IRA men from the South Leitrim Brigade ASU were surrounded in two houses at Selton Hill near Ballinamore by a British

Army patrol. Six IRA men were killed. Their commanding officer, Sean Connolly, was captured but died the following day. On 14 March a patrol of two lorries and an armoured car carrying Auxiliaries was attacked by the IRA on Brunswick Street in Dublin. In the ensuing gun battle two IRA men died, as did two of the Auxiliaries. Two civilians also died having been caught in the crossfire, while two others died of their wounds later. A number of IRA men were captured, one of whom, Thomas Traynor, was hanged on 25 April 1921. On 18–19 March the West Waterford IRA ambushed a convoy of Black and Tans returning to Dungarvan at a place called Burgery. One Black and Tan man was killed, as were two IRA men.

On 19 March the IRA Cork No. 3 Brigade commanded by Tom Barry fought an action against 1,200 British troops in what was the largest military encounter of the War of Independence at Crossbarry in County Cork. Barry's unit of around 100 men managed to escape a near complete encirclement. There were conflicting reports of casualties, with the IRA claiming up to thirty members of the Crown forces were killed while official British figures put the number dead at ten men. The IRA lost four men, Peter Monahan, Charlie Hurley, Con Daly and Jerimiah O'Sullivan. On 21 March the IRA attacked British troops at Headford Railway station in Kerry. The attack resulted in the deaths of eight soldiers. Three civilians died in the ambush, as did two IRA men, and that same day the IRA lost three other men as a result of an altercation with Crown forces at Lispole in Kerry.

Over the following couple of days, three RIC men lost their lives in engagements with the IRA in Mayo and Roscommon. On 23 March six IRA volunteers, Daniel Crowley, William Deasy, Thomas Dennehy, Jerimiah Mullane, Daniel Murphy and Michael O'Sullivan, were shot when they were surrounded in a barn in Clogheen, just outside Cork city. The RIC claimed all six men were killed during a firefight but, according to a *New York Times* report, witnesses claimed the men were ordered to run and then shot in the back to make it appear they were trying to escape. The IRA later learned an informer called Patrick Joseph 'Cruxy' O'Connor was responsible for giving the men's location away to the authorities. It seems he had been arrested for the possession of a revolver and while being questioned he gave the whereabouts of the six men to the police. They were staying on the farm of Cornelius O'Keeffe at Ballycannon on the road leading from Clogheen to Tower. O'Keefe's property was regarded as a safe place to stay and that night the IRA men chose to sleep in the barn. They had safe places to hide their weapons and explosives, which made the place even more convenient. At 4 a.m. O'Keeffe was awakened by the arrival of the RIC and Crown forces, who ordered the family back to their bedrooms as the house was searched. The farmyard was then searched and the six men were discovered sleeping in the barn. What happened next was witnessed by a local schoolteacher whose house overlooked the two fields beside the barn. He went on to say:

> He was awakened by the sound of shots at about half four, while it was still quite dark. He watched the lights moving around the farmyard. He heard one voice scream out and another shout 'run for it'. He could barely see a man breaking away and run across the field. A volley of shots rang out and the man fell. Another man with a light walked towards the body. After ten minutes there were more shots but this time they saw no body fall. Later he saw another man fleeing and more shots rang out. As the light increased he identified the men with guns as police. Later he watched as the police brought down bodies in blankets and laid them outside the house in the boreen, which led from the O'Keeffe farmyard to the public road. At six in the morning, they were placed in lorries, which they then drove away.[113]

The British did conduct a military inquiry but the officers involved concluded the six men had 'been killed by forces of the Crown in the course of their duty' and reached that decision without providing any evidence about gunshot wounds or other injuries suffered by the Volunteers. There was a public outcry but it only served to force the British authorities to whitewash the atrocity even more. The original verdict was expunged and replaced with one that absolved the RIC men involved in the massacre and placed the blame squarely on the victims. According to the new verdict:

> all the deceased, whilst in the custody of the RIC, attempted to escape. The constabulary in the course of their duty fired on them, whereby they suffered various gunshot wounds. The deceased were all killed instantly at the above hour. That no blame attaches itself to the RIC or any other member thereof.[114]

The last three months of the independence conflict saw significantly less in the way of full-scale ambushes of the enemy by the IRA, with a greater concentration on the assassination or execution of individuals. Nevertheless, the intensity of the violence did not relent and every day brought news of shootings often carried out in multiples across the country. In Dublin alone, during April, it was reported the IRA carried out sixty-seven different attacks on British forces in the city. The violence during the month of April began on the first day when the IRA's East Mayo Brigade commander, Sean Corcoran, was killed by British troops near Ballyhaunis. His Vice-Commandant, Maurice Mullins, was captured and beaten severely. Michael Coen, another IRA man from Ballyhaunis, was also captured, tortured and murdered. On 2 April a civilian, Christopher Reynolds, and IRA man Bernard Nolan were shot by Auxiliaries in Dublin. Reynolds later died but Nolan survived.

The early days of April saw the killing by the IRA of a number of alleged spies in Dublin, Cork, Roscommon and Tralee. Two IRA men together with one civilian died during an IRA attack on British soldiers on Dublin's Harcourt Street. Over two days, 6 and 7 April, three civilians, two IRA men and a British Army soldier were killed in varying circumstances in Roscommon. On 8 April, two RIC men were ambushed near Macroom and one constable was killed. That same day, William Hoare, who was Captain of the Ballymacoda company of the Cork No. 1 Brigade, was shot dead in the village by the RIC. On 10 April the violence continued unabated when two RIC men out walking and unarmed were shot dead at Scart, Kildorrery, County Cork, by IRA men from the Castletownroche Battalion. That same day, five RIC constables on their way to church were attacked by an IRA unit led by Frank Aiken. One constable was killed and three others were wounded. In the middle of the month at least three alleged spies were shot by the IRA in different parts of the country. It seemed by then the cycle of violence was never ending and on 16 April two RIC constables were seriously injured in an IRA attack in Ballina, County Mayo. The RIC retaliated by destroying sixteen business premises in the town. The town of Ennis saw violence that same day when off-duty British Army soldiers and RIC men were attacked by the IRA in Shaughnessy's pub on Market Street. One soldier was killed while an RIC man was wounded, as were two women including the proprietor. In retaliation the RIC set fire to a shop, a home and the Old Ground Hotel.

On 17 April, an alleged spy, Kate Carroll, was taken from her home in County Monaghan and shot by the IRA. On 18 April three IRA men, including two brothers, were shot dead near Borris in County Carlow by a combined British Army-RIC patrol. On 19 April, in County Sligo, two

RIC men, both unarmed and in civilian clothes, were taken from a train by an IRA unit and shot dead. Six British soldiers were also captured but they were disarmed and released. That same day a joint British Army-RIC patrol surrounded a house in County Roscommon occupied by four IRA men who attempted to escape. Three IRA men were captured and beaten and two of them were shot dead, while a third man was taken prisoner. The fourth IRA man managed to escape but was wounded. On 20 April the IRA attacked a patrol of Royal Marines from the coastguard station in Ballyvaughan in Clare. Two marines were shot dead and the IRA confiscated four rifles and some ammunition.

On 22 April an IRA flying column of the 3rd South Tipperary Brigade attacked a British Army convoy of fifteen soldiers at Garrymore between Clogheen and Cahir. One British soldier died and two others were wounded in the engagement. In his witness statement, John Nagle, Vice-Commandant of 6th Battalion 3rd Tipperary Brigade, recalled what happened that day:

> On the morning of our arrival at Garrymore, Dan Breen, Sean Hogan, Dinny Lacey, some officers from Lacey's column and myself inspected the proposed ambush position. On account of the proximity of Hyland's house to Garrymore Cross, the position was considered unsuitable and it was decided to call off the attack for the time being. It was also decided that our column would withdraw towards Burncourt and Lacey's column towards Ballyboy in the Ballybacon direction.
>
> Before the rearguard of Lacey's column left the Cahir–Clogheen road, a party of seven or eight British soldiers in a wagon drawn by two horses arrived on the scene coming from the Cahir direction. They were engaged by the rearguard. The horses were shot dead and the soldiers dismounted from the wagon and started to run back towards Cahir. Our column had already moved off towards Burncourt and I should say that we were about 300 yards from the Cahir–Clogheen road when we heard the firing. Not then knowing what exactly had happened, we hurriedly took up the best positions we could and, seeing the soldiers running back along the road, we opened fire on them. The fire of ours held the soldiers on the road and, after a very short time, they surrendered to Lacey's men, who searched them and let them go.

> It was on that day that District Inspector Potter of the RIC was captured. While the captured booty was being examined, he came along the road in a motor car. He was alone and in civilian clothes, but he was recognised by Sean Downey, a member of Lacey's column. Our column had nothing further to do with him after his capture. It was Lacey's column who held him prisoner and who eventually carried out his execution.[115]

On 26 April an IRA man, Thomas Traynor, was hanged in Mountjoy Jail after he had been found guilty of killing Auxiliary Francis Joseph Farrell in a gun battle on Dublin's Brunswick Street in March 1921. That same day the First Southern Division of the IRA was formed at a meeting of senior officers in Kippagh near Millstreet in County Cork. This was, in essence, the first move towards the reorganisation of the IRA into Divisions. The First Southern Division was made up of the three Cork Brigades, three Kerry Brigades, two Waterford Brigades and the West Limerick Brigade. Liam Lynch was appointed Divisional Commander with Florence O'Donoghue named as Divisional Adjutant. The meeting was a wide-ranging one attended by the cream of the IRA leadership, all men of great integrity possessing a determination to see the struggle for their country's independence through to its satisfactory conclusion. One of the appointments was that of Sean Moylan as Commandant of Cork No. 2 Brigade and he recalled the meeting in his witness statement:

> The cold of winter was gone, the sun shone with a comforting warmth, the scent of the furze blossom was heavy in the air, there was a lazy drift of smoke over Claragh as I travelled south from Cullen to Kippagh where the meeting was to be held. Here Paddy McCarthy's body had lain the previous November, and here now were gathered IRA leaders from all the Cork, Kerry, Waterford and West Limerick Brigades. Some were old friends and associates of long standing, others were strangers known to me only by reputation. Sean Hegarty O/C Cork No. 1 Brigade, I hadn't seen for several years. He was now bearded, with homespun trousers and blue coat. The whole ensemble roofed in a bowler hat. He looked like an old-time music hall artist; a stranger seeing him would not be surprised if he broke into song. He was, however, no comedian, but a serious man of keen intellect. If he had a sense of humour, it was of that

> sardonic and devastating type peculiar to Cork. I had heard so much of Tom Barry and of his reputation as a leader of troops in action that I was anxious to see him. Here he was; like Ernie O'Malley, he looked a soldier and didn't care a damn who knew it. He was slight and erect, his smart coat, riding breeches and gaiters giving an impression of uniform. Later as he sat across the table from me, I watched him. His face was that of an intelligent, earnest, determined and intolerant man, one whose mind was closed to all issues other than that, with which he was concerned. I don't think his appearance belied his character. A few weeks before he had at Crossbarry a great success against the British.[116]

The following day the IRA suffered a material loss when an arms dump in Dublin's Baggot Lane was discovered by the British Army. A machine gun, fourteen rifles, fifty-four revolvers and over 12,000 rounds of ammunition were confiscated. The following day was even worse for the IRA as four Volunteers, Maurice Moore, Patrick O'Sullivan, Thomas Mulcahy and Patrick Ronayne, were executed in Cork's Military Detention Barracks. Before the end of the month, the RIC lost three more men in different incidents, while another alleged spy was executed by the IRA in Galway, bringing an end to another violent month.

At beginning of May, Ernie O'Malley set up the 2nd Southern Division with its Divisional Headquarters near Donohill in Tipperary. During the first few days of the month, the IRA lost between fifteen and twenty men in various engagements across the country. The RIC also had casualties, losing up ten men including four in an IRA ambush at Tourmakeady in County Mayo. On 4 May the IRA ambushed a nine-man RIC patrol, resulting in the deaths of eight more men. The patrol came out of Rathmore in Kerry to investigate a body left by the side of the road and, as the RIC men gathered around it, they were fired on by the IRA. Only one constable survived the carnage and he cycled away to raise the alarm. That same day the British Army began a major 'drive' to root out and arrest IRA men in the midlands and, according to some reports, around thirty-five men were taken into military custody.

Between 5 and 7 May the killings continued unabated, with three IRA men losing their lives. Five RIC men died in ambushes and attacks, while two alleged informers were executed by the IRA during the same period. Over the next five days, five more IRA men died at the hands of Crown forces. The RIC also lost four men and at least two civilians died in dubious circumstances at the hands of Crown forces. On 12 May four IRA men were arrested by the RIC as they were returning home from a Redemptorist retreat in Athea, County Limerick. They were ill-treated before being ordered into a field and shot. Three of men died, while one managed to escape and he went on to implicate some of the RIC men involved in the shooting. Over the course of two days, 13–14 May, three IRA men were killed in action, while the RIC lost nine men. The British Army lost six of its men, including three who were captured unarmed by the IRA near Castletownbere in Cork and reportedly shot in reprisal for the execution of the IRA prisoners in Cork prison some weeks earlier.

On 15 May three RIC men were attacked by an IRA unit, including Dan Breen and Ernie O'Malley, as they left a church in Bansha, County Tipperary. One RIC man died, while his colleagues were wounded. Over in Galway, near Gort, District Inspector Cecil Blake of the RIC and his wife, Eliza, as well as two British Army officers, died in an ambush carried out by members of the IRA's South Galway Brigade. The RIC lost two more men that same day when they were captured by the North Tipperary Brigade. They were shot and buried on the instructions of the Brigade's O/C, Sean Gaynor.

On 16 May, Daniel O'Brien, from Liscarroll and a member of the Charleville Battalion, was executed in Cork's Military Detention Barracks, having been captured some days earlier. That day also saw the capture of Sean Moylan near Kiskeam together with thirteen of his men, all of whom were initially taken to Kanturk. The capture of the most wanted IRA man at that time was a major blow to the organisation and a real boost for the Crown forces in Cork, all of whom made a great play of their success. The next day, 17 May, saw no let-up in the violence as seven RIC men died in various engagements with the IRA, while six more men died over the following five days. The violence was not only part of the news cycle in Ireland but it was also a source of concern abroad. On 22 May, Pope Benedict XV issued a letter addressing the situation in Ireland, saying:

> We do not see how the bitter strife can profit either of the parties, when property and homes are being ruthlessly and disgracefully laid waste, when villages and farmsteads are being set aflame … when on both sides a war resulting in deaths of unarmed peoples, even of women and children, is carried on.[117]

One of the biggest IRA operations of the independence conflict took place on 25 May when it attacked the Custom House in Dublin, which housed a number of the British Administration's government departments in Ireland. The operation, which Michael Collins had grave doubts about, was championed by Éamon de Valera. He wanted to stage a spectacular demonstration of IRA strength while at the same time striking at the heart of the British administrative system in Ireland. The planning of the operation was carried out by Oscar Traynor and involved men from the IRA's Dublin Brigade as well as members of the Squad. It went badly wrong as the building was surrounded by hundreds of Auxiliaries and British troops and resulted in the deaths of five IRA men, Edward Dorins, Daniel Head, Patrick O'Reilly, Stephen O'Reilly and Sean Doyle. Four civilians lost their lives in the attack and anywhere between seventy and 130 IRA men were captured, which delivered a huge blow to the organisation in Dublin. In his extensive witness statement to the Bureau of Military History, Traynor went into great detail about the events of that day, saying:

> The plans in general were accepted, but one portion which arranged for the throwing up of barricades in the vicinity of the various city barracks was objected to. This operation was designed to operate only if an attempt was made by the enemy forces to leave these posts during the twenty minutes from 12.55 to 1.20 pm, when it was hoped to have the destruction of the building and its evacuation completed. The Director of Intelligence (Michael Collins) objection to this part of the scheme was very strong. He regarded the throwing up of barricades all over the city as being suggestive of a general uprising, and finally stated, in reply to my arguments, that if it could not be carried out without this precaution it should not be carried out at all. Having withdrawn my arguments in favour of that part of the plan, the date 25 May was agreed upon for the carrying out of the operation.
>
> As the target was in the 2nd Battalion area it was decided the actual destruction of the building would be entrusted to that unit. Commandant Tom Ennis was appointed to take sole control of the party within the building. The 2nd Battalion was reinforced by the addition of the Squad, a party of about twelve men who were attached to the D.I.'s department, as well as some men of the Active Service Unit. To the 1st Battalion was

allotted the task of protecting the outside of the building. In the event of a surprise attack by enemy forces the Battalion was to engage them with grenade, rifle and machine gun fire. To the 5th Battalion, the Engineers, was given the very important task of cutting off from all communications, telephonic or otherwise, the Custom House with the outside world.

The preparation for the main task of destruction brought about the necessity for a number of lesser actions. For instance, I decided right from the beginning that in no circumstances was petrol to be used. This necessitated in the commandeering of a large quantity of paraffin oil and the transferring of the oil from steel casks and tanks to petrol tins. It also necessitated the holding up of an oil concern and their staff for some considerable time, the commandeering of motor lorries to bring the tinned paraffin to the Custom House precisely on time. When this lorry arrived at the back entrance to the building, the men detailed for the inside operation entered, at the same time taking with them from the lorry a tin of paraffin. The building was also entered from the Quays and Beresford Place entrance opposite Liberty Hall. In this way the number going in by any one door was not excessive, and it was hoped would not arouse suspicion. The immediate job of these men on entry was to control all telephonic communications as an added safety device, even though these had been cut by our engineers. Within the building each Captain had been allotted a landing and all the offices on that landing to deal with. His job was to see that every person employed on that floor was sent down to the main hall, where they were kept under the vigilant eyes of the men of the Squad and the ASU. With this part of the task completed, he was then to see that every office on his landing was thoroughly saturated with paraffin oil … When the job of saturation was completed, the officer was to report to Commandant Ennis on the ground floor, and the actual firing was to take place on an order given by him consisting of a single blast on his whistle. Two blasts were to signify the completion of the job and the withdrawal of all men to the ground floor.

Everything went perfectly as per plan, except that just before all the floors had given the Officer Commanding the

> 'OK' or 'All ready' signal, someone blew two blasts on a whistle and all sections retired to the main hall. One officer reported that he had not completed his task of saturation. The Commandant sent him and his men back at once to finish the job. The few minutes loss here was the difference between the successful retirement of all the participants and the arrival of large numbers of enemy forces in lorries and armoured cars. These forces swept into Beresford Place at 1.25 pm, just five minutes after the time allotted in the plan for the completion of the operation. They were immediately engaged on entry to Beresford Place by the 1st Battalion units with volleys of revolver shots and the throwing of a number of hand grenades ... By this time the Squad in the Custom House had gone into action with their parabellums and Mauser automatics, with still further disastrous effects to the Black and Tans who were attempting to storm the main back entrance. Before I managed to get away, I saw several bodies lying around the entrance immovable, and, as far as I could see and judge, dead. Those who were blown out of the lorry with which I was concerned were lying around apparently unconscious on the ground, if not dead. I eventually got out through Gardiner Place and Talbot Street and back into Abbey Street, where I met Captain Daly ... Here we were informed that Tom Ennis, who had shot his way out, was taken away in a lorry, seriously wounded. At this time enemy forces were coming up in lorries, together with additional armoured cars. We then knew that the only hope for the men inside was to escape by the Custom House Docks, a slender enough chance considering the strength of the forces now on the scene. Actually, a goodly number did escape by various ways and ruses. Some were killed in their attempt. All together we lost five killed and about eighty captured.[118]

June was the last full month of the conflict and it began with the IRA ambushing an RIC bicycle patrol near Castlemaine in Kerry. Five RIC men, including a District Inspector, lost their lives in the ambush carried out by men of the 6th Battalion, Kerry No. 2 Brigade. That same day hundreds of men were rounded up in Sligo as part of a British Army operation across the county. In Dublin, two British soldiers were killed in an attack on a transport lorry by the IRA on Parnell Street. Some civilians and other soldiers were wounded. The following day the RIC suffered further casualties with the deaths of six (possibly seven) of their men in an ambush carried out by the IRA's West Mayo Brigade at Carrowkennedy. The IRA also captured substantial amounts of arms and ammunition including rifles, revolvers and a Lewis gun. The ambush initiated a massive response from the Crown forces, with the IRA men having to constantly move around the county to avoid capture. In his witness statement to the Bureau of Military History, Thomas Harvey, Adjutant of the West Mayo Brigade, provided a fascinating account of the events of that day:

> We knew we had little time to prepare as we were a good mile from the main road. We were not yet in position and word came that the convoy was in sight. Fortunately, it stopped at Darby Hastings public house. We knew we had a little more time … picked vantage points and proceeded with all the usual arrangements for attack … Hardly had we made ourselves comfortable when a shout warned us, they were coming. Soon the purr of engines was heard and swiftly into view glided an armoured Crossley tender. At least ten rifles were trained on the driver, whose attention was drawn towards our position for he partly turned his head and looked in our direction … Ten rifles blazed, the tender lurched, laboured, stopped and the fun began. One tall Tan took a flying leap over the side of the tender. He was probably dead before he hit the road. The rest of the crew, however, tumbled out, took up whatever positions they could find and started plastering our position. Rifle, grenades, too, were coming our way, but we were out of range. It was now about 6 p.m. I was watching the tender closely. I had a feeling, a hunch, and suddenly I yelled: 'They are getting out a machine-gun'. Sure enough, one of the fellows in the tender managed to chuck the gun out through the back of the lorry. It fell on the road and was grabbed by an invisible hand, and shortly its horrible notes made hideous the evening which until then had seemed so grand. All rifles in our section were now trained on the spot where the gun was judged to be and, sure enough, it was soon silenced. A second gunner took over. He too was killed. Then the performance was repeated once more, after that the gun was silent for the duration of the fight … After the Lewis gun had been silenced

> for the third time, sporadic firing continued for a long time. There were little lulls during which we passed the time singing or hurling taunts at the enemy, who answered us in kind … At last all firing ceased and our fellows converged on the truck … The fight had lasted four hours. Most of the crew of the tender were dead.[119]

The RIC casualty statistics continued to worsen and four of their number died in an ambush carried out by the IRA at Modreeny in Tipperary on 3 June. Interestingly, that same day Sir Hamar Greenwood, the Chief Secretary for Ireland, issued an order that put an end to official reprisals by Crown forces having come under pressure to do so as the IRA were burning the houses of prominent unionists in response to the British Army burning houses near ambush sites. Between 4 and 7 June thirteen current and ex-British soldiers lost their lives under varying circumstances across the country, while an IRA man, Thomas Keane, of the Limerick Mid-West Brigade, was executed in the Military Detention Barracks in Limerick. On 6 June, Greenwood, in his weekly summary of events in Ireland, highlighted the increasing number of British military casualties since the beginning of May. His comments were indicative of a rising anxiety in British political circles about the conflict in Ireland.

The killings continued unabated into the middle of June, with at least seven RIC men losing their lives in various incidents. A number of British soldiers and ex-soldiers also died during the period, while the IRA executed at least two alleged spies. On 16 June the IRA's Cork No. 2 Brigade ambushed four lorries carrying twenty-five Auxiliaries at Rathcoole near Millstreet, during which two Auxiliaries were killed. Between that day and 25 June at least six RIC men lost their lives in different attacks and ambushes, while eight IRA men died in various incidents around the country. The IRA also executed a number of alleged spies during that time including a man called Patrick Darcy, a school teacher in Doonbeg, County Clare, who was shot for allegedly supplying information that led to the capture and deaths of two local IRA men. The violence continued up the end of the month, with at least seven IRA men dying in a number of incidents across the country, while the Crown forces lost around fifteen men.

The early days of July saw a continuation of the conflict before a truce came into being on the 11th day of the month. During those days up to twenty members of the Crown forces lost their lives, while the IRA lost around six men. About ten people were shot on the basis of being spies and about a dozen civilians lost their lives in various other incidents. On 10 July four unarmed British soldiers stationed at Cork's Victoria Barracks were captured by the IRA and executed. That same day saw the last major incident of the War of Independence before the calling of a truce. A gun battle erupted between the IRA and the British Army in Castleisland, County Kerry. Accounts vary as to the number of casualties, with reports claiming between four and five soldiers lost their lives while three IRA men died in the engagement.

The following day, 11 July, a truce was announced, officially ending the War of Independence that had inflicted so much suffering and destruction on the country. According to Eunan O'Halpin and Daithi O'Corrain in their book *The Dead of the Irish Revolution,* some 2,346 people died between 1917 and 1921. That figure was broken down into 919 civilians, 491 Irish republicans, 523 police and 413 from the military. In a country with a relatively small population, the casualty figures were shocking but they did reflect the ferocity of the conflict. While the truce was welcomed by many people, especially the civilian population and no doubt by many of the combatants, everyone was aware Ireland's future had yet to be settled. The hope was that an agreement could be arrived at when the politicians took centre stage and agreed to sit down to discuss a way forward. That process soon got under way and was watched intensely not only in Ireland and in Britain but also by many people across the world.

CHAPTER THIRTEEN

Cumann na mBan

THE UNSUNG HEROINES OF THE REVOLUTION

Over the past century much of what has been written about the Irish revolutionary era has, very naturally, concentrated on the exploits of the Irish Volunteers, the Irish Republican Army and its Flying Columns as well as Michael Collins's infamous group of young men known as the Squad. The courage of the men who took on the might of the British Empire knew no bounds and today the Irish revere them as the heroes they undoubtedly are. Their actions brought the British to the negotiating table for the first time in Ireland's history and set in motion a process that delivered to the Irish people the freedom they craved for so long. However, while the men of the revolutionary era rightly received the gratitude of the nation, the women who made a significant contribution to the republican cause during that tumultuous time have not always been afforded the credit they also richly deserve. As such, no recounting of the country's revolutionary era would be complete without due recognition being given to the many women who were prepared to put their futures and, in many instances their lives, on the line for a cause they were as committed to as their menfolk.

In 1913, a number of republican-minded women came together in Wynn's Hotel in Dublin to discuss the possibility of forming an organisation for women to work in tandem with the recently formed Irish Volunteers. The die was cast that evening and, on 2 April 1914, a further meeting was called, chaired by Agnes O'Farrelly, which marked the foundation of Cumann na mBan. Soon after, numerous branches were formed across the country and members pledged themselves to the constitution of the organisation. The first branch was called the Ard Craobh and it held its meetings in Dublin's Brunswick Street. The constitution had very clear references to the use of force, by arms if necessary, in order to achieve the goal of independence. The primary aim of the organisation as set out by the constitution was to,

> advance the cause of Irish liberty and to organise Irish women in the furtherance of this object and to assist in arming and equipping a body of Irish men for the defence of Ireland … and to form a fund for the purposes to be called 'The Defence of Ireland Fund'.[120]

Those who joined the organisation mainly came from a middle-class background and were white collar workers and professional women, but there was also a good cohort of working-class members.

When the Irish Volunteers famously split in September 1914, after John Redmond's speech to thousands of men in Woodenbridge, County Wicklow, the majority of Cumann na mBan members sided with the ten thousand or so Volunteers who rejected Redmond's call to join the British Army and fight in the Great War. A small number of Cumann na mBan women chose to follow Redmond but they made little impact and quickly faded into obscurity. On 23 April 1916 the Military Council of the Irish Republican Brotherhood completed arrangements for the Easter Rising and while doing so integrated Cumann na mBan into the Army of the Irish Republic, allowing it to take its place alongside the Irish Volunteers and the Irish Citizen Army in the conflict.

Prior to the Rising, the Cumann na mBan women prepared medical kits and worked as couriers conveying messages across Dublin and beyond. At the outset of the fighting on Easter Monday, the women turned up at all the major Volunteers strongholds across the city, with the exception of the South Dublin Union and Boland's Mills, where Éamon de Valera refused to have any women in his garrison. During the fighting, the women placed themselves in grave danger as they continued to work as couriers carrying despatches and as medical assistants. Some even went out on scouting missions to gather intelligence while others transferred arms and ammunition from secret dumps to various outposts across the city. Some individuals went above and beyond what was expected of them, including Winifred Carney, who was James Connolly's secretary in his trade union work. She reported for duty to the GPO at the beginning of the Rising and stayed for the duration of the fighting, tending to the wounded and cooking meals. She was eventually evacuated with the stricken Connolly from the burning building on the day prior to the general surrender.

Other Cumann na mBan women, like Countess Markievicz, Mary Hyland and Lilly Kempson, were part of a small group under the command of Frank Robbins that took over the College of Surgeons on St Stephen's Green. Markievicz was reputed to have shot and killed a policeman during the early stages of the conflict. Another prominent woman, Helena Molony, was a member of the Citizen Army garrison that attacked Dublin Castle and eventually took over City Hall. It is believed she and other women sniped at British soldiers from that position. When the fighting ended, P.H. Pearse asked Cumann na mBan member Elizabeth O'Farrell to convey his surrender note to the rebel units still fighting across the city. She also accompanied Pearse when he surrendered to General Lowe, bringing the conflict to an end. Around seventy republican women were arrested after the Rising and initially imprisoned in Kilmainham Jail. All, with the exception of about twelve individuals, were released within a couple of weeks. Those who continued to be held were deported to British prisons for a number of months before being released.

All the women were very loyal to the independence cause and were committed to seeing the Rising to its conclusion. Some of the Cumann na mBan women later contributed statements to the Bureau of Military History Archive, many of which vividly illustrate the immense courage they displayed during a very difficult and intense week of fighting. One such statement was provided by Aine Ni Riain, a member of Cumann na mBan, and is indicative of similar statements to be found in the archive. Miss Ni Riain, who was from Longford but working in Tullamore, had travelled to Dublin to visit her sister for the Easter Bank Holiday weekend. However, she eventually found herself unexpectedly embroiled in the conflict. In her statement she recounted the part she played in the Rising:

> On Monday morning the Cumann na mBan mobilised in Palmerstown Place near Broadstone. I went up with my sister … I left them there and I came away with the intention of visiting a friend … I was waiting for a bus at Parnell Street to take me to the quays when some shots were fired. That was the shooting at the Lancers. There was terrible confusion and running about and I gave up on the idea of visiting my friend. I returned to Joseph's Street. All the people there were standing at the doors. Some were giving out about the Volunteers, and some saying nothing. I stayed at Mrs Clery's on St Joseph Street for the rest of the evening. The following

morning, I got up very early and, after Mass, Mrs Clery and myself were standing at the door and there was a girl living opposite, Margaret Derham, who was in Cumann na mBan, she was very anxious to see her young brother who had been mobilised with his section of the Volunteers … We went to Reis's Chambers, gave the password and got in. My sister, the Elliots, and a crowd of Cumann na mBan and some Volunteers were filling up the small space. During the day a message came from the Four Courts asking for some Cumann na mBan girls. My sister and her friends went there.

Later that day most of the people in Reis's Chambers went into the Hibernian Bank and we with them. We got busy then filling baths of water and sterilising it for First Aid instruments.

At this stage I met a marvellous lady, Mrs English, with whom I got pally (I have to thank her for my certificates for service in Easter Week).

Before nightfall two fellows came across from Reis's Chambers and asked for two girls to go back there to prepare meals, etc, as they had no girl at all. Mrs English immediately volunteered and I said I would go with her. When we said that the fellows said 'Remember now, it is a death trap'. My heart fell to my boots but I did not pretend anything. We went and tidied up the place. There was a lot of shooting that night and we were all taking cover.

Mrs English was giving out the Rosary and we were answering it. My memory tells me that some of the British occupied McBirney's roof during the night because the boys were looking over there. At daybreak things got quiet and Mrs English cooked a breakfast for the men. She gave them chops and we drank tea. During the morning, we girls went back to the Hibernian Hotel. What was going on there was that they were boring into the next building, a chemist's shop which is now Hamilton Longs. The place was choked with dust. All that time there was dreadful shooting from the Helga. We could not hear each other talking.

I don't know how it came about but I found myself and another girl carrying a zinc bath full of food from Reis's Chambers across to the GPO with our heads bent down to the ground. We did this at least twice and were admitted through

> the side door in Princess Street. I finally went to stay in the GPO with the other girls. We were employed upstairs in the restaurant where there was a huge range. I remember Desmond Fitzgerald, who was in charge of the cooking arrangements. I remember the British Tommy – a Dublin man – who was cooking all the time and joking with the girls. He was in great humour and he had rosary beads around his neck. There were British prisoners there – some of them officers – to whom we brought meals.
>
> On Thursday it was much the same only that the bombarding was much heavier and I thought the place would come down around us every minute. That was the day the Imperial Hotel and other buildings near it came down. That night some of us at least lay down on mattresses in the basement. On Friday morning, Patrick Pearse sent for us and he made a nice speech to us. He said he wished that everyone of us who was not qualified in First Aid should leave as the fighting would get very severe and it would probably come to using bayonets to fight their way out.
>
> Leslie Price took charge of us who were to leave. She carried a Red Cross flag. We came out through the wall of the building into Henry Street. Sean McDermott and Patrick Pearse were standing inside the wall of the building and shook hands with each one of us as we passed out. Leslie brought us down Henry Street to Jervis Street Hospital … We were not admitted but a nun spoke to Leslie and we marched on to Capel Street … We turned right from Capel Street into Parnell Street … We had to go along Parnell Street and Summerhill where we got plenty of abuse and were called all sorts of names by the ladies who were standing in the doorways.[121]

After the Rising, the women of Cumann na mBan were not prepared to stand down and allow their organisation to fade away. Indeed, they were even more determined to continue with their role in the struggle for independence and, in time, they excelled to an even greater degree. By 1917 individuals such as Countess Markievicz had come to the fore in the Cumann na mBan leadership and they set about revitalising the organisation. Markievicz insisted on popularising the memory of those who died in the Rising and she and other prominent women organised prisoner relief funds. When the conscription crisis came along in 1917, the women of Cumann na mBan were quick to get out and support Sinn Fein's campaign of opposition to it. They also enthusiastically campaigned for Sinn Fein candidates in the pivotal general election of December 1918. In fact, one of their number, Markievicz, managed to win a seat, while Winifred Carney narrowly missed out when she stood in a Belfast constituency. However, as much as the women of Cumann na mBan and the Irish Citizen Army contributed to the Easter Rising, many of them really came to the fore in the run up to and during the War of Independence.

When that conflict began in earnest, the Cumann na mBan women were again not found wanting and volunteered for all kinds of tasks. During the war they undertook the very dangerous work of transporting arms and explosives as well as conveying messages across the country. They were also on hand to glean intelligence information from wherever they could and were to the fore in tending to the wounds and injuries of the fighting men of the IRA. The women were not, however, permitted to take any part in the attacks on or ambushes of the Crown forces, although there is some evidence of at least one breech of that rule. What was evident throughout the conflict was the sheer enthusiasm displayed by all of the Cumann na mBan women for the cause of Ireland's independence and their willingness to take extraordinary risks in the pursuance of it.

After the Easter Rising there was a lull in republican activities but the women, conscious that hostilities were likely to be reactivated at a near future date, continued their work and prepared medical and field kits for the Volunteers. In April 1918, some nine months prior to the War of Independence, Gortatlea RIC Barracks in County Kerry was attacked and two Volunteers were killed. Their comrades, all of whom escaped, were forced to seek shelter and the local Cumann na mBan were called upon to assist the men in any way they could. As a result, the Ballymacelligott branch became the first in Ireland to look after active Volunteers on the run. From the beginning of the War of Independence, every Cumann na mBan branch turned its attention to the task of providing medical aid to the injured and wounded. A number of women from each branch were chosen to attend first aid classes and, once the course was completed, the women were examined for their competency by a local doctor sympathetic to the republican cause before being awarded a certificate. As the war progressed, almost every Cumann na mBan branch, most especially in rural areas, was asked to arrange for flying column members to be billeted and fed nourishing meals in order that their ability to prosecute the war was maintained.

Many Cumann na mBan women and their families were often placed in invidious and dangerous situations throughout the conflict. They never knew when their homesteads might be surrounded by Crown forces and always had to be on their guard and prepared for all eventualities. One Cumann na mBan member, Mary Walsh (nee O'Neill), Captain of the South Bandon area, provided a fine example of the dangers faced by members of the organisation and their families in a witness statement to the Bureau of Military History when she related a story from 4 February 1921:

> Volunteer P. Crowley remained at this time in our district. He was awaiting an appendix operation. A dump was prepared for him by us. (He had his meals in our house after being told there was no raiding). Unfortunately, the place was surrounded this morning by military in single formation which closed in on suspected houses. When word came, Paddy and my brother ran by a fence to cover, only to run into Percival (Commander of the British garrison in Bandon) himself. They retraced their steps, Percival following and firing. My sister and I ran after the two boys hoping to save them from the firing as we felt sure he would not fire on us. My brother then gave up hoping that Paddy could get out as he had to be held prisoner, but another soldier was called on to cover him. Then my sister caught Percival by the legs (he was on a gate) and held him fast, even though he beat her knuckles with a gun.
>
> When he could not release himself, he pointed the gun at our brother, and said he would shoot him dead if she did not let him go. We had hoped that by this time Paddy had got well away. He was followed by Percival and found stretched dead about a quarter of a mile from our home by a Cumann na mBan girl that was crossing to let us know of the raid. My sister and I with a few others, brought the body back to our house before the military had time to collect it. They came along with a local RIC man to identify the body, but did not interfere again. He was waked and buried from our house in Clogagh and was given full military honours.[122]

As well as engaging in drilling, attending first aid classes and doing anything else required of them to help their menfolk, the women of Cumann na mBan had no problem in appearing in public to show their support for the cause of an Irish republic. They also took every opportunity to make life difficult for the British administration in Dublin Castle as well as the government in London. For example, during the years 1917 and 1918 when the British launched a recruitment campaign in Ireland, the Cumann na mBan women were always eager to disrupt the many meetings that took place across the country. They did so by moving through the crowd singing nationalist songs until the meeting either collapsed or they were ejected. Some of the women were asked by the Volunteers to engage in intelligence work, which mainly consisted of keeping an eye out for RIC patrols and carrying despatches. The women were also entrusted with distributing bundles of the Volunteers newspaper, *An tOglach.* After the general election of December 1918, the women began to take drilling much more seriously and they also engaged in military training exercises in the countryside. In her witness statement to the Bureau of Military History, Margaret (Peg) Broderick, Section Commander in the Galway Cumann na mBan, recalled one particular exercise, saying:

> We were working day and night in preparation for the very memorable general election of 1918. This being over, we started to drill and have exercises out in the country. On one occasion when on a Field Day at Barna, we were being instructed by an officer of the brigade or battalion. I think his name was Shiels. We were marching back through the village when we met a Volunteer's scout, who said he thought there were a few RIC outside the barracks waiting for us. Shortly afterwards two RIC on bicycles approached us, dismounted and walked along our flanks. When we reached the barracks, I noticed a sergeant with six or seven men, who then made a charge out to arrest the Volunteer officer. We immediately pounced on the police. I remember getting up on one policeman's back and getting my two hands around his throat. He wriggled to knock me off and let his grip on the prisoner relax.
>
> Another RIC man intervened and pulled me off. I grabbed the second fellow's cap and beat him on the head with the hard peak, and the other fellow swung round and struck me with his revolver on the side of the head, above my ear. I was half stunned and staggered against the wall, when someone shouted, 'This is no time for fainting'. I shook myself back to life, but by this time, they had Sheils inside the barracks and came out firing shots in the air to frighten us, and using vile language.

> We collected all the stones, of which there were plenty, and broke every window in the barracks. We then reformed and commenced our march back very 'bronach' indeed.[123]

Peg Broderick was typical of many Cumann na mBan women; determined and in many ways fearless. She and her comrades were always willing to stand up for the Irish republic they dearly wished to see established. Such was Peg's standing within the republican movement she was assigned in 1920 to the Irish Volunteers Brigade Staff to carry out intelligence work. She also delivered and collected revolvers and ammunition as required and conveyed despatches on a regular basis. Broderick, like many other Cumann na mBan women, was always in constant danger and, in the autumn of 1920, the RIC attempted to burn down her family's home, which was only saved with the help of her neighbours. During the attack the family was forced to endure shots being fired by the police and her brother was arrested and held for a time before being released.

During the War of Independence, it was not uncommon for Cumann na mBan women to be threatened by members of the RIC and the British military but they all displayed an inordinate amount of bravery in the face of such severe intimidation. The republican women were truly heroic and their actions during Ireland's revolutionary era deserve universal recognition. Their extraordinary stories now occupy a deserved place in the public domain and serve to remind modern generations of the sacrifices made by all of the women. From the outset of the Easter Rising, they played a heroic role in the struggle for Irish freedom and their endeavours were even more impressive during the War of Independence. Many of the Cumann na mBan women went on to repudiate the Anglo-Irish Treaty as a matter of principle and conscience, and vowed to continue the struggle as they saw it for an Irish Republic. Like their male counterparts, who also repudiated the Treaty, they fully believed they had every right to do so.

PART FOUR

The Aftermath of the Revolution

CHAPTER FOURTEEN

The Truce

PEACE COMES AT LAST

In the last weeks of 1920, the Prime Minister David Lloyd George openly and very bluntly put an end to any possible peace overtures when he insisted on the IRA laying down their arms and surrendering them up to the authorities. That demand fell on deaf ears in Ireland and the struggle for independence continued uninterrupted. However, after two and a half years of conflict between the IRA and the forces of the Crown, both sides came to the conclusion in July 1921 that the military stalemate that had set in over the previous few months looked destined to continue indefinitely. By early summer the government in London was coming under increasing public and political pressure to bring about an end to the conflict in Ireland. Since 1914 and the outbreak of the Great War, the daily news in Britain was dominated by conflict and, most especially, the losses sustained by the British military across Europe. For most British people the time had come for a settlement to the 'Irish question' and there was a general desire to see the troops return home and for the country to settle into a period of peace, free from any hostilities in Ireland and elsewhere across the world.

On the other hand, it was clear to Michael Collins and others in the IRA leadership that it was becoming more difficult to sustain the struggle against the Crown forces. The supplies of arms and ammunition were running out and the streams of finance necessary to continue the conflict were also drying up. The view that a military struggle alone would deliver on the long-cherished Irish republic was dissipating and attention turned to achieving that aim through a political process. Fresh contacts between Dublin and London emerged in the spring of 1921 and in June the British ended the policy of house burnings, which had been in place since the turn of the year as reprisals for IRA attacks and ambushes.

The move towards some type of settlement gathered impetus during the second half of June when King George V was scheduled to address the opening of the Northern Ireland parliament in Belfast. The government in London prepared a 'war to the hilt' speech for the King to deliver but he had a different view on Ireland and expressed his deep unease about the speech to Jan Smuts, the South African Prime Minister, who happened to be in London. The King told Smuts he disagreed with the contents of the speech written by his ministers and, it seems, Smuts was in lock step with him. The King then asked Smuts to write a new speech, which he duly did and it was presented by the King to the government in London. This, of course, caused consternation in Downing Street and Smuts, who was very highly thought of in British government circles, was called in to offer advice. He was told the country was facing a constitutional crisis because the King had not only refused to deliver the speech prepared by the government but had produced his own draft. Smuts pretended he knew nothing about these developments and asked to see the King's draft. It was given to him and he made a pretence of reading over it carefully, twice. Then he said he thought the speech was a good one and the government might do worse than accept it. Ultimately, the British government did accept Smuts' advice and the speech, with a few minor adjustments, was delivered on 22 June by the King at the opening of the Belfast parliament. In general, the speech went down well and during it he called on:

> All Irishmen to pause, to stretch out the hand of forbearance and conciliation, to forgive and to forget, and to join in making for the land they love a new era of peace, contentment, and good will.[124]

As the speech called for negotiations on the Irish question, the government in London had no option but to initiate steps to accommodate peace talks.

In essence, the King in his speech set the ball rolling and the move towards a truce gathered pace on 24 June when the cabinet in London decided to ask for talks with the Sinn Fein leadership. That same day, Lloyd George wrote to Éamon de Valera as 'the chosen leader of the great majority in Southern Ireland' with a view to organising peace talks. De Valera, after some consultations with other republican leaders, agreed to the talks proposals. Despite James Craig, the Northern Ireland unionist leader, refusing to enter into discussions with him, de Valera spoke with prominent southern unionists and after those discussions he telegraphed Lloyd George indicating he was ready to talk.

The peace talks began in earnest on the week beginning 4 July and Smuts arrived in Dublin as an emissary of the British government to speak with de Valera. He quickly reminded the Irish leader of all the compromises that had brought about an end to the Boer War and how he and his fellow Boers fashioned a relationship between Britain and South Africa. The discussions in Dublin's Mansion House were joined by General Sir Nevil Macready, who was at the time commanding the British forces in Ireland, and the terms of the truce were agreed on 9 July to come into effect at noon on 11 July. Though somewhat surprised, there was a general welcome for the news among the civilian population across the country.

It has to be acknowledged that by July 1921 the civilian population was, by that stage, displaying distinct signs of war weariness, having endured the impact of conflicts since 1914. Many young Irishmen went to the front during the Great War while, in the middle of that conflict, the Easter Rising took place and from January 1919 the War of Independence began to overshadow the lives of all citizens. The promise of peace appealed to so many and the prospect of not having to hear news of further deaths every day on both sides of the divide was an opportunity too important to pass up. There was, without doubt, widespread happiness across the country and T. Ryle Dwyer referred to it in his book *Tans Terror and Troubles, Kerry's Real Fighting Story* when he wrote,

> the people of Tralee were so overjoyed they milled out onto the streets and fired off some rockets in celebration. A band, made up of ex-British soldiers played popular Irish tunes.
>
> People who had never openly engaged in the conflict against the British or publicly supported it got in on the act of celebration and wore Sinn Fein colours for the first time ever.[125]

However, for the IRA commanders in the field like Ernie O'Malley and Tom Barry as well as Sean Moylan, who was by that time incarcerated in Spike Island prison, the truce came as a complete surprise. The notification of it came in a message signed by Richard Mulcahy, the IRA Chief of Staff, and ordered all men to lay down their arms by lunch time on Monday, 11 July. O'Malley, who was at the time Commander of the Second Southern Division, was less than pleased when he heard about the truce. He was in Tipperary when a young Dublin boy, Paddy O'Connor, arrived with Mulcahy's directive, which famously read,

> in view of the conversations now being entered into by our government with the Government of Great Britain, and in pursuance of mutual conversations, active operations by our forces will be suspended as from noon, Monday, 11 July.[126]

O'Malley, as he later wrote in his book *On Another Man's Wound*, was 'bewildered' by the news, which nevertheless was an order and had to be obeyed, bringing about an end to what he later called 'the scrap'. Interestingly, the numbers in IRA Volunteer units across the country increased as soon the truce was announced, which irritated many men who had been to the forefront of the fighting during the previous two and half years. Those who joined up after the truce were somewhat ridiculed by the veteran Volunteers and were known as 'flagwaggers'. There was, it seems, a lot of ill feeling between both factions, and the Clare IRA leader Michael Brennan was particularly scathing of the 'flagwaggers', all of whom, he believed, 'kept under the bed while the war was on'.

With a cessation of the fighting imminent, the final weekend of the conflict turned out to be a rather deadly one, with the deaths of over forty people being recorded. It seems many local IRA units who had been somewhat inactive up to then, or who had been drawing up plans to engage with Crown forces, decided to spring into action. Some of the units did not relish the prospect of being remembered for not having played their part in the conflict to secure Ireland's independence. They also knew, of course, that there was little chance of reprisals in their areas prior to the ceasefire coming into effect on the following Monday. However, when the time came to officially lay down their arms, the fighting men who made up the flying columns returned to their homes and were welcomed back as heroes. The British, it seems, also adhered to the spirit of the truce and ended their military presence on the streets of cities and towns. Military lorries and cars disappeared from view and all troops were generally confined to barracks, though a few took a little while to accept the new order in the country. A report in *The New York Times* on 12 July relayed how a republican supporter in Kingstown harbour unfurled an Irish tricolour over his yacht to celebrate the signing of the truce. Some British troops rowed out to the yacht to force the man to take the flag down but were ordered back by their commanding officer as the gathering crowd on the pier cheered wildly.

When the truce came into effect on Monday, 11 July there was an outpouring of joy and one of the first impacts was the lifting of martial law that had been imposed in Munster and in other counties such as Kilkenny and Wexford. People could look forward again to attending marts, fairs and sports matches as well as a return to normal life. Socialising, which was curtailed so much, would once again become an integral element of Irish life. The lifting of the curfew was welcomed by everyone and the requirement of having to be in one's home before sunset no longer applied. This was a welcome development and as the summer of 1921 in Ireland was a very pleasant one weather wise, people quickly took advantage of their new-found freedoms to be out and about in the evenings. While the civilian population took advantage of the cessation of the fighting and violence, members of the Crown forces did likewise once they were no longer confined to barracks.

On the stroke of noon on Monday, 11 July church bells all around the country peeled in celebration of the end of the conflict. In Dublin, ships anchored at the docks sounded their sirens and whistles, while railway engines in the vicinity also sounded their sirens. Most people working on the docks as well as Corporation workers were given the afternoon off from work. There were reports of members of the Crown forces in the city seen out shopping in civilian clothes on thoroughfares like Grafton Street, while some of their comrades went swimming in Dun Laoghaire. Business was very brisk on the streets of Dublin as market traders took advantage of the crowds willing to spend some money. Plans were made by many communities to light bonfires that night. Ernest Blythe, by then a member of de Valera's Provisional Government and a leading republican, recalled the joy and sense of goodwill that evening in the area of the city in which he lived:

> I remember that in the lane at the back of the house where I lived a couple of huge bonfires were lit and the people remained around them half the night, dancing and singing.[127]

That afternoon and evening, bands marched in the centre of the city and the fact that a curfew was no longer in place meant people could, for the first time in a long while, stay out on the streets for as long as they wished.

Similar scenes were acted out around the country as 'Truce Night' became a night to party and celebrate. Dances were held, bonfires were lit, songs were sung and stories were told. In Midleton in County Cork the citizens got back to normal life at noon, as soon as the ceasefire came into effect, when a cattle and horse fair began. Many shops and business were quick to make bargains available to shoppers, while all around the country shops stayed open until midnight hoping to cash in on the willingness of shoppers to spend money. It seemed that all at once the country came alive again and the economy, which had been depressed for over two years, suddenly sprang into life as soon as the joyful peel of the bells were heard that day.

The next few months saw a delay before meaningful discussions got under way. The British continued to insist on the IRA decommissioning its arms and ammunition. That demand was dismissed by the republican leadership and eventually the British dropped it. Many of the local IRA officers across the country, however, regarded the truce as being a temporary halt to hostilities as they did not fully trust the British. As a result, they ensured their men maintained their discipline and insisted on them being ready to resume hostilities if called upon to do so. Ernest Blythe, writing in his witness statement to the Bureau of Military History some years later, confirmed the sense of unease that continued to weigh on the minds of many republicans between July and October 1921. He went on to say:

> The long correspondence which ensued between Mr de Valera and Lloyd George, before negotiations really began, delayed a decision so much and produced such a change in feeling at home that the danger of ultimate civil war began to manifest. I remember within two months of the beginning of the Truce meeting a university professor who was a Sinn Feiner but not active in politics – the late Professor J.J Nolan – who had paid a visit to West Cork. He told me that there was such an attitude amongst certain sections of the Volunteers, and particularly amongst the truce leaders who were in some places behaving like an army of occupation in a foreign country, that he felt certain that peace with Britain was bound to be followed by a new struggle amongst ourselves.[128]

Nevertheless, despite the ominous prediction of Professor Nolan, the cessation of hostilities on 11 July 1921 brought about a real sense of relief across the country. It was accompanied by a sense of pride that a small nation had, against all the odds, stood stoutly and determinedly against the powerful forces of the Crown for two and a half years. The Irish people were also able to find glory in the knowledge that for the first time in history, they were about to bring their British suppressors and overlords of the last 700 years to the negotiating table. For all republicans, the long-held and much-cherished independence ideal was now one step closer. The cost of pursuing that ideal had been great and the campaign left a long trail of sorrow as it claimed many military and civilian lives. So, in July 1921, with the truce in place, the job of the military men was done and it was left to the politicians to secure the country's future. That same task, unfortunately, proved to be a very difficult one for those involved in the process of finding a political way forward for the country. Their well-intentioned endeavours, which culminated in the signing of the Anglo-Irish Treaty in December 1921, unhappily plunged the country into a further period of turbulence in the form of catastrophic civil war. However, for the time being, the knowledge that the War of Independence had come to an end was enough for most people to celebrate one important fact: that peace, albeit an uneasy one, had at last come to the country.

CHAPTER FIFTEEN

The Anglo-Irish Treaty

The Anglo-Irish Treaty of December 1921 marked the official end of hostilities between Ireland and England. It was, however, to have profound implications for the future of Ireland in the sense that it not only divided the country but also plunged it into a vicious civil war. That conflict cost many lives and left a toxic political legacy that lasted for decades. The period between the truce and the signing of the Treaty was fraught with difficulties for those involved in the republican movement. The more hard-line individuals were not convinced by the cessation of hostilities agreed by Éamon de Valera and Lloyd George in July 1921 and they hugely distrusted the British and their intentions. On the other hand, the more moderate faction of Irish republicanism was of the opinion the military stalemate that had set in during the first half of 1921 looked destined to continue and the chances of defeating the British in a military struggle were receding quickly.

Over the course of time spanning from mid-July to the first week of October in 1921, a debate raged in Ireland about the next steps to be taken in relation to the country's future. The politicians eventually won out over the military men and Dail Eireann agreed to send a delegation to London on behalf of the Irish people to negotiate a future for a new Ireland. Before the negotiations got under way, a storm of controversy blew up when de Valera announced he would not be part of the Irish delegation travelling to the British capital. A stunned populace hardly knew what to make of the decision because it viewed de Valera as not only the undisputed leader of Irish republicanism, but also the one individual with the capabilities to forcefully articulate the republican ideal to the British.

De Valera's decision to remain at home in Dublin became one of the great imponderable questions in modern Irish history. Many theories have been offered up as to why he made that momentous decision. For his part, he always maintained it was necessary for him to remain at home to keep the more militant faction of republicanism in check, while it also enabled him to be the final arbiter once an agreement had been struck with the British. Many historians and observers believe he decided to stay at home because he knew from his personal discussions with Lloyd George prior to the negotiations in London that a thirty-two county, independent Ireland was unattainable at that stage and he did not want to be blamed when such a scenario became a reality. During the negotiations, de Valera insisted on regular reports from London, which led to his many disagreements with Michael Collins and Arthur Griffith.

Besides Collins and Griffith, the Irish delegation was made up of Éamonn Duggan and George Gavan Duffy, both lawyers who were there to oversee the legalities of anything agreed with the British and, Robert Barton. The delegation was accompanied by Erskine Childers in his capacity as its secretary, though there is no doubt his main task was to regularly report back to de Valera in Dublin, which caused a great deal of tension within the delegation. We now know, of course, that there was a high degree of antipathy between Griffith and Childers throughout the negotiations in London. Barton was also a 'de Valera' man and, like Childers, he was included in the delegation to counterbalance Collins and Griffith. Essentially, the Irish delegation was a divided one from the outset, which did not help its cause during the negotiations and, unfortunately, that sense of division continued to beset Irish republicanism over the following years and decades. It has to be acknowledged also that the Irish delegation was an inexperienced one, initially devoid of any knowledge of the art of negotiation. As the members left for London, they were well aware their task was going to be a difficult one. They were, in every sense, on a hiding to nothing while in London, most especially because their leader was back in Dublin often undermining their every move.

The Irish delegation had been granted the authority of plenipotentiaries by Dail Eireann, which meant they could agree and sign a deal with the British if they felt it was in the interest of the Irish people. That arrangement was overridden by de Valera, who told the delegation in no uncertain terms they were not to sign anything until he had given permission to do so. As it transpired, the delegation was forced to refer everything back to de Valera, which not only undermined the confidence of Collins, Griffith, Duggan and

Gavan Duffy, but also placed them in a difficult position with the British, who constantly reminded them that they were, in fact, plenipotentiaries with the authority to make a deal. Prior to the negotiations, the cabinet in Dublin decided the delegation should seek a thirty-two county, independent republic, but as soon as the negotiations began, Collins and Griffith realised this aspiration was unattainable. The remaining members of cabinet in Dublin then decided the delegation should emphasise the question of unity and indicated the delegates should inform the British they were prepared to give up some independence in return.

Unfortunately, the cabinet did not settle on how much independence to give up, which complicated matters further for the delegation in London. De Valera was of the opinion the unionists in Northern Ireland would not really matter in the final equation and they would have to accept whatever the British agreed to. However, de Valera failed to take into account Northern Ireland already had its own parliament by that time and the unionists were unlikely to give that up. Of course, the Conservatives in the British coalition government were also unlikely to do anything to jeopardise the Union of Great Britain and Ireland. The British delegation was a very experienced one, probably the most experienced in the world at that time. It was made up of big-name politicians, all well-known on the world stage and, it included the Prime Minister, David Lloyd George, Austen Chamberlain, F.E. Smith (Lord Birkenhead) and Winston Churchill. They were a formidable opposition to the Irish delegation and proved to be very tough and determined negotiators.

On 11 October 1921, Michael Collins travelled to London and arrived separately to the rest of the delegation. He saw himself as a soldier rather than a politician and he would have refused to go to London for anyone other than de Valera. During the negotiations he resided separately from the rest of delegation and was accompanied by Liam Tobin, Tom Cullen and Ned Broy, all members of his Intelligence Staff. While Griffith was the nominal head of the delegation, it quickly became obvious to the British that Collins was the dominant personality on the Irish side and he went on to forge a good relationship with Churchill and Lord Birkenhead. Early on in the negotiations, the British offered a 'twenty-six county dominion', which included conditions like perpetual free trade between Ireland and England, as well as Ireland contributing to the national debt repayments. The British were also to be given free access to certain Irish ports for naval purposes. De Valera rejected the proposals out of hand, though both sides were anxious to continue the negotiations. As the negotiations progressed, the members of the Irish delegation seemed like fish out water at times as they took part in seven plenary sessions, twenty-four sub-conferences and nine meetings of special committees.

It soon emerged Lloyd George's main concern revolved around the defence of Britain and he feared a hostile Ireland might ally herself later with one of Britain's great adversaries, Germany. He also wanted to keep Ireland in the Empire and insisted on the Irish people pledging their allegiance to the Crown. The early days of the negotiations saw a general agreement on issues like trade, defence and national debt. The main problem to surface concerned Northern Ireland and the need to convince the unionists to accept the outcome of the negotiations and any subsequent agreement. Lloyd George made it clear to Griffith he needed some concessions from the Irish delegation in order to keep the unionists onside and prevent a backlash from them. He claimed if he did not get the concessions, it would end the negotiations and also hasten the demise of his government. He believed it would be replaced by a government dominated by the Conservative Party, which would not hesitate to subdue Ireland by force.

This, of course, was a scare tactic of huge proportions and typical of how the wily 'Welsh Wizard' operated. On 2 November 1921, Arthur Griffith assented to Lloyd George's demand and gave the Prime Minister a written promise he would recommend recognition of the British Crown if he and his colleagues were satisfied on all other issues. The following week, Griffith agreed to a new and further demand from Lloyd George. It was made through Tom Jones (Assistant-Secretary to the Cabinet), who asked the Irish delegation to consider the setting up of a Boundary Commission if the unionists in Northern Ireland refused to accept subordination to an all-Ireland parliament in Dublin. Initially, both Griffith and Collins harboured doubts about the proposal, believing the Prime Minister intended it as a tactic against Sir James Craig and his unionist colleagues. Jones made it clear Lloyd George was not prepared to continue the talks unless Griffith gave an assurance he would not publicly repudiate his commitment to the recognition of the Crown. Griffith felt he had no choice but to provide that undertaking.

Tom Jones wrote in 1971 that by acceding to Lloyd George's request, Griffith allowed the Prime Minister to bring the two staunch unionist supporters, Chamberlain and Birkenhead, back on his side during the negotiations. The ploy worked, according to Jones, and the two men managed to face down the more strident members of their own Conservative Party and persuade the majority to back the strategy and the talks. Eventually, the Irish delegation consented to the idea of a Boundary Commission, believing the unionists had no choice but to agree to its recommendations and that it would in time bring about a united Ireland. Griffith wrote to de Valera explaining the concept of the Boundary Commission and suggested it would remove all of two counties and parts of others from the Northern Ireland state, thereby rendering it almost unviable. Privately, the British did not disabuse Griffith of that notion, though they were at pains not to do so in public.

There is also evidence that confirms Lloyd George told his cabinet colleagues in early November that if Northern Ireland remained outside the jurisdiction of the proposed all-Ireland parliament, it would not be able to retain the predominantly nationalist counties of Fermanagh and Tyrone. De Valera and the rest of his cabinet, all of whom had remained in Dublin, eventually agreed to the setting up of the Boundary Commission, realising that by doing so they were openly admitting to the concept of partition, thereby ditching the aspiration, for the time being, of a thirty-two county, independent Ireland. The negotiations in London continued on until December 1921, not helped by the Irish delegation making several trips to Dublin to converse, often acrimoniously, with de Valera. This exasperated the British and eventually Lloyd George lost patience with the process.

On 5 December, reminding the members of the Irish delegation that they had the power of plenipotentiaries, Lloyd George put an ultimatum before them and insisted they sign it immediately. He also made it clear that if it was not signed, Ireland would once again face the wrath of the British military, though most historians and observers now regard that threat as nothing more than a bluff because the British public would not have countenanced such an action. The final British proposal included the establishment of the Irish Free State as a dominion of the Empire with the King as Head of State. Members of the Dublin parliament would have to swear an Oath of Allegiance to the Crown. De Valera had earlier dismissed that demand and instructed his delegation put forward a proposal that he called 'External Association', whereby Ireland would not be part of the Empire but would have a special relationship with Britain. Griffith pointed out to de Valera that the British had already rejected that very same proposal.

The final proposals also included giving Ireland the same constitutional status as Canada and other dominions. It also insisted on the Governor General being the King's representative in Ireland. The British would also have access to three specified ports, Cobh, Berehaven and Lough Swilly. The British ultimatum gave the Irish delegation two choices; either accept the final proposals or reject them and gamble the British would not revert to military action against Ireland. The delegation chose the former option and, in the early hours of 6 December signed the Anglo-Irish Treaty. It truly was a difficult decision and, though not satisfied with all of its contents, the Irish delegation probably believed it was the best deal it was going to achieve. Winston Churchill later wrote:

> Michael Collins rose looking as though he were going to shoot someone, preferably himself. In all my life, I have never seen so much pain and suffering in restraint.[129]

After the signing of the Treaty, Lord Birkenhead, a staunch believer in the Empire and the Union, is reputed to have said; 'I may have signed my death warrant tonight.' Collins is reported to have replied, 'I have signed my actual death warrant.' The delegation returned to Dublin to a bitterly divided Dail Eireann and country. The cabinet discussed the Treaty and de Valera rejected it in tandem with Austin Stack and Cathal Brugha. On the other hand, the Treaty was accepted by Collins, Griffith and Barton, leaving W.T. Cosgrave to cast the deciding vote to send it to Dail Eireann for debate and ratification.

The Anglo-Irish Treaty was debated for three weeks by Dail Eireann, with a break for the Christmas holidays. Had a vote been taken before the break it is very likely the agreement with the British would have been rejected. However, when the deputies returned to their constituencies for Christmas, they were told in no uncertain terms by their constituents they should consider voting in favour of the agreement. It was very clear by then that much of the population wanted peace and did not wish to see a resumption of hostilities. On 7 January 1922 the Dail voted on the Anglo-Irish Treaty and it was ratified by sixty-four votes to fifty-seven. This caused de Valera and his supporters to stage a brief but symbolic walkout of the chamber. Ireland's destiny had finally been put in the hands of her own politicians and the first rule of democracy prevailed. The majority of deputies decided, there and then, that the Anglo-Irish Treaty, which had been so painstakingly put together, should be accepted as the basis for Ireland's immediate future.

The Anglo-Irish Treaty has continued to exercise the minds of many historians since its ratification. Many commentators have pondered if it should ever have been signed at all, considering the divisive impact it had on the country and the people. Some have contended Irish republicans should have called Lloyd George's bluff and resumed hostilities, because signing the agreement repudiated the ideal of a thirty-two county, independent Ireland and negated everything that had been fought for in the Easter Rising and in the War of Independence. Other historians and commentators still remain convinced the delegation chose the best course of action and saved the country from a military debacle that would have resulted in an even more hard-line British subjugation of Ireland. By making the decision they did, the delegation was always going to be damned by a cohort of people back home and lauded by many others. In general, the Anglo-Irish Treaty was welcomed by the majority of the Irish people because, in their minds, it brought about an end to years of conflict. However, little did they realise the agreement with the British would eventually become a very contentious one and, a source of much bloodshed and chaos in the form of a civil war. It turned out to be a brutal, unforgiving conflict that cost many lives and left a bitter legacy which tainted the country for the best part of the twentieth century.

References

Introduction

1. The North Began. Eoin MacNeill, An Claidheamh Soluis. November 1913.
2. Bulmer Hobson. Witness Statement to Bureau of Military History. No. 51, p.5.
3. Sean T. O'Kelly. Witness Statement to Bureau of Military History. No. 1765, p.110.
4. Bulmer Hobson. Witness Statement to Bureau of Military History No. 53, p.2.
5. Ibid., pp.2–3.
6. Redmond. A Life Undone. Chris Dooley. Gilland MacMillan, p.237.

Chapter One

7. Sean Moylan. Witness Statement to Bureau of Military History. No. 838, p.14.
8. Charles Townsend. Easter 1916. The Irish Rebellion. p.71.
9. Ernest Blythe. Witness Statement to Bureau of Military History. No. 939, pp.44–45.
10. Sean T. O'Kelly. Witness Statement to Bureau of Military History. No. 1765, pp.208–209.
11. Charles Townsend. Easter 1916. The Irish Rebellion. p.116.
12. Sean T. O'Kelly. Witness Statement to Bureau of Military History. No. 1765, p.209.

Chapter Two

13. Mortimer O'Leary. Witness Statement to Bureau of Military History. No. 107, pp.1–2.
14. Bernard Reilly. Witness Statement to Bureau of Military History. No. 349, pp.2–3.
15. Bulmer Hobson. Witness Statement to Bureau of Military History. No. 81, pp.11–12.
16. Ibid., p.12.
17. Ibid., p.13.
18. Ibid., p.13.
19. Captain R. Henderson. Witness Statement to Bureau of Military History. No. 1686, pp.3–4.

Chapter Three

20. Helena Molony. Witness Statement to Bureau of Military History. No. 391, pp.34–35.
21. Ibid., pp.35–37.
22. Ibid., pp.37–39.
23. Frank Henderson. Witness Statement to Bureau of Military History. No. 249, p.34.
24. Harry Colley. Witness Statement to Bureau of Military History. No. 1687, p.10.
25. Ibid., p.11.

Chapter Four

26. Harry Colley. Witness Statement to Bureau of Military History. No. 1687, pp.12–13.
27. Frank Henderson. Witness Statement to Bureau of Military History. No. 249, pp.41–42.
28. Ibid., p.42–43.
29. Frank Thornton. Witness Statement to Bureau of Military History. No. 510, p.15.
30. Ibid., p.16.

Chapter Five

31. W.T. Cosgrave. Witness Statement to Bureau of Military History. No. 268, p.8.

32. Ibid., p.9.
33. Frank Thornton. Witness Statement to Bureau of Military History. No. 510, p.15.
34. Michael Staines. Witness Statement to Bureau of Military History. No. 284, p.17.
35. National Museum of Ireland. 1916 Stories.

Chapter Six

36. Sean Moylan. Witness Statement to Bureau of Military History. No. 838, p.16.
37. Ibid.
38. Thomas Doyle. Witness Statement to Bureau of Military History. No. 1041, pp.20–21.
39. Michael McAllister. Witness Statement to Bureau of Military History. No. 1494, pp.9–14.
40. Michael Newell. Witness Statement to Bureau of Military History. No. 342, pp.6–7.

Chapter Seven

41. Frank Henderson. Witness Statement to Bureau of Military History. No. 249, pp.57–64.
42. Kilmainham Tales. Women Imprisoned in Kilmainham Gaol After the Easter Rising.
43. Ireland's Own. Women of the Revolution Pt 2. Éamonn Duggan, August 2016.
44. Kilmainham Tales. Women Imprisoned in Kilmainham Gaol after the Easter Rising.
45. Kathleen Lynn. Witness Statement to Bureau of Military History. No. 357 (Pt 2) p.3.
46. Ibid., pp.4–5.
47. We Go Into Action Today at Noon. P115. Éamonn Duggan, O'Brien Press, 2021.
48. Ibid., p.116.
49. Robert Holland. Witness Statement to Bureau of Military History. No. 280, p.43.
50. Ibid., p.44–45.

51. Ireland's Own. Ireland in 1916. Jeers Turn to Cheers. Éamonn Duggan, 3 June 2016.
52. Ibid.

Chapter Eight

53. Liam de Roiste. Witness Statement to Bureau of Military History. No. 1698, (Pt 2), p.362.
54. Thomas Donnelly. Witness Statement to Bureau of Military History. No. 519, pp.1–2.

Chapter Nine

55. Joseph P. Lawless. Witness Statement to Bureau of Military History. No. 1043, pp.229–233.
56. Frank Henderson. Witness Statement to Bureau of Military History. No. 821, pp.2–3.
57. Sean Moylan. An Irish Revolutionary at War, p.7, Éamonn Duggan, Pen and Sword, 2024.
58. Nicholas Laffan. Witness Statement to Bureau of Military History. No. 703, p.3.
59. Ibid., pp.5–6.
60. Patrick Joseph McElligott. Witness Statement to Bureau of Military History. No. 1013, p.4.
61. Matthew O'Callaghan. Witness Statement to Bureau of Military History. No. 561, p.1.
62. George Fitzgerald. Witness Statement to Bureau of Military History. No. 684, pp.6–7.
63. Michael Healy. Witness Statement to Bureau of Military History. No. 1064, p.3.
64. Ibid., p.3.
65. Michael Fahy. Witness Statement to Bureau of Military History. No. 1018, p.3.
66. Joseph P. Lawless. Witness Statement to Bureau of Military History. No. 1043, p.243.
67. Ibid., p.243.
68. Joseph Kinsella. Witness Statement to Bureau of Military History. No. 476, p.7.

Chapter Ten

69. Patrick O'Dwyer. Witness Statement to Bureau of Military History. No. 1432, pp.10–11.
70. Patrick McCrea. Witness Statement to Bureau of Military History. No. 413, pp.6–7.
71. Dr Joseph Kearney. Witness Statement to Bureau of Military History. No. 704, pp.2–3.
72. Ibid., p.4.
73. James Slattery. Witness Statement to Bureau of Military History. No. 445, p.2.
74. Ibid., p.5.
75. Patrick Ahern. Witness Statement to Bureau of Military History. No. 1003, pp.9–10.
76. Ibid., pp.9–10.
77. James Slattery. Witness Statement to Bureau of Military History. No. 445, p.6.
78. Ibid., pp.6–7.
79. Vincent Byrne. Witness Statement to Bureau of Military History. No. 423, pp.15–18.

Chapter Eleven

80. Michael Leahy. Witness Statement to Bureau of Military History. No. 1421, pp.16–17.
81. Ibid., pp.17–18.
82. Joseph Dolan. Witness Statement to Bureau of Military History. No. 663, pp.1–2.
83. Vincent Byrne. Witness Statement to Bureau of Military History. No. 423, pp.36–37.
84. The Funeral of Tomas MacCurtain. *Cork Independent*, 23 March 2020.
85. Vincent Byrne. Witness Statement to Bureau of Military History. No. 423, pp.37–38.
86. James Slattery. Witness Statement to Bureau of Military History. No. 445, pp.7–8.
87. Thomas Malone. Witness Statement to Bureau of Military History. No. 845, pp.36–38.
88. John O'Brien. Witness Statement to Bureau of Military History. No. 1647, pp.16–18.

89. Daniel Healy. Witness Statement to Bureau of Military History. No. 1656, pp.9–11.
90. James Slattery. Witness Statement to Bureau of Military History. No. 445, p.9.
91. Sean Moylan. An IRA Revolutionary at War, p.33.
92. Ibid., p.33.
93. We Go Into Action Today at Noon, pp.171–172.
94. Ibid., p.172.
95. Ibid., pp.173–174.
96. Century Ireland. World Pays Tribute to MacSwiney as Funeral Brings Cork to a Standstill.
97. Ibid.
98. Bloody Sunday. A Day of Terror and Death in Dublin. E. Duggan, Ireland's Own, 20 November 2020.
99. Ibid.
100. Ibid.
101. Ibid.
102. Ambush at Kilmichael. An Iconic Republican Victory. E Duggan, Ireland's Own, Annual 2020.
103. Jack Hennessy. Witness Statement to Bureau of Military History. No. 1234, p.4.
104. Ibid., p.6.
105. When Cork City Burned. Mary Rose McCarthy, Ireland's Own, 11 November 2020.

Chapter Twelve

106. Michael Brennan. Witness Statement to Bureau of Military History. No. 1068, pp.73–74.
107. James Murphy. Witness Statement to Bureau of Military History. No. 1684, pp.12–13.
108. Sean Moylan. An IRA Revolutionary at War, pp.76–77.
109. Lt Colonel J. O'Connell. Witness Statement to Bureau of Military History. No. 1444, pp.10–13.
110. James Cashman. Witness Statement to Bureau of Military History. No. 1270, p.8.
111. Irish Republican Bulletin, Volume V, No. 48, p.2.
112. Sean Moylan. An IRA Revolutionary at War. pp.84–85.

113. The Auxiliaries.com/incidents/Ballycannon-Ambush/Ballycannon.html. 28 June 2025.
114. The Irish Revolution Project. UCC, Cork's War of Independence Fatality Register. 1921–167.
115. John Nagle. Witness Statement to Bureau of Military History. No. 1394, pp.10–11.
116. Sean Moylan. An IRA Revolutionary at War, pp.100–101.
117. Paper Past. Irish History. 1919–1923, Chronology.ie
118. Oscar Traynor. Witness Statement to Bureau of Military History. No. 340, pp.70–75.
119. Thomas Harvey. Witness Statement to Bureau of Military History. No. 1668, pp.45–48.

Chapter Thirteen

120. Cumann na mBan. The Unsung Heroines of the Revolutionary Era. Ireland's Own. 6 June 2020.
121. Aine Ni Riain. Witness Statement to Bureau of Military History. No. 887, pp.4–9.
122. Mary Walsh. Witness Statement to Bureau of Military History. No. 556, p.5.
123. Margaret (Peg) Broderick. Witness Statement to Bureau of Military History. No. 1682, pp.2–3.

Chapter Fourteen

124. The Truce. Peace Comes at Last. Ireland's Own Centenary Annual 2021. Éamonn Duggan.
125. T Ryle Dwyer. Tans, Terror and Troubles. Kerry's Real Fighting Story. Mercier Press, 1996.
126. The Truce. Peace Comes at Last. Ireland's Own Centenary Annual 2021. Éamonn Duggan.
127. Ernest Blythe. Witness Statement to Bureau of Military History. No. 939, p.131.
128. Ibid.

Chapter Fifteen

129. The Anglo-Irish Treaty. Ireland's Destiny in the Hands of the Politicians. Ireland's Own Centenary Annual 2021. Éamonn Duggan.

Reference Books

Redmond. A Life Undone. Chris Dooley, Gill and Macmillan, 2015.

Easter 1916, The Irish Rebellion. Charles Townsend, Allen Lane History, 2015.

We Go Into Action Today at Noon. Éamonn Duggan, O'Brien Press, 2021.

Sean Moylan, An IRA Revolutionary at War. Éamonn Duggan, Pen and Sword, 2024.

Guerrilla Days in Ireland. Tom Barry, Anvil Books, 1981.

The Irish War of Independence. The Definitive Account of the Anglo-Irish War of 1919–1921. Michael Hopkinson, Gill Books, 2004.

The Dead of the Irish Revolution. Eunan O'Halpin and Daithi O'Corrain, Yale University Press, 2020.

Tans, Terror and Troubles, Kerry's Real Fighting Story. T. Ryle Dwyer, Mercier Press, 1996.

On Another Man's Wound. Dan Breen, Mercier Press, 2013.

Index

A
Ahern, Patrick 126-127
Ashbourne, Battle of 61-64
Ashe, Thomas 61, 91, 99, 100
Aud 20-23

B
Ballylanders RIC Barracks Attack 139-140
Barry, Tom 156, 158, 164, 177, 198
Barton, Robert 96, 204, 208
Bell, Alan 138-139
Bloody Sunday 153-156
Blythe, Ernest 13-15, 93, 96, 200, 201
Boland, Harry 3, 36, 40, 96
Boland's Mills 31, 40, 56
Bowen-Colthurst Captain J.C. 42, 46
Bradfield, Thomas 164-165
Breen, Liam 36-37
Breen, Dan 116-119, 120, 122, 131, 150, 179
Brennan, Michael 162-163
Broderick, Peg 193-194
Brooke, Frank 145-146
Brugha, Cathal 50, 87-88, 98-99, 103-105, 208
Byrne, John Charles 135-136
Byrne, Robert 121-122
Byrne, Vincent 129, 130, 134, 136, 138

C
Carney, Winifred 55, 73
Carrowkennedy Ambush 183-184
Casement, Roger 7, 8, 11, 20-23
Ceannt, Eamonn 4, 7, 11, 19-20, 30, 38, 50, 76, 80
Childers, Erskine 7-9, 204
Clarke, Kathleen 92, 99
Clarke, Tom 16, 19, 30, 55, 68-69, 75
Clery's 38, 43
Clogheen Ambush 173-174
Clonbanin Ambush 171-172
Clonmult Ambush 169-170
Colbert, Con 76-79
Colley, Harry 6, 35-37, 40
Collins, Michael 65, 85-88, 96-99, 102,105, 111-112, 120, 124, 128, 196, 204,208

Connolly, James 19, 29-30, 32, 34-35, 38, 40-49, 54-59, 61, 73-77, 80
Cosgrave, W.T. 50, 87, 91, 96, 208
Crossbarry Ambush 173
Custom House Attack 180-182

D
Daly, Edward 30, 38, 40, 52-56, 68, 75, 80
Daly, Paddy 134-135, 145
De Valera, Eamon 20, 31, 47, 56, 80, 91-96, 103, 117-124, 197, 203-204, 207-208
Dolan, Joseph 134-135
Dublin Castle 32, 34
Dublin City Hall 32, 38
Duggan, Eamonn 96, 103, 204

E
Ennis, Tom 125, 128

F
French, Lord 129-131
ffrench-mullen, Madeleine 72,73
Figgis, Darrell 7-8
First Southern Division Inaugural Meeting 177-178
Fitzgerald, George 108-109
Frongoch Internment Camp 85-87

G
Galligan, Paul 59-60
Gavan-Duffy, George 96, 204
General Post Office 30, 34, 49, 52-55, 61
Griffith, Arthur 87-96, 120, 204-208

H
Hayes, Dr Richard 61-64
Henderson, Frank 14, 20, 34-36, 42-46, 67-68, 104
Henderson, Leo 36, 45, 69
Heron, Archie 110-111
Heuston, Sean 38, 46
Hobson, Bulmer 2-10, 24, 25, 26
Holland, Robert 78-79
Hurley, Charlie 140,167

I
Imperial Hotel 38, 43, 45
Irish Citizen Army 19, 28-29, 34, 38
Irish Republican Brotherhood 2-3
Irish Volunteers 6-14, 17, 24-29
Irish Volunteer Newspaper 6, 14, 23

J
Jacobs Biscuit Factory 29, 41-42, 56

K
Kearney, Dr Joseph 122-123
Keogh, Tom 125, 129, 134-135, 139, 145
Kent, Thomas 75-76
Kettle, Laurence 4-5
Kilmichael Ambush 156-158
Knocklong Ambush 122-123

L
Laffan, Nicholas 106-107
Lawless, Col Joseph 101,110-111
Leahy, Michael 132-134
Lloyd George, David 92-94, 196-197, 203-207

Lynch, Diarmuid 99, 103
Lynch, Fionan 68, 69, 100
Lynch, Liam 127, 148, 177
Lynch, Mick 110-111
Lynn, Dr Kathleen 33, 72, 73

M

Mallin, Michael 32, 57, 71-72, 76
Mallow Barracks Attack 148-150
Mansion House 89-90, 97
Markievicz, Countess 57, 71-73, 92, 96
Marrowbone Lane Distillery 38, 48
Maxwell, General Sir John 48, 52, 54, 74
Mellows, Liam 65-66
Mendicity Institute 38, 46
Military Council IRB 19, 24, 26, 28-29, 30
Molony, Helena 32-33, 72
Mourne Abbey Ambush 168-169,
Moylan, Sean 58-59, 96, 104-105, 146-148, 166-167, 170, 198
Mulcahy, Richard 63, 99, 105, 198

Mc

MacCurtain, Thomas 13-14, 136-137
McDermott, Sean 4, 19, 25, 30, 55, 67-69, 76
MacDonagh, Thomas 11, 19, 25, 30, 56, 59, 75-76
McDonnell, Mick 125, 128, 131, 139
McElligott, P.J. 107-108
McEoin, Sean 153, 161, 165, 171
McGarry, Sean 69, 103, 120
McKee, Dick 103, 110-111
MacNeill, Eoin 3-4, 8,10, 14, 20, 24-25, 29, 32, 96
McSwiney, Terence 13-14, 96, 146, 151-152

N

Nadd British Army Raid 172-173
Nathan, Matthew 84-85
National Volunteers 10-14
North King Street 52-53, 57

O

O'Brien, Conor 7, 8, 9
O'Connell, J.J. 10, 24, 25
O'Connor, Rory 88, 103, 105, 111
O'Donovan Rossa, Jerimiah 15-18, 101-103
O'Duffy. Eoin 103, 135, 147
O'Dwyer, Paddy 117, 118
O'Farrell, Elizabeth 56, 57
O'Kelly, Sean. T. 4, 11, 17, 26, 96, 120
O'Malley, Ernie 135, 143, 148, 177-179, 198-199
O'Rahilly, The 3, 7, 8, 11, 25, 52, 55

P

Pearse, P.H. 11, 14, 15, 17, 19, 23-25, 28, 29, 30-31, 40, 44, 52, 54, 59, 67, 75
Pearse, William 27, 54, 75
Plunkett, Count 87-89, 90, 91, 96
Plunkett, Joseph 11, 19, 30, 59, 67, 69, 75

R

Redmond, John 6, 8, 9, 10, 11, 13, 86, 92
Rian, Aine Ni 188-190

Robinson, Seumas 116, 117, 118, 119, 120, 122
Royal Dublin Fusiliers 38, 42
Royal Irish Fusiliers 42, 46
Ryan, Dr James 49, 55

S

Savage, Martin 130, 131
Sheehy-Skeffington, Francis 42, 46
Slattery, James 129, 145
Smyth, Col Gerald 143-145
South Dublin Union 29, 34, 38, 40, 42, 50, 56
Stack, Austin 96, 100, 103, 208
Staines, Michael 54, 99, 103, 105
Squad, The 124, 125

T

Thornton, Frank 45, 51
Traynor, Oscar 36, 43, 45, 80, 180
Treacy, Sean 116, 117, 118, 119, 122, 150
Truce, The 185, 199-201
Tureengarriffe Ambush 170-171

U

Upton Train Ambush 168

W

Weafer, Thomas 20, 35, 36
Weston, Charles 61, 63
Woodenbridge Speech, John Redmond 8, 9